Social Policy

T. H. Marshall's
Social Policy
in the twentieth century

5th edition by
A. M. Rees

London
UNWIN HYMAN
Boston   Sydney   Wellington

Published by the Academic Division of
Unwin Hyman Ltd
15/17 Broadwick Street, London W1V 1FP, UK

Unwin Hyman Inc.
955 Massachusetts Avenue, Cambridge, MA 02139, USA

Allen & Unwin (Australia) Ltd
8 Napier Street, North Sydney, NSW 2060, Australia

Allen & Unwin (New Zealand) Ltd
in association with the Port Nicholson Press Ltd
Compusales Building, 75 Ghuznee Street, Wellington 1, New Zealand

First published in 1965 by Hutchinson and Co. (Publishers) Ltd
Second edition 1967
Third (revised) edition 1970
Fourth (revised) edition 1975
Fifth edition 1985
Second impression 1990

British Library Cataloguing in Publication Data

Marshall, T. H.
    Social policy in the twentieth century. – 5th ed.
1. Great Britain – social policy
I. Title   II. Rees, A. M.
361.6′1′0941   HN 385.5
ISBN 0-04-445912-2

Library of Congress Cataloging in Publication Data

Marshall, T. H. (Thomas Humphrey)
    Social policy
Rev. ed. of: Social policy in the twentieth century. – 4th ed. 1975
Bibliography: p.
Includes index
1. Social policy
I. Rees, Anthony M.   II. Marshall, T. H. (Thomas Humphrey)
Social policy in the twentieth century   III. Title
ISBN 0-04-445912-2

Typeset in 10 on 12 point Times Roman by
Words & Pictures Limited, Thornton Heath, Surrey
and printed in Great Britain by Courier International Ltd, Tiptree, Essex

Contents

Preface to the fifth edition

The first editions of this book, including two substantial revisions of the original text, were entirely the product of the amazingly fruitful retirement of Professor T. H. Marshall. The fourth and last of these editions came out in 1975, and, such is the pace of change in social policy, was already in some respects out of date by the end of the 1970s. A decision therefore had to be taken about whether a fifth edition should be prepared. One possible argument was that textbooks, like items of domestic equipment, have a useful life which should not be prolonged indefinitely. On the other hand, *Social Policy* was no ordinary textbook; Tom Marshall's gift for rigorous compression and lucid exposition had ensured that. Moreover, his distinctive perspective had helped several generations of students to an understanding of the policy dilemmas and choices involved in the promotion of welfare values. As the 1970s passed into the 1980s, these values were being more insistently questioned than for many years past, and he was anxious to grapple with the challenge posed by the change in the climate of political and economic opinion. It was therefore decided to go ahead with a fresh edition.

However, Tom Marshall had always doubted his ability to undertake the arduous task of a further revision single-handedly. He there therefore sought a sympathetic collaborator, and in 1980 it was agreed that I should work with him in preparation of the new edition. Some decisions were taken early on: in particular, in order to give continuity, to concentrate, as in previous revisions, on the second half of the book, concerned with development since the Second World War. Alterations to the historical sections of the book have therefore been relatively slight and few in number, although it should be noted that, should at some time in the future a sixth edition be contemplated, a priority would be a more extensive recasting of these pages in the light of modern historiography.

Unfortunately, this collaboration was not destined to last long. Professor Marshall died in November 1981, at the age of 86. He had

had time to read early drafts of the revised Chapters 7 and 8, and had set out his ideas for the remaining chapters. Apart from that, however, I was thereafter on my own. I have tried to retain as much as possible of the original text, and, although I cannot claim to emulate the compactness and elegance of Professor Marshall's prose style, to dovetail new and old together so that the joins do not show. I hope that the finished product fairly represents Tom Marshall's intentions.

A draft of this book was completed at the end of 1983, and has subsequently been further revised to take account of developments to the end of 1984. There is never a perfect place to stop, but social policy seems to be set on courses which will last some years, although it may well be that the present government will have some surprises in store, perhaps particularly in the field of social security.

I would like to thank Professors John Martin and Bob Pinker for reading through the drafts, and making helpful suggestions, most of which I have incorporated. Thanks are due, too, to Doreen Davies, Glynis Evans and Sally Johnson for typing successive versions of my script. Lastly I would like to thank Professor Marshall's widow, Nadine, for her help and patience over what turned out to be a rather extended period of time.

Anthony M. Rees
January 1985

Preface to the first edition

As this book is based not on original research but on secondary authorities and official publications, my debt to those who have worked in this field is enormous and obvious. I am particularly grateful to my former colleagues at the London School of Economics, most of whom are now members of the remarkable team headed by Professor Titmuss, for what I learned from working with them and for the response I received from the inquiries I addressed to some of them – from Dame Eileen Younghusband on social workers, Mrs Cockburn on housing, Mrs McDougall on mental health, Mr Carrier on demographic problems, and Mr Bird on some intricacies of our tax system.

Conscious as I was of my lack of first-hand knowledge of the major social services, I decided to seek interviews with some of those actually engaged in the work and I chose for this purpose three very different areas – London (the LCC), Leicester, and the County of Cambridgeshire. I was fortunate in obtaining introductions in the first case from Mrs Peggy Jay, in the second from Professor Neustadt, and in the third from Lady Adrian and Mr Michael Pease. All those I approached were generous in giving me their time and took great trouble in telling me the things I wanted to know, for all of which I here express my gratitude. They are in *London*, in addition to Mrs Jay herself (Vice-Chairman of the Welfare Committee and member of the Children's Committee), Mrs Durbin (member of the Housing Committee, a Rent Tribunal, and other bodies), Mr Lloyd Jacob (Head of the General Division of the Welfare Department), Miss Taylor (Chief Inspector of Child Care), and Mr Balchin (Assistant Director of Housing); in *Leicester* Dr Moss (Medical Officer of Health), Mr Powell (Director of Welfare Services), Mr Evans (Children's Officer), and Mr Hadfield (City Housing Manager); in *Cambridge* Dr Tyser (Medical Officer of Health, Miss Valentine (Children's Officer), and Mr Hitch (County Welfare Officer).

Last, but by no means least, I am indebted to Professor W. A. Robson who first proposed that I should write this book and without whose initiative and encouragement it would never have been written.

Introduction:
what is social policy?

'Social policy' is a term which is widely used but does not lend itself to precise definition. The meaning given to it in any particular context is largely a matter of convenience or of convention. The conventional approach will tell us which areas of government action are generally accepted as belonging to the 'social' sphere. Convenience, in this case, will determine what it is possible to deal with adequately in this book. Neither will explain what the subject is really about. For that we must look, not simply at the measures adopted, since these are but means to an end, but at the nature of the end itself – at the objectives which 'social' policy pursues in a way in which other policies do not. Let us begin with convention, then plunge into the deep waters of objectives and leave convenience to the end.

Convention in this matter is international, at least in part. It is most decisive in its inclusion, and definition, of social security. A convention adopted by the International Labour Organization in 1952 specified, under 'social security', measures for maintaining income during sickness, unemployment and old age, family allowances and the provision of medical care. The last item was, presumably, included because in most countries this requirement is met, not by a national health service, but by social insurance to cover the greater part of medical costs. The British custom is to treat what we now call *health care* as a separate item outside of *social security* which thus becomes synonymous with the system of cash benefits. This makes good sense, because it allows health to move over to the place where it properly belongs, next to social work and allied *welfare* services. A fourth item, which has a prominent place in, for instance, the social reports of the European Economic Community, is *housing*. Here definition becomes more difficult, partly because of the intricate involvement of public action with private enterprise in the housing market, and partly because housing policy merges into town and country planning which, if studied in depth, would lead us beyond the frontiers of social policy, as conventionally understood. As a fifth

item we can add *community services*. In these, although they exist for
the benefit of individuals, the services themselves are not personal.
Their aim is to contribute to the creation or maintenance of a
neighbourhood, both physical and social, fit to satisfy the needs of its
inhabitants. This category of social policy has gained in prominence
in recent years and there is much talk today of 'community health' and
'community development'. Finally there is one other major service
which has every right to be classed as 'social', namely *education*,
but convention does not usually admit it into the fold, perhaps
because it is too large a subject, or because it raises too many issues
peculiar to itself.

The objectives of these policies are indicated by the words used to
designate them – security, health and welfare. Of these welfare, in its
most general sense, is the only true end product, one to which an
assured cash income, a healthy body and, one could add, a house to
live in are among the most important contributors. This was
recognized when we coined the phrase 'the welfare state' to describe
the post-war social and political order. The term was meant to refer to
the end achieved, not to the means employed, and when critics speak
of it as 'the social service state' they rather suggest that the means
employed have become more important than the ends at which they
aim. Be that as it may, the avowed objective of twentieth-century
social policy is welfare. So what can we say about it? We are
concerned here, not with etymology or historical usage, but simply
with the meaning given to the word today in the context of social
policy. This meaning is undoubtedly more personal, more subjective
than that of its sister-word 'wealth'. It has a mixed reference which
embraces both the experience of well-being and the conditions which
produce it. To say that a man* 'fares well' implies that he is both doing
well and feeling well. A programme which takes welfare as its
objective must be planned on the assumption that there is normally
some correlation between these two aspects – the external conditions
and the internal experience. It can then operate on the external
conditions. But when action reaches the level of personal contact with
the intended beneficiary, as it does at some point almost everywhere
in the social policy world, then it becomes possible to modify the
initial assumption so as to take account of individual differences in
respect both of the needs to be met and of the response to the kinds of

*Throughout we have used the words 'man' and 'he' when referring to both men and
women.

help offered. The parts played by these two approaches, the assumed correlation and the assessment of the individual case, vary from service to service.

Ever since the invention of social insurance standard cash benefits have been assessed according to a *presumption* as to the amount of income needed to enable the *average* beneficiary to achieve the level of welfare to which he is held to be entitled. Hence the attempts to draw a poverty line, to define the subsistence level, to estimate what is needed to sustain family welfare as the children arrive and grow up, or to decide what the relationship should be between a man's retirement pension and his previous earnings. Only those cases which are overlooked or inadequately provided for by the general system are treated individually and, since they are marked out as exceptions, this individual treatment is felt to be invidious. So twentieth-century social policy in the matter of cash benefits has been under constant pressure to reduce to a minimum the number of cases requiring individual investigation of an invidious kind while seeking ways of bringing the approximations closer to the realities. But this problem has proved to be very intractable, and policy-makers in the 1980s are still looking for the answer.

The pressure in the health and welfare services has been, on the whole, in the opposite direction, towards personalizing the service as much as possible and protecting the individual from the harsh impact of those institutions, organizations, rules and regulations without which no personal service could be provided on a national, or even on a local, scale. Success in this endeavour depends greatly on the intervention of the professional, or the expert, between the bureaucratic machine and the individual client, or patient. The bureaucrat tends to assign cases to appropriate categories and order the prescribed treatment; this has a depersonalizing effect on the relationship. The professional, by contrast, claims the right to judge each case on its merits and then to prescribe, or to recommend, what is in his opinion the best treatment for it, within the limits of the service of which he or she is the agent. The distinction between these roles is important, both in theory and in practice. But any authority, whether bureaucratic or professional, which touches on such intimate personal matters as health and welfare should be exercised with great circumspection and restraint. The relationship is in some ways easier to handle in medicine than in the personal social services. The concept of health is sufficiently precise and the standing of the medical profession is sufficiently high to win general agreement that the doctor knows best, nor need there be anything humiliating about his intervention. Welfare, by comparison, is a vaguer concept, the professional standing of the social worker is less eminent, the element of uncertainty when decisions must be taken is likely to be greater, and the intervention of the social worker can be felt to be humiliating. But decisions must be made, and made by the 'outsider' on behalf of the patient or client, though the decision may often consist in accepting and endorsing the client's own expressed preferences.

The purpose of this brief analysis is to identify to two most fundamental problems which confront a social policy which chooses welfare as its objective. The first, briefly and crudely expressed, is how to enable a mass-produced service to distribute a highly individualized product by means which are neither invidious, humiliating nor presumptuous. The second is how to manage its dual role of being both the servant and the master of its intended beneficiaries. A social service exists for the benefit of those it serves, but in the course of its operation a host of decisions must be taken, not by them, but on their behalf by 'outsiders' from policy-makers at the top to physicians and social workers at the point of impact. This discharge of a vicarious responsibility is often described – with derogatory intent – as 'paternalism'. But a social service cannot function without it, since it must be guided by a consistent system of values and it must take its own decisions about priorities. There is inevitably in social services a danger of excessive vicarious paternalism, which is enhanced by the imbalance of authority between the providers and the recipients of the service. In other spheres the antidote to a lopsided power situation has been found (or sought) in the organization of the weaker party, as in the case of trade unions. There has been relatively little of this in the social service world, where, until recently, the only effective pressure groups were themselves run by 'outsiders', not by, but on behalf of, those immediately concerned. But recent years have seen a rapid expansion of activities of this kind, both defensive and aggressive, among those at the receiving end of social policy, of which the 'claimants' unions' are a good example. It is very much on the progress of this movement that many people build their faith in 'community development'.

To return to welfare as an objective of social policy, it might be argued that it is in fact the ultimate objective of all policy, and also of the economic system as a whole. This is true in a sense, but in the case of social policy the relation between programme and objective is a more immediate one. The general pattern is one of action carried through until, so to speak, the product has been delivered into the hands of the person for whom it is intended; till then the job has not been finished. That is why we can speak of *individual* rights (or in some cases, more accurately, claims) to welfare. Economic policy, on the other hand, is concerned more with the 'common weal' than with individual welfare. Second, it has been represented by the present authors and others that social policy uses political power to supersede, supplement or modify operations of the economic system in order to achieve results which the economic system would not achieve on its own, and that in doing so it is guided by values other than those determined by open market forces.

Finally we come to the question of convenience – the limitations this book imposes on this extensive subject. We shall try to cover: first, social security, in the sense of income maintenance, whether through social insurance or other methods of providing cash benefits; second, health care, whether it takes the form of a health service or of health insurance or a combination of the two; third, social welfare, or personal social services; and fourth, housing policy, particularly in so far as it aims at enabling less well-off families to obtain a home on terms that they can afford. Policies directed towards the health and welfare of communities rather than immediately of individuals will be considered in the context of those policy areas, as will also the roles of the agents through whom the policies are carried out. A novelty in the last edition was a chapter on poverty in Part Two. This has been retained because of the key position the subject continues to occupy in the 1980s, and also because it is a problem area on which all other subjects converge – income, health, welfare and housing. The question of delinquency and its treatment will be dealt with only as it concerns juveniles and merges with the welfare services for children. Education, unfortunately, must be omitted. Finally, although the bias in both parts of the book is towards British history and policy, as much consideration as possible has been given to the affairs of other countries at a similar stage of development, and every effort has been made to examine problems and policies in general, and not in purely national, terms.

Part One

The First Fifty Years

1 The legacy of the Victorian era

In the first volume of his autobiography Leonard Woolf writes: 'our youth, the years of my generation at Cambridge, coincided with the end and the beginning of a century which was also the end of one era and the beginning of another. . . . We found ourselves living in the springtime of a conscious revolt against the social, political, religious, moral, intellectual and artistic institutions, beliefs and standards of our fathers and grandfathers. . . . The battle, which was against what for short one may call Victorianism, had not yet been won, and what was so exciting was our feeling that we ourselves were part of the revolution'.[1]* This is a personal recollection of the authenticity of which there can be no doubt, and it is supported by many historians who have maintained that the death of Queen Victoria marked the close not only of a reign but of an epoch.[2] But when we pause to consider these sweeping generalizations we remember how often young men of one generation have believed that they were waging a revolutionary war against the generation of their elders, and how many 'epochs' with profoundly significant opening and closing dates historians have discovered, and subsequently discarded. So it behoves us to be cautious; and it is the purpose of this chapter and the next to look at the situation in or around the year 1900 in order to see in what respects if any it really did mark the birth of a new era, especially in the field of social policy.

That year falls midway between what Trevelyan has called 'the two mid-Victorian decades of quiet politics and roaring prosperity'[3] and the appearance of what we have become accustomed to call the welfare state. For Leonard Woolf it was the time of *Sowing* (the title of his book). Can we transfer the metaphor from his personal life to our social and political history? This would imply that the seed was sown, around the turn of the century, in land that had been ploughed by an earlier generation, and that the harvest was gathered by a later

---

*Superior figures refer to References section p. 267.

one. We shall see, as we follow the passage of events from the first period to the last, that the metaphor is, in many ways, a very appropriate one indeed.

The industrial revolution, whatever may be the truth about its beginning, most certainly had no end. For it is the essence of industrialization that, once you are well 'over the hump', and fully committed to the industrial way of life, the movement never stops and (in all probability) the pace will get continually hotter. It takes a society a little time to get accustomed to the motion and to tidy up the bits and pieces which were thrown out of place when the acceleration started. The thesis, just quoted, about the mid Victorian decades signifies that by then Britain had achieved this adaptation and found its balance, or at least that most of the people who mattered believed that this was so. In a sense they were right, but in another sense they were wrong. It was true that by the 1850s the old order had vanished and a new order had taken its place. It was true, also, that the more violent disturbances which had accompanied its birth were over and that relative harmony prevailed. But much still remained to be done to enable the immanent principles of the new order to reach fulfilment. And when Victorian society, in its age of confidence, embarked upon this task of fulfilment, it set in motion forces within the system itself which led, by natural and logical processes, to its transformation into something totally unforeseen and unfamiliar. In fact the transformation, when it came, was shaped by a conscious effort on the part of twentieth-century policy to create a social order essentially different from that of the Victorians.

So far as industry was concerned, the triumph of the Victorian society was beyond dispute. 'The country regarded itself,' says Ensor, 'as "the workshop of the world" – a phrase then universal which expressed not an aspiration but a fact'.[4] The boast was justified, but there were, nevertheless, two vital matters to be settled within the industrial system itself, namely the structure of the large business unit and the status of the organizations of the workers that these business units employed. A decisive step towards the settlement of the former was taken when Parliament, in 1855–6, established the legal basis for the operation of joint-stock companies with limited liability. There were some exclamations of horror from *The Times*, but the new shape of things was soon generally accepted. Some years later legislation, culminating in the Act of 1875, legalized collective bargaining by trade unions including (so it seemed) the right to strike. This too appeared to be in tune with the spirit of the age. For did not the Royal

Commission on Labour, of 1894, express the view that the 'occasional great trade conflict' to settle a major issue represented 'a higher stage of civilization' than continued local bickerings?[5] But when the trade unions began to make powerful use of their new liberties, these were challenged by the courts, and had to be reaffirmed, and strengthened, by Parliament in 1906. The truth, not fully realized at the time, was that an industrial system characterized by the consolidation of business into vast impersonal units and the combination of workers into national trade unions was a very different thing from the paradise of individual enterprise, free competition, and self-help which the Victorians imagined they had established. The logical elaboration of the principles of the Victorians, and the natural growth of the institutions they had founded, were leading to something which, though it might at first look like a fulfilment, was in fact a transformation; the seed sown in the ground which the Victorians had ploughed produced a crop unlike anything they had known or could easily imagine.

If capitalist industry was one of the pillars upholding the Victorian system, the other was responsible government, both central and local. After 1832 the cabinet was responsible to a House of Commons which in turn was aware of its responsibilities to the electorate, but it did not represent the people. The franchise was far too restricted for that. Only about 19 per cent of the adult males in the population had the vote, but the principle that men were sent to Parliament by votes of their fellow-citizens had been accepted, and it was logically inevitable that, by a process of natural growth, parliamentary government should become representative as well as responsible. The mid Victorians themselves took the crucial step in 1867 when they passed the Reform Act which just about doubled the proportion of the enfranchised. By the end of the century the system fell little short of manhood suffrage, but it was still based ostensibly on the idea that a man was qualified for the franchise by virtue of his substance as reflected in the annual value of his home. It was not until after the First World War that the right to vote was recognized as being a right of citizenship as such, to be enjoyed by men and women alike. However, in 1900 there was a legislative organ in sensitive touch with the public conscience and with the new streams of political thought flowing through the minds and from the pens of the radicals and socialists. And in the year 1906 the Labour Party first entered the political arena as a fully qualified competitor in the party game. Even contemporaries, without the help that historical perspective gives, saw, and said, that a new era of party politics had begun. Here, too, natural growth and logical processes were on the way to produce a transformation.

In local government, a matter of great importance in the history of social policy, the picture is not so clear nor the story so simple. The reformed Parliament had cleaned up what *The Times* once referred to as the 'chartered hogsties' of municipal government as early as 1835,[6] but no comparable reform had been undertaken in rural areas when the mid Victorian age of prosperity and confidence began. Nor did the mid Victorians make good this defect. When a new task emerged which required a firm hand and an honest mind to guide it they created new machinery for the purpose, first the Poor Law Guardians (with their special administrative areas) and then in 1870 the School Boards, while the urban sanitary authorities, under the permissive Act of 1848, largely created themselves by private bill very much as the fancy moved them. It is tempting to imagine that the 'sowing' could not have taken place had the ground not been prepared by the legislation which, between the years 1882 and 1894, brought the municipal corporations up to date and established a uniform and effective system of rural administration in the hands of the county, urban district, and rural district councils. But this interpretation cannot really be sustained. For, although a fair measure of concentration of functions in the hands of these bodies did eventually take place, the old tangle remained in being at least till 1929, by which time a new tangle was growing up to take its place, and heated debates about the reform of local government have continued to the present day. In fact, in the years around 1900 the only local government that could be counted as a power in the land was municipal government in the cities together with the specialized bodies just mentioned.

Turning now to the social policy which was enacted and executed by these political organs, it is convenient – since space does not allow a comprehensive survey – to group the salient features of the picture under four headings: education, industry, poverty, and health. Education falls outside the scope of this book, but a word must be said about it here, if only because it illustrates so well the thesis that natural growth in the second half of the nineteenth century prepared the way for transformation in the twentieth. For the Victorians, democracy and education were partners. A free society could not be orderly unless it was literate, and a self-governing society could not progress in peace unless it was educated. Since, therefore, education was required as much for the benefit of the society as for that of the individual, it was not too difficult to establish the case for holding the state responsible for seeing that it was both offered and accepted. Universal, compulsory, and therefore free elementary education was the corollary; it was implicit in the Act of 1870 and was made explicit in subsequent legislation. Thereupon some people concluded that, with democracy and education securely established, there was little more to be done in the way of social policy. But they were wrong even as regards education itself. Attention was next turned, naturally and logically, to technical and secondary education. And then the story of trade unionism repeated itself. The authorities which tried tentatively to invade the field of secondary education were told by the courts that they had no legal power to use public money in this way. In the counter-attack of the Act of 1902 they not only won back the ground they had lost but established a base for further advances in great depth. The eventual result was, once more, a transformation. The public elementary education of the nineteenth century was an inferior commodity provided for an inferior class, and it led straight into the lower reaches of the labour market. The twentieth century created an educational ladder from the primary school to the university, and adopted, in principle, the ideal of equal opportunity. It is true that it remained a good deal easier to mount the ladder from half-way up than to start from the bottom rung, but education in 1985 was profoundly different, both in structure and in quality, from what it had been when Queen Victoria died, and also from what the reformers of those days had had in mind.

When we look at industry, we see that the mid Victorian state had already accepted its duty and asserted its right to intervene directly for the protection of workers in factories. It is true that, in accordance with the pure doctrine of individualism as understood at the time, it did not 'interfere' with the liberty of adult male workers but confined its attention (in theory) to women and children. In effect, as was quite clearly appreciated, the men benefited indirectly from some of the measures designed for the protection of others. As the need to guard the workers not only against moving machinery but also against such insidious menaces to health as lead poisoning and noxious dust became more and more apparent, this principle was quietly dropped in the legislation of the 1890s dealing with matters of this kind. The significance of this departure from doctrinaire individualism is considerable, but it should not be misinterpreted. It did not mean that in future individualism was to be replaced by paternalism every-where. Far from it. It meant only that paternalism was deemed acceptable in cases where the individual was powerless to protect himself, even if he wanted to, and where the ill-judged acts of the few might cause grave injury to the many. Each case must be judged on its merits, and many important instances could be cited, from that time to the present, in which the choice betwen individualism and paternalism proved difficult and the judgement was not unanimous. We shall meet such instances shortly in the field of public health.

But the other two aspects of factory legislation are still more important. The first is the creation of the inspectorate, acting under the orders of the central government. We shall return later to the role of inspectors in nineteenth-century social administration. The point about the factory inspectors is that there was no local authority for them to work through; all power was concentrated at the centre, and this was done because it was clearly realized that 'conflicting interests, local influences, indisposition to carrying the law into effect, and other circumstances' might well make administration by local authorities ineffective, as indeed it proved to be when it was tried briefly in the case of workshops as distinct from factories.[7] Second, under this legislation first the factories, then the workshops, and eventually even the domestic premises of the manufacturers – that is to say their private property, their real estate, and, in certain circumstances, their homes – were treated as things for the use of which they could be publicly answerable and into which public officials had the right of entry in the ordinary course of their duty. In this way the second great principle of Victorian individualism, the principle of the inviolability of private property, was put on trial and found wanting. Certainly it was not overthrown, but it was dislodged from its position as a sacred dogma and made to submit like other humbler principles, to the modifications required by the circumstances in which it was applied.

Poverty is a subject that will figure so extensively in the later parts of this book that little need be said about it here. We can confine ourselves to identifying the concepts of poverty and of the Poor Law which prevailed during the period of Victorian confidence, within the framework of the concept of competitive capitalism. Poverty, one might venture to say, was regarded more as a social fact than a social problem. The problem was how to reduce the mass of apparent or self-declared poverty to the hard core of the genuine article. This was done by means of the deterrent effect of the workhouse test and the principle of 'less eligibility' (the condition of the pauper must be less attractive than that of the poorest person outside this category). This remained the accepted doctrine in official circles right through the period of confidence and for some time afterwards. But on the question what to do with the hard core of the genuine poor there were some doubts and some disagreement. Should they be treated harshly or generously, in the workhouse or outside it, as unfortunate citizens or as social outcasts? The answers were not clear, and in the soil of this perturbation of mind lay the seeds of the first great social reforms of the twentieth century.

There are two points of general significance which must be grasped if the events that followed are to be understood. The Victorians, we have just suggested, regarded poverty as a social fact. The poor, they reflected, are always with us, always have been and always will be. In the prosperous nineteenth century there should be fewer, rather than more, of them than at previous times. Their ever-present need was traditionally relieved by their families, the church, the religious orders, and the neighbours. It was only in a supplementary way, to co-ordinate or to provide special types of service, that the public authorities stepped in. This is what one sees very clearly when one looks at a country like France in which religious institutions operated at full strength, or at the United States, particularly in the early years of its independence, where the neighbourhood generally felt quite capable of looking after its own affairs. But in Britain the power of religious institutions had been greatly curtailed by the Reformation, and the strength of the neighbourhood had been extensively undermined by the industrial revolution. In addition, for centuries the neighbourhood had been personified, for major administrative purposes, in the Justice of the Peace, who, though a genuine neighbour, was at the same time a public official and the agent of the central government. Now the Justices had been replaced by the Poor Law Guardians who, although still local worthies, seemed to have even less of the neighbourly spirit in them. Thus the traditional philosophy of poverty still persisted, but the social and institutional structure through which the philosophy could be translated into action had passed away.

The second point to grasp is that we must think in terms not of the poor but of the paupers. Pauperism was a status, entry into which affected not merely a part of a man's life, but the whole of it. He became a pauper for all purposes, and he carried his family with him. Paupers formed a distinct group of second-class citizens, deprived of most of the important rights of citizenship. The principal officer of the Poor Law Division of the Local Government Board, giving evidence before the Royal Commission of 1905–9, said that the status of pauper implied 'firstly, the loss of personal reputation (what is understood as the stigma of pauperism); secondly, the loss of personal freedom, which is secured by detention in a workhouse; and thirdly the loss of political freedom by suffering disfranchisement'. The pauper, he added, has in practice a right of relief, but 'his right is not a complete right for the necessary sanctions are lacking . . . he cannot sue for his relief', and that is precisely why it is the duty of the state to see that he gets his rights.[8] The comprehensive character of the status meant that certain essential services, especially those of health and education, were split in two. Sick and infirm paupers were attended by the Poor Law Medical Officer or entered the Poor Law Infirmary, and their children were sent to the Poor Law Schools or other establishments certified as available to them, while the other needy members of the society were provided for by the local sanitary authority and its Medical Officer of Health and the local School Board. The anomalies that resulted, as well as the hardships induced by the workhouse test and the rigid conception of pauperism, caused growing uneasiness as the nineteenth century drew towards its close, and provoked a frontal attack on the system in the early years of the twentieth.

Our fourth category of social policy, health, will also figure extensively in this book, but in some respects it is the most critical of all to the understanding of the period under review, and must therefore receive careful attention here. It is critical for two reasons: first, because it was most conspicuously in the field of public health that the battle was fought over the relative roles of central and local government and, one might almost say, even over the role of government as such, in the pursuit of welfare. Second, whereas the developments in the machinery of democratic government, in education, in the structure of industry and the processes of collective bargaining, and in factory legislation, can properly be regarded as the natural growth and logical evolution of the mid Victorian system, it is a debatable question whether the measures taken in the field of public health were a natural fulfilment of Victorian democratic capitalism or an attack launched against it. Aneurin Bevan took the latter view, but he qualified it by adding that the system was quick to claim the credit for what had been imposed upon it by its attackers. Public health measures, he said, have become part of the system, 'but they do not flow from it. They have come in spite of it. . . . In claiming them, capitalism proudly displays medals won in the battles it has lost'.[9] The question having been posed, one must make haste to admit that it cannot be answered. There are no valid arguments by which one interpretation can be proved right and the other wrong. And yet even a cursory glance at British history leaves the impression that the public health measures were much less of a natural growth from within the system than any of the items listed above. They sprang from the determined efforts of a small number of men – doctors and civil servants – of outstanding ability, courage, and energy who can easily be identified as the pioneers of this great advance. They had to instil into the circles that controlled affairs both in industry and in local government something of their own knowledge and understanding and of their own attitude to life; their understanding not only of the medical but also of the social factors involved, and their attitude towards man's environment, which refused to treat it as something given, as something to be accepted as an expression of the unalterable laws of nature. It was equally necessary in this conceptualization of the environment, both physical and social, to see in it something different from a mere aggregation of individual actions and circumstances to which the principles of individual rights and freedoms could be applied. The physical environment created by men and the social environment composed of men must be handled according to principles peculiar to themselves, and it was for the recognition and general application of these principles that men like Chadwick and Southwood Smith were fighting. One of the most notable examples of the utter failure to grasp this point is the leading article in *The Times* of 1 August 1854, celebrating the downfall of these two men and the suppression of the Board of Health. 'If there is such a thing as a political certainty among us, it is that nothing autocratic can exist in this country. The British nature abhors absolute power. . . . The Board of Health has fallen.' And it continues: 'We all of us claim the privilege of changing our doctors, throwing away their medicine when we are sick of it, or doing without them altogether whenever we feel tolerably well. . . . Esculapius and Chiron, in the form of Mr Chadwick and Dr Southwood Smith, have been deposed, and we prefer to take our chance of cholera and the rest than be bullied into health.'

This passage covers three distinct points. The first is concerned with the limits of bureaucratic power and in particular with the relations between the central bureaucracy and the allegedly democratic local authority; we shall return to this in a moment. The second refers to the right of the individual to choose for himself. But this is a right which, as we saw in the case of the Factory Acts, applies only where there is a real power to choose and when the choice made by one man cannot endanger the health and welfare of others. The third point concerns the environment and is a complete *non sequitur*. It would have been impossible to cope with 'cholera and the rest' without the help of bureaucracy guided by the best scientific knowledge of the age, and the man who decided to 'take his chance' was a menace to the health of his neighbours. Fortunately *The Times*'s song of victory was premature, and the public health movement continued to advance.

Before we close this chapter there is one question to be considered which is relevant to all areas of social policy. It is the question of the means by which a central government: 1 gathers information about the social problems with which the policy is to deal; 2 having decided on its policy, explains to its local executives, whether they are its own servants or autonomous local authorities, what they are to do; 3 keeps a watch to see if they are doing it, and 4 puts pressure on them, if they are not, to make them do it. Some provision to meet these needs is a prerequisite of any social policy, and it is therefore important to know whether the twentieth century inherited from the nineteenth a serviceable equipment for these purposes. The answer to 1 is the almost fabulous list of reports of Royal Commissions and Select Committees, admittedly somewhat unequal in quality, which were one of the outstanding contributions of the period to the apparatus of government. The answer to questions 2 and 3 is, apart from routine ministry circulars, the inspectorate. There were inspectors for the Factory Acts, for education, for the Poor Law (Assistant Commissioners), and for public health. Their relations with the local executives of policy varied. The factory inspectors had no local agents to work through. For education and the Poor Law there were the *ad hoc* boards created by government for the purpose, and therefore having something of the character of government agents. In public health the sanitary authorities were an integral part of general local government, and often showed the independence characteristic of its institutions. But, whoever it was that they were dealing with, the inspectors occupied a key position which they exploited as fully as contemporary ideas about the liberty of the subject and local dislike of bureaucratic interference permitted. The procedure laid down for them consisted of inspection, report and advice; it did not include dictation. So the answer to question 4 above is that the pressure on local agents to implement central policy was exerted rather patchily, often indirectly and not always effectively. But the result was better than one might have expected.

In the mid Victorian age of confidence there was a continuous resistance to the encroachment of the central government in local affairs, but the encroachment went on. The machinery at the centre was steadily expanding, and we are told that the twenty years ending in 1854 saw the addition of twenty permanent central agencies to the apparatus. Also, even when no uniform pattern could be imposed by authority on local administration, the device was used with considerable effect of designing models which most of the local authorities were only too glad to copy. So, by the time the period of confidence ended and the nineteenth century drew to a close, the ideas, the habits, and the machinery of government had developed to a point at which the obstacles to the new urge in social policy were not insuperable. Whatever we may think about the exact interpretation of the phrase 'the welfare state', we can appreciate the force in David Robert's judgement that during the mid Victorian epoch the ordinary Englishman had become 'the beneficiary of a state that assumed a responsibility for the well-being of its citizens. However limited that responsibility, however meagre compared to the responsibilities assumed by Whitehall today, it did mark the beginning of the Welfare State'.[10]

2 Problems and policies at the turn of the century

It was argued in the last chapter that during the period of Victorian confidence in the social order the ground was being prepared for the new developments of the twentieth century in part by the natural and logical evolution of the social order itself. But in the last quarter of the nineteenth century the situation was changed by a series of events and discoveries which severely shook the confidence of the Victorians and seemed to betray unsuspected weaknesses in their society. One of the most important effects was to provide fresh ammunition and a more receptive audience for the various critics of the system whose utterances until then had not greatly disturbed the general calm, but who were now in a position to challenge the dominant orthodoxy. The distinction here made between events and discoveries may be a little arbitrary, but it is useful. It serves to distinguish between occurrences which struck society with a new impact, and the fruits of deliberate, planned inquiries which revealed conditions that had existed for some time, and thus convicted the public mind of having been lulled into a false complacency.

The principal event was the depression which attacked the economy of the Western world in the last quarter of the century. In Britain it came at a time when the competition of foreign industries had made manufacturers doubt whether the country was still entitled to call itself the 'workshop of the world', and it was accompanied by the new and alarming phenomenon of mass unemployment. In 1882, in spite of the gathering clouds, the *Spectator* could write: 'Britain as a whole never was more tranquil and happy. No class is at war with society or the government: there is no disaffection anywhere, the Treasury is fairly full, the accumulations of capital are vast.'[1] Very soon, however, the unemployed were demonstrating in Hyde Park, and in 1886 Hyndman, leader of the Marxist wing of the socialist forces, was addressing packed crowds in Trafalgar Square, with John Burns waving a red flag and shouting, 'When we give the word for a rising will you join us?' There followed rioting, arrests, prosecutions, and – most significantly – acquittals. The Mansion House fund for the unemployed, 'which had long lingered, half moribund, at about £3000, rose in the four days after the riot to £20,000', and a fortnight later reached £60,000.[2] This was tangible evidence of the extent of public sympathy. The corresponding crisis in the United States came a little later, in the years 1894 to 1898, when the percentage of unemployed in manufacturing industry and transport rose from a level of around 5 per cent to a maximum of 16.7 per cent and the depression was described as 'extreme', 'deep', 'severe', and 'intense'.[3] The comments of historians on events in the two countries are very similar. In England, says Ensor, 'the slump gave Victorian courage and optimism the severest shock that it had yet received'.[4] In the United States, we are told, 'it was very clear that the country was profoundly shaken, that men everywhere were beginning to envisage a turning-point in national development'.[5]

The shaking engendered a new attitude to social problems. According to the old orthodoxy the prime cause of social distress and destitution was to be found in the persons or individual circumstances of the victims, and it was usually identifiable as moral weakness. There was considerable resistance to admitting the presence of impersonal social causes, because this implied an inherent defect in the system itself. The shock administered by the spectacle of mass unemployment did much to break this resistance, because it was evident that the unemployed in Trafalgar Square were not a collection of weaklings or idlers, but the product of an impersonal phenomenon called 'unemployment', a word that had only recently been introduced into the vocabulary. Close on the heels of these events came the famous strikes of the match-girls and the dockers, in 1888–92, in which once more public sympathy was on the side of those protesting against their lot. And this time it was not a question of people who had been ejected from an economic system which, for the moment at least, had no use for them. The complaints were voiced by men and women whose labour was in demand but who were not thereby enabled to rescue themselves from conditions of extreme poverty.

In this sense these strikes were not only events; they were also discoveries. They brought to light new facts about the standard of living of the unskilled workers. And they coincided in time with other discoveries of still wider import. The new enlightenment about the depth and extent of urban poverty erupted in the 1880s with the publication, first of *The Bitter Cry of Outcast London* (1883), and then of the more widely publicized studies by Charles Booth of the people of London (1889) and Seebohm Rowntree of the people of

York (1901).[6] These books created a sensation, and the facts reported in them passed immediately into general currency as established truths, and were quoted with telling effect in the highest circles. 'We know, thanks to the patience and accurate scientific investigations of Mr Rowntree and Mr Charles Booth, that there is about 30 per cent of our population underfed, on the verge of hunger.' So wrote Leo Chiozza Money in his widely read and very influential book *Riches and Poverty*.[7] The tone is typical; it is that of a man announcing a discovery, not quoting an opinion. And yet these two local studies provided only a slender basis for a general statement of this kind. A little later Lloyd George, at the outset of his campaign for social reform, was equally emphatic. Booth and Rowntree, he said, have 'revealed a state of things, especially in the towns, which it would be difficult even for the orators of discontent to exaggerate. There are ten millions in this country enduring year after year the torture of living while lacking a sufficiency of the bare necessities of life'.[8] This was in 1906, when the road to old-age pensions and national insurance still lay ahead of him, beset with hazards both known and unknown; he needed the popular support that these shocking truths might win for his social programme.

A second source of new information to which historians frequently refer is the Report of the Interdepartmental Committee on Physical Deterioration of 1904. It is indeed relevant to the story, but not so much because it administered a shock as because it was set up to investigate a shocking discovery which had already been announced. This was the report of the military authorities on the high rate of rejection, on medical and physical grounds, of recruits during the South African War. They concluded from this experience that the physical state of the population had deteriorated. The Inter-departmental Committee, on the contrary, decided that it had not. The statistics, they said, had been mishandled and misinterpreted, and they expressed the hope that their work might have some effect in 'allaying the apprehensions of those who, as it appears on insufficient grounds, have made up their minds that progressive deterioration is to be found among the people generally'.[9] But, on the basis of quite different evidence, they showed that some very shocking conditions existed in certain sections of the population, especially in the poorer parts of the big cities. They made a strong appeal for action to alleviate overcrowding, pollution of the atmosphere and under-feeding, and for the medical inspection of school children.

A third disclosure concerned the sweated industries. It was not so much the report of the House of Lords Committee of 1888 on sweating, though the mere fact of its appointment was full of significance, nor the brilliant study made by Beatrice Webb, that administered a sudden shock to the public mind, but rather the Sweated Industries Exhibition organized by the *Daily News* in 1906. Here could be seen particulars about the hours of work and the earnings of the sweated workers (mostly women and children), examples of the work they produced, demonstrations of the skill and labour they put into it, and models of the rooms in which they toiled. The effect was irresistible. Finally one might add the growing body of knowledge about the housing of the people, although here the story lacks the element of sudden discovery. However, for those who knew the facts, the situation was sufficiently alarming. As far back as 1885 a Royal Commission had reported that, although the improvement in the housing of the poor in the past thirty years had been enormous, 'yet the evils of overcrowding, especially in London, were still a public scandal, and were becoming in certain localities more serious than they ever were'.[10] In 1900 the Prime Minister was telling the Conservative Party that they should 'devote all the power they possess to getting rid of that which is really a scandal to our civilization ... I would earnestly press upon all over whom my opinion may have any weight that the subject which should occupy their attention more than any other social subject is that of providing adequate and healthy accommodation for the working classes'.[11]

Thus the pride of Britain was assaulted from all directions. Her cities were breeding young men unfit to fight for her, there were workers in her industries reduced to conditions to which only a Dickens could do justice, a third of her inhabitants were living in absolute poverty or on the edge of it, and the slums of her towns were a public disgrace. The combined effect of these discoveries was great enough to change the political atmosphere and to create possibilities for new and more determined action. The previous generation had realized that these problems existed, but had not grasped their magnitude. Consequently their treatment of them remained, as it were, peripheral, as though concerned only with the fringes of society and not with large sections of its ordinary members. The new situation demanded a reappraisal of the rights of the citizen and of the obligations of the state towards him.

The recognition of the need for such a reappraisal and the attempts made to meet this need deeply disturbed the political thinking of the period and left their mark on the programmes of the political parties. It is remarkable how often in the speeches and writings of these years one meets the words 'socialist' and 'socialism'. It is obvious that the representatives of the old orthodoxy felt it necessary to take up some position with regard to this new doctrine – to belittle it, to appropriate it, or to fight it. And it is equally obvious that many of them had only the vaguest idea what it was; which was not surprising, since even those who called themselves socialists were not in agreement on this point. Definitions of socialism varied greatly. Dicey, in his book *Law and Public Opinion in England*, published in 1905, called the years from 1865 to 1900 'The Period of Collectivism', and he defined collectivism as 'the school of opinion often termed (and generally by more or less hostile critics) Socialism, which favours the intervention of the State, even at some sacrifice of individual freedom, for the purpose of conferring benefit upon the mass of the people'.[12] He elaborated the definition by specifying the types of state action he had in mind, and giving examples.

This definition is broad enough to cover practically all the policies of social reform that were taking shape at the turn of the century. For they all sprang from the belief that the state was responsible (in some measure) for the welfare of 'the mass of the people' and that it was endowed with the authority to interfere (to some extent) with individual freedom and economic liberty in order to promote it. The novelty of this idea lay in its divergence from the former view that the state was concerned only with the destitute and the helpless, and that its action on their behalf must not impinge upon the ordinary life of the community. And Dicey was quite right in saying that this was what most people meant by 'socialism' – except, of course, for the real socialists, who meant much more by it. But he was wrong in suggesting that the term was used mostly by the hostile critics of socialism. It is true that 'Tory socialist' was originally a term of abuse applied to those Conservatives whose humanitarian feelings had enticed them along those paths which seemed to lead straight to Radicalism.[13] But the Radicals themselves frankly admitted, or one might almost say proudly proclaimed, that their programme was compounded of socialism. To Dicey the 1885 programme was merely moving 'in the direction of socialism',[14] but Joseph Chamberlain, its principal author, was more emphatic. The aim of the radicals was, he said, a government 'in which all shall co-operate in order to secure to every man his natural rights, his right to existence, and to a fair enjoyment of it. I shall be told tomorrow that this is Socialism . . . of course it is Socialism. The Poor Law is Socialism; the Education Act is Socialism; the greater part of the municipal work is Socialism; and every kindly act of legislation, by which the community has sought to discharge its responsibilities and obligations to the poor, is Socialism; but it is none the worse for that'.[15]

The thinking behind this statement is confused, but the sentiment and the intention are clear. It was becoming necessary to assert a belief in the responsibility of government for the welfare of the people and to deny to the official socialists any monopoly of good intentions by borrowing their name and rendering it innocuous. Hubert Bland, the Fabian, put the point very clearly in his comment on the famous utterance of a leading Liberal. 'Why does that extremely well oiled and accurately poised weathercock, Sir William Harcourt, pointing to the dawn, crow out that "we are all Socialists now"?' And his answer to his own question was that no politician could address a political meeting at that time without making some reference 'of a socialist sort to the social problem'.[16] Naturally this kind of talk angered the socialists proper, because it obscured the real nature of the conflict of opinion. They were not at war with Tory socialists or radical socialists, and were even prepared to support them when they agreed on particular measures. But they were the implacable enemies of the traditional Liberalism of the nineteenth century, the Liberalism of Gladstone and *laissez-faire*. And they thought, and hoped, that it was dying.

In 1889 the *Nineteenth Century* published a symposium of articles on the 'Liberal Collapse'. 'The Liberal Party', wrote Sidney Low, 'is once more in trouble about its soul', and Keir Hardie and Ramsay MacDonald, speaking for the Independent Labour Party, explained what the trouble was. Liberalism had assumed that 'the man politically enfranchised would be economically free; but experience was proving that the hope was thoroughly false, and Liberalism had nothing else to put in its place'.[17] And three years later Sidney Webb returned to this theme in the same journal. Gladstonian Liberalism, he said, was extinct because it had an 'atomic conception of society'. 'Its worship of individual liberty evokes no enthusiasm. Its reliance on "freedom of contract" and "supply and demand" . . . now seems to work out disastrously for the masses', because they lack the means to make their demand effective even for the minimum conditions of well-being. The freedom which the ordinary man now wants 'is not individual but corporate freedom'.[18]

But, though Gladstonian Liberalism might be defunct, a new Liberalism was arising which, under the leadership of Asquith, Lloyd

George, and Winston Churchill, was destined to carry social policy forward on the first stage of its journey towards the welfare state. It accepted fully that common element in the new outlook which Chamberlain and others called 'socialist'. Churchill, in 1906, declared that 'the fortunes and the interests of Liberalism and Labour are inseparably interwoven; they rise from the same forces'. And he urged his followers not to be discouraged if some old woman came along and told them their measures were 'socialistic'. He even admitted that 'the whole tendency of civilization is . . . towards the multiplication of the collective functions of society', but he insisted nevertheless that the Liberalism he championed was in essence the very antithesis of socialism, because Liberalism wanted only to humanize the system of free enterprise, whereas socialism would destroy it.[19] By 1906 the question was no longer whether the state was responsible for the welfare of the masses, instead of merely for the relief of the destitute. This was generally agreed, and after all the masses now had the vote. The problem was to decide on the extent of the responsibility and above all on the means by which it should be discharged. And here consensus ended and political conflict began. And when we look more closely at the clash of opinions we shall see that the issues raised were fundamentally the same then as they are now.

We can identify three main schools of thought. First there is the genuine socialist school. This starts from the belief that the 'capitalist system' of private enterprise and a free market economy is inefficient and unjust. It is a kind of anarchy that should be replaced by a rational order of things planned and directed by the political power. In such an order, not only would the normal needs of everybody be met automatically by the operation of the system itself, but many of the needs that now clamour for satisfaction would no longer exist, since their cause – primarily poverty, squalor, and insanitary conditions of life – would be eliminated. Social progress, therefore, should be marked by a reduction, not an increase, in the special social services which are extraneous and supplementary to the working of the social and economic system itself.

This was the line of thought pursued at first by the Fabians. They had so much faith in the efficiency of a socialist economy that they paid little attention to social policy as such. They thought that under socialism, most of our social problems would disappear. Sidney Webb, looking back in 1920 at those early pioneering days of simple enthusiasm, admitted that he and his friends had behaved 'as if society were, or ought to be, composed entirely of healthy adults, free from accidents and exempt, if not from death, at any rate from senility'.[20] This is, no doubt, a piece of deliberate self-parody, but it is true that Graham Wallas, in his chapter in the original *Fabian Essays*, had dismissed very lightly the whole question of those who, in a social society, would be unable to provide for themselves. 'There would always remain the sick, and infirm, and the school children, whose wants would be satisfied from the general stock without asking them to bear any part of the general burden.'[21] The essential thing was to socialize the system itself.

The second school of thought was the most strongly represented at the time. Its adherents admitted that the economic system left many needs unsatisfied and distributed its rewards inequitably, but held that in the purely economic tasks of production and distribution of goods it was superior to anything else that might be put in its place. They therefore did not wish to see any drastic change in the system. But, since they believed that the system could not cure its social defects itself, they recognized the responsibility and the right of the state to interfere and compulsorily to modify and supplement its operations. For the members of this school of thought, therefore, the first task of the twentieth century was to extend the social services and increase what Churchill called the 'collective functions' of society, until the ideal balance between private enterprise and public provision and control was attained. The outstanding examples of this approach to the problem are the radical programme of 1885 and the Liberal programme of 1906.

The third school of thought was of less importance, because its influence was declining. It was that of those Conservatives who thought that there was nothing seriously wrong with the economic system and that the main concern of government should be to see that it had every facility and encouragement to continue its good work. If everybody worked hard, cared for their children, and saved up for sickness and old age, the volume of cases requiring, and deserving, outside help would be small. Public social services, except for a strictly administered Poor Law, were likely to diminish the incentive to work and save. Therefore it would be best to leave as much as possible of the welfare work to the voluntary agencies. This was the basic philosophy of the Charity Organisation Society, the most important voluntary agency of the time. It rested on the belief that England was a rich and prosperous country, and that, where wealth abounded, poverty must be unnecessary. Mrs Bosanquet, a leading exponent of the doctrine, asserted that all who were not genuinely incapable of work should be held responsible for their own maintenance and that of their dependent relatives. It may be asked, she said, 'what if the social conditions will not permit them to meet the responsibility?' And her answer was – 'It is a vain and idle hypothesis. The social conditions *will* permit them.'[22]

These three points of view are deeply rooted in the very nature of modern society and the issues they raise have therefore remained alive to this day, though in a setting that has gradually changed. The dividing line between the first and the second – the 'revolutionary' and the 'reformist' – came to fall, not between the socialists and the rest, but within the socialist movement itself. On the one hand were those who continued to maintain that the only policy acceptable to socialism was one that aimed at the elimination of the capitalist system. Social welfare measures were merely palliatives, which sapped the strength of the attack on capitalism. On the other side were those who became increasingly interested in, and favourable to, social legislation that humanized the capitalist system without overthrowing it.

The second point of view, which favoured welfare measures, was of course held also by many non-socialists; by radicals in general and by those Liberals who had escaped from the strait-jacket of nineteenth-century dogmatism. They had been given a lead by the distinguished economist Stanley Jevons, who argued in favour of judging practical issues on their merits and not by appealing to the authority of some doctrine. 'In social philosophy', he wrote, 'or rather in practical legislation, the first step is to throw aside all supposed absolute rights or inflexible principles', even the principles of liberty and property. 'I conceive', he continued, 'that the State is justified in passing any law, or even in doing any single act which, without ulterior consequences, adds to the sum total of happiness.'[23] The view was also held by many Conservatives for humanitarian reasons, and by some, perhaps, for the rather more subtle reason given by Arthur Balfour. 'Social legislation, as I conceive it', he said, 'is not merely to be distinguished from Socialist legislation, but it is its most direct opposite and its most effective antidote.'[24]

The third point of view carried diminishing weight as the social policy of the twentieth century developed, but it reappeared in a modified form as a result of the alleged arrival on the scene of the Affluent Society. It was argued that amid so much affluence poverty could be only an exceptional phenomenon, and that now it really was possible (as Mrs Bosanquet wrongly believed it to be half a century earlier) for all but a few to win for themselves all the amenities of a civilized existence. However, in the 1970s and the 1980s the view that social policy interventions distorted the workings of the economy once again came to be put forward with a vigour and a conviction not seen for a century: hostile critics talked of the Thatcher government attempting to put the clock back to the 1930s, or to 1904, or some other date before the Liberal social reforms. Ironically this resurgence in pre-Keynesian beliefs was a response to a crisis in British economic performance not so different from that which had troubled sensitive thinkers at the turn of the century.

3 The problem of poverty

It is not surprising that most countries of the Western world should have felt, towards the end of the nineteenth century, that their methods of dealing with poverty were in urgent need of revision. The new information which was being accumulated revealed not only the true magnitude of the problem but also the great heterogeneity of the company of paupers. Where the Poor Law had been for centuries the only public agency for giving assistance to the helpless and destitute, as well as 'correcting' the idle and insubordinate, it had become a multi-purpose affair without having developed a variety of methods corresponding to the variety of cases with which it had to deal. The relief of poverty, too, was a field of action in which both public and voluntary bodies were active, often with a fairly equal distribution of responsibility between the two. And the public authorities concerned were mostly local ones. Thus there was a need both to co-ordinate the services and to standardize the procedures of the various agencies, and this was particularly necessary where urbanization was changing the nature of the problems and making some of the old methods of dealing with them obsolete.

In facing this task Britain suffered more acutely than any other country from the unhappy legacy of its nineteenth-century system. Nowhere else could you find quite the same combination of harsh deterrent principles, centralized policy control, and administration by an isolated authority, detached from the normal organs of local government, specializing in the treatment of paupers and nothing but paupers, and functioning in regions peculiar to itself. The Poor Law Guardians lacked both the incentive to modify and humanize the ideas which the central government obtained from the contemplation of its overall responsibilities, and also the personal touch that one might expect to find in true representatives of a neighbourhood. In fact it was precisely because the parish authorities had been too weak or too fearful to check the spread of indiscriminate relief in the early years of the century that the Poor Law Guardians and their unions had been invented in 1834. Although in most countries of the Western world there had at one time been a tendency to lump rogues, vagabonds, and paupers together in a single category, and to treat them all in semi-penal institutions, the concept of pauperism as both an inferior and a shameful status persisted longer and penetrated more deeply into the public mind in England than elsewhere. It was kept alive, and deliberately reinforced, by the bureaucratic machinery created to translate it into action.

The situation was different in countries where the dominating influences were those of voluntary and charitable bodies, especially the churches, or of the accepted leaders of local communities. In France, for example, the protagonists in the story were the church and the commune. It had been declared by Louis XIV that the estates of the church were the patrimony of the poor, and ideas about poverty were still coloured by this tradition. The central government recognized that the secular power and initiative in this matter should be located in the commune. At this level there was an Office of Charity (*Bureau de Bienfaisance*), usually headed by the mayor. It was described as the 'representative' of the poor, and it alone was authorized to receive gifts and legacies on their behalf. This notion of 'representation' of the poor was inimical to the concept of poverty as a degradation, but it was entirely in harmony with the principle that all relief was a kind of charity. Another circumstance favouring a higher status for the paupers than in Britain was the acceptance of the rule that relief should be given in the home, whenever possible, which is almost exactly the reverse of the British practice. The idea was that, if the pauper remained at home, his relatives would care for him; if he was put into an institution, they would wash their hands of all responsibility.[1] We find the same principle adopted later in the Scandinavian countries.[2]

Debates about the problem of poverty in twentieth-century Britain revolved around the notion of 'the break-up of the Poor Law', a phrase popularized by the Webbs to denote the recommendations of the Minority Report of the Poor Law Commission of 1909. But, though the phrase may have been invented by the Webbs, they did not originate the process, which had been going on with gathering force throughout the Western world for some years before the Commission came into existence. It did not, however, at that time aim, as the Webbs did, at the total dissolution of the Poor Law and the authorities that administered it. The purpose of the movement was to provide special services for distinct categories, and to do this outside the ambit of the Poor Law. The categories of persons who were being gradually extracted from the heterogeneous company of paupers were the children, the old, the sick, and the unemployed.

The case for the special treatment of children was an obvious one and had long been recognized in most countries by the provision made for their education and for their exclusion from, or protection in, industrial employment. Measures of this kind applied to all children, whether paupers or not, though the education of paupers might be given, as it often was in Britain, in special pauper schools. At the same time steps were being taken by the Poor Law authorities to get children out of pauper institutions by boarding them out in families or putting them in cottage homes or entrusting them to voluntary organizations. These practices were encouraged in Britain by the strong recommendations made by Mrs Nassau Senior in her report to the Local Government Board in 1873.[3] The combined effect of these two lines of development was to build up the status of children as a special category among paupers, even when they remained technically in the care of the Poor Law. To them must be added the important legislation which initiated the school medical service in 1907 and authorized local authorities to provide meals for school children in 1906. These were clearly seen as an encroachment by the education authorities on the preserves of the Poor Law and were therefore the most definite moves in the direction of its 'break-up' so far as children were concerned.

At the turn of the century most countries of the Western world suffered from a guilty conscience about the aged poor. In Britain a whole series of commissions and committees were set up to study the problem, and a survey made for the government in 1899, with a supplement in 1908, described the action taken in Russia, Norway, Sweden, Denmark, Germany, Holland, Belgium, France, Italy, Austria, Romania, and New Zealand.[4] We shall be concerned with the results of this awakening interest in old people in the next chapter. The point to be noted here is that by the end of the nineteenth century it was universally agreed that respectable, 'deserving' old people, who had worked while they could and were now without means, should not be treated as paupers. But the only action that had been taken in Britain by 1900 was to instruct Guardians not to force such people into the workhouse, and to see that the relief given them in their homes was adequate to their needs.[5]

As regards the sick, it had for some time been noticed in Britain that the services rendered to the paupers by the District Medical Officer, the poor Law Dispensary, and the Poor Law Infirmary were not very different from those offered to the general public by the Medical Officer of Health and the municipal and voluntary hospitals. The government had recognized the special character of medical relief and treatment by enacting, in 1885, that its receipt through the Poor Law should not carry the stigma of disfranchisement; this implied that the sick poor were not necessarily to be regarded as paupers. It went on, a few years later, to state officially that it had no objection to the Poor Law Infirmaries being used as general hospitals for ordinary citizens, when no other equivalent facilities were available. As in the case of school meals and the school medical service, some of the Guardians saw this as an encroachment on their preserves, and complained that it blurred the distinction between the pauper and the independent citizen. In Manchester, in order to keep this distinction alive, they instructed their officers when speaking of Poor Law institutions for the sick 'to avoid the word "hospital" or "infirmary", and simply to use the word "workhouse"'.[6]

The fourth distinct type of poverty was that caused by unemployment. We have already seen how sharply public attention had been drawn to this in the 1880s and how substantial were the emergency relief funds raised by voluntary subscription. The first clear indication of a new official attitude came when Chamberlain, at the Local Government Board, issued a circular in 1886 to local authorities and Boards of Guardians urging the former to utilize voluntary funds to set to work unemployed men referred to them by the latter. The wording of the circular is significant. The men selected by the Guardians were to be those whom 'it is undesirable to send to the workhouse or to treat as subjects for pauper relief', and they were to be given 'work which shall not involve the stigma of pauperism'.[7] Chamberlain's successor, Walter Long, revived this policy and prepared a bill which became the Unemployed Workmen's Act of 1905. This rendered obligatory in towns of over 50,000 inhabitants what till then had been only permissible. The task was to be undertaken by Distress Committees representing the Councils and the Guardians; but the act was a failure. The experience showed that temporary work could not confer any permanent benefit.

Such, in brief, were the trends leading towards the break-up of the Poor Law which were visible at the beginning of the new century, and they were common to the Western world as a whole. Even in the United States, where the resistance of the States to Federal interference in domestic matters and the passionate belief in individual liberty combined to check the development of social legislation, the same tendency was noted by those devoted to the cause of social welfare. One of these observed that 'the movement to analyse the relief load and to substitute for a general assistance programme appropriate provision for certain groups or categories was making real headway before the war',[8] that is to say the First World War. And we must also bear in mind that, already in the 1880s, Bismarck had initiated in Germany the first programme of compulsory social insurance, covering sickness, invalidity, and old-age pensions, and had thus introduced the world to what was destined to be the principal alternative to the Poor Law as a means of maintaining the personal incomes of those unable to earn.

The Royal Commission on the Poor Laws and Relief of Distress was appointed by the Conservative government in 1905, shortly before it fell, and reported to the Liberal government in 1909. Its creators intended it, we are told, to suggest administrative improvements which might make it easier to keep the 'principles of 1834' in operation. But it issued two reports, the more conservative of which (the Majority Report) recommended a substantial modification of those principles, while the more radical Minority Report called loudly for their total rejection. Both reports delved deeply into matters of policy concerning every social problem in which poverty was a factor, and made a host of practical proposals about all of them. But the immediate effect of their labours on policy was very small indeed. The Liberal government had planned most of its social programme, and already put part of it (old-age pensions) into effect before the reports appeared. In fact it was not until March 1911, we are told, that Lloyd George began to read the reports. By then he was well on with the preparation of his National Insurance Bill and, since both reports were opposed to compulsory social insurance against sickness and unemployment, they could not help him very much.[9] Nevertheless the two reports are historical documents of great importance. They give us a picture of informed opinion on the major social problems of the day, and they present most of the arguments that were being advanced for and against new proposals current at the time. In addition the Minority Report, written by Beatrice Webb with the able off-stage help of her husband, planted an idea in the minds of British politicians which was first translated into action when the Poor Law Guardians were abolished in 1929, and finally triumphed – or appeared to do so – when Parliament passed the National Assistance Act (1948) with its opening sentence – the 'existing poor law shall cease to have effect'.

The two reports of the Commission had much in common, as the Webbs admitted. They listed the points of agreement, which included the transfer of the administration of the Poor Law to the ordinary local authorities, the abolition of the general mixed workhouse, the abandonment of the principle of deterrence, the adoption of preventive and curative measures in addition to palliatives (or mere relief), the extension of the public medical services, and the introduction of old-age pensions and some kind of facilities for insurance against unemployment.[10] As a matter of fact they were somewhat over-generous to the Majority. For these, while rejecting deterrence in its old form, with its associations of 'harshness and still more of hopelessness', favoured a mild kind of 'less eligibility' even for the aged, and they did not want medical treatment to be 'so attractive that it may become a species of honourable self-indulgence'.[11] Their view on unemployment insurance was the same as that of the Minority. They recognized very clearly the need for more insurance than was as yet provided by the trade unions and other voluntary bodies, but they were opposed to a compulsory scheme, mainly because of the very unequal distribution of the risk among the various occupations. So they recommended the encouragement of voluntary insurance by state subsidies.[12] Pensions for the old and incapacitated worried them a lot, as their instinct was to rely on personal savings. But the evidence was too strong. They expressed their final view in the rather odd sentence – 'we almost seem driven to the conclusion that a new form of insurance is required, which, for want of a better name, we may call Invalidity Insurance', but they left it to others to work out a plan.[13] They said it should be contributory, unlike the scheme just enacted by Parliament, and one must assume that they meant it to be compulsory. The Minority, on the other hand, wanted a more generous non-contributory scheme for pensions at the age of 65.[14]

There were two major points of disagreement between the two groups. The first concerned the respective roles of the state and the voluntary agencies. The Majority wanted the latter to be the front line of the attack on poverty, with the public service following behind and taking care of the cases with which voluntary action could not deal. And public assistance was to be deliberately made less attractive than voluntary assistance. The Minority objected strongly to these proposals on two grounds. First, because they held that full responsibility for policy and its execution must rest on the public authority, which should make use of voluntary helpers and the voluntary agencies as it thought fit. This reflected the Fabian belief in the virtues of scientific planning at the centre. Second, they could not accept the principle of discrimination between the deserving poor, who would be the charge of the voluntary agencies, and the less deserving, who would be passed on to the Guardians or their successors. This savoured too much of the attitude characteristic of what Beatrice Webb called 'my friend the enemy – the Charity Organisation Society – one of the most typical of mid-Victorian offsprings'.[15]

The second point of disagreement was more fundamental. While both groups favoured the extension of the special public services for the care of the old, the sick, the children, and the unemployed, the Majority believed that there would always remain a residual class of destitute persons who could only be looked after by a destitution authority, which they proposed to re-name the 'Public Assistance Committee'. It would not only distribute relief in cash or kind, but would provide for all the needs of those entrusted to its guardianship. The Minority maintained that if the public services were properly developed there would be no such residue, and it would be possible to get rid of both the separate category of pauper and the destitution authority. There would be only a temporary and miscellaneous collection of 'omitted cases' deposited through the meshes of the administrative net, which could be disposed of by an official whom they proposed to call the Registrar of Public Assistance, because he would also keep a record of all those receiving assistance of any kind from public funds.

The issues raised here are so vital to our subject that we must look carefully into them and see what arguments were, or could be, advanced in support of the two opposed points of view. It is best to begin with the Minority, because their motives are easier to identify. They had three main reasons for wishing to dispense with a destitution authority. The first sprang from the determination of the Webbs to apply scientific principles to social administration. It was unscientific to treat the poor as an operational category, since poverty was of many different kinds and resulted from many different causes. Scientific administration would split up this heterogeneous mass for purposes of treatment into its distinct component parts.

Second, they maintained that social policy should never be satisfied merely to relieve distress; its primary aim must be to prevent it and, failing that, to cure it. A destitution authority could never prevent distress, and could rarely cure it, because it could only touch those who were already destitute; and even the destitute often tried to evade its clutches as long as possible, for fear of the stigma its assistance carried with it. And their third reason was that a destitution authority that catered for all the needs of those entrusted to its care would duplicate the general public services in a wasteful and inefficient way, as indeed the Poor Law services for the children and the sick were already doing.

The Minority envisaged a widely ranging system of public services, co-ordinated at the local level by the Registrar of Public Assistance. For 'public assistance' for them had nothing to do with the relief of the poor as such, but referred to every kind of benefit offered to any class of person by a public agency financed (apart from what the recipients might pay) from public funds. It included, as they explained, the case of the paying patient in the County Lunatic Asylum, of the poor man's wife receiving milk at a nominal charge, of the County Bursary to Oxford, and of compulsory admission to an industrial school.[16] They were not offering everything for nothing, nor did they shrink from the need to empower those administering the services to discipline the unruly. The unemployed man, for instance, who could not at once be placed by a Labour Exchange, would be assigned to a training establishment, and for the 'industrial malingerer', who kept coming back for relief after he had been given several chances of work, there would be 'judicial commitment to a Detention Colony'.[17] This was the alternative the Minority preferred to the mass assignment of the undeserving to an inferior category and an inferior status, and it was one with its own characteristic brand of harshness.

The Majority were, no doubt, influenced by the natural inclination to cling to the familiar. A dozen of them had been personally active either in the public service or the voluntary agencies and might be expected to defend what they believed to be good in them. It must also be remembered that a proposal to transfer Poor Law functions to the general public services was a proposal to put your faith in what did not yet exist, or what was in the process of being created while the Commission was sitting. When they began their debates there were no old-age pensions, no health insurance, no unemployment insurance, few homes for the aged (except for the workhouses), few general hospitals under public control (except for the infirmaries); the treatment of mental defectives was in its infancy and was being studied by another Commission; free meals for poor school children as offered in London, were a novelty regarded with suspicion (until the Act of 1906); Care Committees under the education authorities were only just beginning to appear; the powers to deal with cruel or negligent parents were quite inadequate (until improved by the Children Act of 1908). The picture drawn by the Minority, or rather by the Webbs, was in fact a brilliant anticipation of the eventual results of a movement which had only just started and of which they sensed the nature, except for their rejection of the instrument of compulsory social insurance.

It is not surprising that the Majority should believe that the residue of cases left untended by the specialized public services would be, at least for a long time to come, a large and unimportant one, and that consequently there must continue to be a general assistance agency to deal with them. When one asks what would be the common characteristics of these cases, one comes to the crux of the matter. And here it is best not to try to establish what actually were the motives that influenced the minds of the Majority but rather to see what their proposals seemed to imply.

One of the most common characteristics was, of course, extreme poverty. But there was another, closely associated with it, which we might call helplessness, and the Majority were much concerned about this more personal factor. It must be interpreted as covering not only the old, sick, feeble-minded, feckless, idle, and (if children) neglected, but also the incorrigibles who were apparently incapable of living a decent life but were not criminals. All these needed something more than cash benefits, because poverty was not their only problem, and also something more than a specialized service, because their trouble was aggravated by poverty. They were cases, it might be argued, where it was necessary, either for their own benefit or in the public interest or both, that somebody should take charge of their lives. The Majority made it clear that the authority accepting this responsibility should try, not merely to relieve their distress, but also to overcome their helplessness. They also made it clear that even if helplessness were a common characteristic of these cases, they must also be poor. They did not wish the public assistance authority to extend its range of activities beyond those afflicted by poverty. But they proposed a certain enlargement of the definition of the class eligible for assistance by suggesting that it be described as 'necessitous' instead of 'destitute'.[18]

The Majority were also much concerned that the family, in which several different factors might be at work to produce distress, should be treated as a unit. It was a part of the ancient tradition of the Poor Law in Britain and elsewhere that it should deal with families, and not merely with individuals; hence the basic principle, dating from Elizabethan times, that the resources of the family must be taken into account in deciding whether poor relief should be given and, if so, how much. It is true that this principle had some bad consequences, such as the practice of treating the whole family as paupers if the head became a pauper. But it also had its good side, potentially at least, since welfare work is most effective if based upon the family unit. This was coming to be recognized by the voluntary agencies to which the Majority wished to assign so important a role. They were developing the techniques of 'family case-work', which came to be one of the most highly esteemed forms of social work in the mid twentieth century. The Minority's plan, with its reliance on specialized services for different individual needs, would, said its critics, militate against family-based welfare work. The Webbs were aware of this criticism, and tried to answer it in a long footnote in one of their books. It might be objected, they said, that in 'directing attention to the fact that it is always an individual who is attacked, not, at first, the family as a whole', they were ignoring the case of families which were 'as whole families, in a state of destitution'. Their reply was that 'each member of such a family requires, for restoration, specialized treatment according to his or her need'.[19] But this really missed the point. It was not only a question of what we should now call 'problem families' but also the much wider one of treating all individual cases with due attention to their family setting. And the fear that the specialized services might fail to do this was not groundless. It is generally agreed that the most glaring defects of the policy of the next few decades was the failure to help parents of large families (by family allowances) and the failure to provide medical care for the families of insured persons.

But all this does not necessarily lead to the conclusion that the old Poor Law Guardians had to be preserved under a new name. What was there about them that the Majority considered to be so indispensable? Was it, perhaps, precisely the fact that they were not a 'service'? A public service is run by public servants who minister to the needs of those who are ultimately, though very indirectly, their masters, and who have the right to demand what the public servants are there to supply. But the person for whom a guardian cares is not his master, but his ward. And a ward is placed, or places himself, in the hands of his guardian, who accepts the responsibility of making decisions on his behalf. Thus the 'wards in poverty', as we might call the paupers, had no clear-cut right to demand any particular benefits or attentions from the Poor Law Guardians. The guarantee that their needs would be met rested, not on their right to insist, but on the Guardian's obligation to provide. The only difference between this and charity was that the obligations of the Guardians were legal and those of the purveyors of charity, moral or religious. It was this relationship of dependence, or of ward to guardian, that the Majority appear to have considered necessary for the proper treatment of the 'necessitous', and it was precisely this feature of public assistance that the Minority most intensely disliked and wished to abolish.

What we have touched on here is the whole question of the role and the organization of welfare services in modern society and in particular their relationship with services for the relief of poverty. The British Poor Law had the functions, but not the spirit, of a welfare service, and the authors of the Minority Report were quite right in urging that it must be uprooted. But when the 'break-up' for which they had campaigned eventually took place, it was found, as we shall see later, that in the process something had disappeared which it was necessary to re-create in a new form. The consequence was that in Britain, unlike most other countries, welfare and the relief of poverty were placed in separate administrative compartments, and we shall in due course be concerned to explore the advantages and disadvantages of this solution of a very difficult problem.

When the reports appeared, the Webbs launched a nationwide campaign in support of their plan for the 'break-up of the Poor Law', but, as they later admitted, it was a failure. The changes which actually took place at that time amounted to little more than a chipping away of the fringes of the Poor Law, accompanied by a certain humanization of the services retained within it. But a new note was struck by the Liberal leaders after their spectacular victory in the 1906 election. They spoke as the heralds of a new age of social reform, and insisted that their programme, though necessarily introduced piece by piece, was an integral whole whose total effect would be of momentous importance. It was, said Churchill in 1908, a programme that 'marks the assertion of an entirely new principle in regard to poverty; and the principle, once asserted, cannot possibly be confined within existing limits'.[20] He could not know that he would live to see it culminate some forty years later in the creation of the welfare state.

4 The coming of social insurance

It was during the first forty years of the twentieth century that compulsory social insurance was generally adopted by the countries of the Western world as one of the main instruments of social policy. Voluntary social insurance had, of course, been practised by Friendly Societies and various kinds of industrial and social clubs for a very long time. Schemes of this kind were often supported by government subsidies and made to conform to regulations imposed by law to ensure their sound administration. In the case of certain classes of workers, such as miners and seamen, regulation by government was common, and Prussia had made the insurance of miners compulsory as early as 1854. But the first decisive step in the establishment of compulsory social insurance on a more general basis was taken by Bismarck in the 1880s. By 1910 it was possible for two American observers to write that 'in all countries of Europe the beginnings are readily discernible of a movement towards a complete and connected system under which working-men will be insured against all contingencies where support from wages is lost or interrupted by any cause other than voluntary cessation of labour'.[1] But, though the principle was universally accepted, it was not used in the same way by all countries, and 'complete and connected' systems did not appear everywhere quite as soon as these authors expected.

Compulsory social insurance was a novelty in three respects. It involved a new kind of interference in the affairs of industry, a new type of relationship between the citizen and the government, and new problems of finance and administration. When introduced by Bismarck it had the character of a request to industry to join with him in making concessions to meet the legitimate claims of the workers, in order to make it easier both for him and for it to resist their illegitimate ones. But as presented by an aggressive figure like Lloyd George it had more the character of an attack, not against industrialists personally, but against the capitalist economy of the nineteenth century and against the 'establishment' which had tolerated its inhumanity. 'No one', he said, 'can honestly defend the present system.' Side by side with great wealth there were multitudes who were not assured of even a bare subsistence. And the Liberal government aimed at something more than subsistence, namely at an income large enough to maintain efficiency for every man, woman, and child. 'The individual demands it, the State needs it, humanity cries for it, religion insists upon it.'[2] But the economy did not provide it; hence the need for the political power, backed by morality and religion, to interfere and make good the defect.

There is a curious passage in the Majority Report of the Poor Law Commission on this point. They were discussing the need for pensions, and they said: 'the evidence shows that, with very few exceptions, what working-men desire is the "cash nexus" – the bare wage contract uninfluenced by any but purely economic considerations – and the employing classes generally have accepted the situation and consider their obligations fulfilled when they pay the wage'. Most wages, they added, were fixed by collective bargaining, and the result was a 'maximum wage during the prime of life, and no wage at all when the prime is passed'.[3] They were quite right to describe the wage system in this way, but one wonders where they found the evidence that the working men wished it to be so. It does not appear in the appendices to their report, and it is in conflict with what many labour leaders were saying when they denounced a system that treated labour as a commodity. But the passage brings out clearly the exact way in which compulsory insurance interfered in the affairs of industry. It inserted something into the relationship between the employer and employed which was not just the cash nexus; it interfered with the contract of employment, the very keystone of the free market economy, by writing into it a new mutual obligation. The contributions paid by and on behalf of the insured workman, and the benefits he earned thereby, became an integral part of his status as an employee.

Compulsory insurance also created a kind of contractual relationship between the insured and the state, which was a new political phenomenon. The benefits were due, as specified, because the contributions had been paid, and the government was a party to the contract, being responsible for its terms and for their faithful fulfilment. It was thought that this contractual element in social insurance would prevent it from becoming the plaything of party politics. Governments, out of respect for the sanctity of contract, would not feel free either to cut the benefits in the interest of economy or to increase them in a bid for votes. But in the event mass unemployment between the wars and then the fall in the value of money made constant revision of the terms of insurance necessary, affecting the rights and obligations of those already in the scheme as well as new entrants, so that hardly any subject was more constantly at the centre of political strife. It was also believed that the beneficiaries would be happy to feel that they had won their benefits by their own action (even though they had no choice in the matter), while appreciation of the fact that larger benefits must mean larger contributions would put the brake on extravagant demands.

This emphasis on the binding, contractual character of social insurance had some subtle and probably unforeseen effects. It led people to exaggerate the distinction between social insurance and social assistance, and helped to maintain the flavour of inferiority and shame that clung to the latter. Second it caused, or at least was accompanied by, a widespread misunderstanding of the nature of social insurance which bedevilled discussions of social policy for many years. And this brings us to the new problems of finance and administration that social insurance brought with it.

The prominence given to the term 'insurance', with all its associations of security, respectability, and virtuous providence, implied that the schemes were modelled on the current practice of insurance companies. Friendly Societies and others engaged in similar operations. But this was true only to a very limited extent even at the beginning, and it became less true as time went on, as Beveridge explained very clearly in his report.[4]

In private insurance the income consists of the premiums paid by policy-holders and the interest on accumulated funds. The premiums are assessed in relation to the risks covered, by a process of actuarial calculation. The same terms are offered to those exposed to the same risk, but anyone whose circumstances raise the risk above the average is required to pay a higher premium. The tubercular must pay more for life insurance than the healthy, or 'good-life'. The policy-holder can, therefore, claim that he is paying the true price of the coverage he receives, and if the price seems too high, he is free to take it or leave it. With public social insurance the position is different. If the state makes insurance compulsory for a large section of the community, it has a responsibility towards the insured greater than that of a private company, just because they are not free to 'take it or leave it'. The terms enforced must be such as they can afford to meet and the benefits must bear some relation to their real needs. The only way in which they can protest against terms which they consider unfair is by political action, through Parliament; consequently the fixing of the terms is primarily a political decision and only secondarily an actuarial one. The state can accept this responsibility because it is free to diverge from the strict actuarial principles of commercial insurance. And it enjoys this freedom because it has the power to draw on money other than the subscriptions of the beneficiaries; it can compel their employers to contribute and it can transfer sums from public revenue to the insurance fund. The ultimate guarantee of the solvency of any public scheme is the power of the state to levy taxes.

The part played by the state, and the nature and basis of the rights acquired by the citizen, differ according to the purpose of the insurance and the kind of risk it is designed to cover. A special position was occupied from the beginning by measures for the compensation of workmen for industrial injury, because they involve the legal liability of the employer. British law originally recognized a claim by the workman only where there was proof of negligence on the part of the employer or (by the Act of 1880) of one of his employees. But the Workmen's Compensation Act of 1897 brought British practice into line with that on the continent of Europe by accepting the principle of 'occupational risk'. This meant that it was not necessary to prove negligence, but only that the accident arose 'out of and in the course of the employment' – since the risk was inherent in the occupation – and the principle was extended in 1906 to certain industrial diseases.

But there are different steps which a government may take to ensure that the worker in fact receives the compensation due to him. In a majority of countries this aim was achieved by making it compulsory for employers to insure their employees, at their own expense, against occupational risks, either in a central state scheme or, as in Germany, in Mutual Associations set up for the purpose by the various industries, or (exceptionally) with such insurance companies as they chose. It followed that the injured worker received compensation, at standardized rates, as a benefit provided by a form of social insurance of which employers bore the cost. It is true that most British employers insured voluntarily, but this was not insurance of the workmen against occupational risk; it was insurance of the employer against his liability to meet such claims as he could not rebut. Consequently the injured workman had to establish his claim for compensation, not with an insurance policy, but against his employer,

if necessary in a court of law. It was not until after the Beveridge
Report that compensation for industrial injury was included among
the social insurance benefits.

In the case of other risks – old age, sickness, unemployment, etc. – it
was the potential beneficiary who was compulsorily insured, and
contributions were usually levied both on him and on his employer.
In some countries social insurance was treated as being fundamentally a bipartite affair, between employer and employed, with the
state only supporting the scheme from outside, as it were. Since it had
set it up and made it compulsory, the least it could do was to guarantee
its solvency. But it might go beyond this and contribute a lump sum
annually to the funds (as in France), or add a fixed amount to each
benefit paid out (as in Germany), or help to finance some special
branch of the scheme which was least able to be self-supporting. But
Britain, and some other countries, adopted a tri-partite system in
which employers, employed, and the state (or the taxpayer) are all
full partners, and all make regular contributions, though not
necessarily of the same amount. In British thinking this partnership
was not simply an administrative convenience, but a matter of
political principle, because it reflected truly the distribution of
responsibility in the society.

Whatever system was adopted, it is evident that social insurance
lacked the qualities that gave to private insurance its respected status
as an expression of personal thrift, since the contributions of the
beneficiaries were neither voluntary nor sufficient to cover the
benefits. But this did not prevent people, dazzled by the magic word
'insurance', from asserting that they had a right to their benefits
because they had paid for them. Or, rather less crudely, they might
claim that they had paid their fair share of the price. This was true,
provided that it was realized (as generally it was not) that their 'fair
share' was not something that an actuary could calculate, since he
could estimate only the total income needed to cover the risks. The
decision as to what proportion of that total should be charged to the
beneficiaries was a purely political one. The contribution of the
insured person should, in fact, be regarded, not as paying for the
benefits, but as qualifying to receive them, and the state is entirely free
to fix whatever qualifying conditions it may think desirable. And it
has generally fixed them, for political, fiscal, and psychological
reasons, in such a way as to create the appearance of some logical
relationship between contributions and benefits, although in fact
no relationship exists.

This is true in particular of statutory old age pensions to which it is peculiarly difficult to apply the principles of insurance in their classic form. For old age is not a misfortune which may fall at any time on any member of an insured population; it is a normal phase of life to which people can look forward and which they may hope to enjoy, and it comes to all, at the appointed time, provided they live long enough. So, whereas one *insures* against sickness or unemployment, one *saves* for old age, and the saving process must continue throughout one's working life. In the case of insurance against a risk, like sickness or a motor accident, what one draws out in return for a given premium depends on the extent of the damage suffered, and may be more than one had paid in; those on whom the misfortune falls benefit from the contributions of the lucky ones who escape it. And this is for the 'mutual benefit' of all, because all are equally protected against the risk. But in the case of saving for old age one can draw out, when the time comes, only what one has paid in together with the interest it has earned, and perhaps a share in the capital appreciation. This gives rise to special problems.

First, it is difficult to persuade people to keep up their payments continuously over a long period, so there is a strong case for compulsion. Second, the value of money may fall and make the pension, when eventually it falls due, quite inadequate. And third, when a new scheme is introduced, those who are already in middle life would, if they were allowed to join it, have to pay much larger premiums than younger men in order to earn the same pension. It is in order to overcome these difficulties that the state has so often found it necessary to 'boost the benefits' to a level above that which corresponds to the contributions made by, or on behalf of, the insured.

Voluntary insurance for old age had been practised for some time in most countries, but because of these difficulties the societies had run into trouble. In France there were so many cases of insolvency that in 1850 a ban was placed on private insurance for pensions, and public savings banks were set up instead to receive the contributions of individuals and of societies, and the state added a subvention to guarantee their stability. Belgium and Italy followed suit before the end of the century.[5] In Britain, although Gladstone had expressed alarm at the number of companies that failed and of policies that lapsed, and had established the Savings Bank and a Post Office insurance scheme for the benefit of small savers,[6] no proposal was made that private savings should be subsidized by the state until

Joseph Chamberlain put forward this idea in the 1890s. Its attraction for the Victorians was that the state would be helping only those who helped themselves; but it was pointed out that unfortunately the most urgent need was that of those who were far too poor to save anything at all. The suggestion was not adopted.[7]

By this time Germany had, in 1889, introduced a fully-fledged scheme of compulsory contributory insurance for pensions. It covered practically all wage-earners and other employees earning less than the equivalent of £100 a year, and it provided pensions for old age (at 70), for invalidity (i.e. permanent disability), and for widows and orphans. Employers and employees contributed equal amounts, and the state added a fixed sum to each pension. Both contributions and benefits were scaled to correspond to some extent to the level of earnings, the insured being divided for this purpose into five income classes, each with its own rates. German policy, in deciding that pensions should reflect economic inequalities, underlined the difference between insurance and assistance. In the former, the more you had the more you would receive (and also contribute), but in the latter, where a means test was used, the more you had the less you would be given.[8]

In spite of the German example, British opinion was on the whole opposed to a contributory pension scheme. The Minority Report of the Poor Law Commission had been emphatic on this point. 'The insuperable difficulties inherent in contributory schemes of Old Age Pensions', they said, had been expressed in the reports of previous commissions 'in a manner and with an authority that we take to be conclusive'.[9] Even Bismarck himself had not intended that the employees should be obliged to contribute towards their pensions.[10] But when the Act was passed he was no longer in power, and by then all the machinery for compulsory insurance had been created to deal with sickness and accidents, and could be used for pensions. Also, since the total pension (including the state subvention) was something between 2s. 6d. and 3s. a week, the contributions could be small.

There had been so much discussion in Britain about the needs of the aged poor that the Liberal government had to put pensions in the forefront of the programme it announced in 1906. But, argued Asquith when he introduced the bill, it was not possible to have a contributory scheme. In the first place the administrative machinery for this did not exist. Second, the immediate task was to save old people from falling into the clutches of the Poor Law, and a contributory scheme could not do that, because 'none of its benefits would come into actual enjoyment until after the lapse of twenty or more years'. Finally a regular insurance scheme would antagonize the private agencies already engaged in the business. The government had therefore prepared a non-contributory scheme, to be financed directly out of taxes. By caring for the needs of the old in this way they would make insurance against other risks much easier. But if pensions were not to be given as an insurance benefit there must be 'some kind of discrimination' by which to select the pensioners, and the possible criteria were age, means, status, and character. The qualifying age was to be 70, the qualifying income (for the full pension of 5s. a week) was fixed at £21 a year and the status was that of a British subject who had not suffered imprisonment during the last ten years and was not in receipt of poor relief. As to character, Asquith thought that the less said the better, but he was overruled and the act stated that the pensioner must have worked to the best of his ability to maintain himself and his family. In New Zealand, where a similar scheme had been introduced in 1898, the pensioner had to be 'of good character and have for five years preceding application led a sober and reputable life'; so great was the anxiety lest the stigma of pauperism be lifted from those who did not deserve to be free of it.[11]

We have examined two ways in which the state can, in its management of social insurance, deviate from the orthodox principles of commercial insurance – namely by participating in the basic contributions, and by 'boosting the benefits' above the actuarial level. A third method (to which we referred briefly above) may be called the 'pooling of risks'. It is best seen in health insurance and in unemployment insurance. While all health insurance schemes at this time included cash benefits to compensate for loss of income during sickness, their major task was to bring medical care to the insured. In the period we are considering the concern of the state with the health of the people was being extended from the environmental to the personal services. This was in part a result of the growing sense of public responsibility for the welfare of the citizen, but there were special reasons for it as well. The evidence that was being accumulated made it clear that, although it was certainly true that bad sanitation and slum conditions were a potent cause of sickness, it was undeniable that the inadequacy of the medical services for detecting and treating illness, and for teaching people how to look after their own health and that of their children, made things worse than they need have been. If steps were to be taken to provide the cost of medical service for a large part of the population, it was essential that thought should be given to the question of how that service should be organized. A start had been made in England with the school medical service, and there was a great interest in the possibility of fighting tuberculosis by individual treatment in special institutions. Professor Mackintosh in fact claimed that 'the cause of the tuberculous was the spearhead of the campaign for a personal service at the beginning of the century'.[12] And Lloyd George, when preparing his plans for health insurance, was deeply impressed by what Germany was doing for the tubercular.[13]

At the same time the Friendly Societies and clubs which provided medical treatment as an insurance benefit were in trouble, and this was true of many European countries. The doctors whom they employed complained that they were not paid enough, that they often had to provide the medicines themselves, and that they were being expected to treat, not only the insured persons, but their whole families, as well as many well-to-do people, who, they said, ought to come to them as private paying patients. In many places these disputes broke out into open warfare. As early as 1895 the *Lancet* had appointed a Special Commissioner to study the matter at home and abroad, and it published his reports under the general title of 'The Battle of the Clubs'. He had found, not only that there was much discontent in England, but also that 'the situation across the Channel is identical with what exists in Great Britain and Ireland'.[14] In Germany the conflict continued to rage between the doctors and the societies operating under the health insurance scheme. Each such society negotiated its own terms of service with the association of doctors, and one of the main points of contention was the principle of the 'free choice of doctor', which the societies were unwilling to concede. In Leipzig in 1904 mounting grievances drove the doctors to go on strike, and 'blackleg' labour of very dubious quality was brought in to take their place. After a settlement of a sort had been reached, the association of doctors closed its ranks and called on its members to 'accumulate a heavy war chest' in readiness for the next battle.[15] The German Act of 1911 did not exaggerate when it said that 'for many years keen dissensions have occurred between the doctors and the sickness insurance authorities, resulting in many places in bitter disputes and a state of open conflict'.[16]

It is perhaps not surprising that Lloyd George should have come to the conclusion that the voluntary societies must not be entrusted with the provision of medical care for the insured. But he decided to let them handle the cash benefits. Those that satisfied his conditions would be listed as 'Approved Societies' and authorized to seek the custom of those covered by the Act. The government would hand over to each Approved Society the appropriate proportion of the contributions received in respect of its clients, and the society would undertake to pay them the statutory benefits when they fell sick. We have here an example of the 'pooling of risks' in one of its forms. It was recognized that the state, when making insurance against sickness compulsory, could not discriminate, in the terms it offered between the sickly and the robust, or between those living in unhealthy conditions and those in healthy ones. These unequal risks must be 'pooled', even though it meant that some people would be getting what was by strict actuarial standards more for their money than others. But the government wanted nevertheless to preserve as much as possible of the spirit of voluntary, or commercial, insurance, and it allowed Approved Societies, if their finances permitted, to give additional benefits, such as medical appliances, dental and ophthalmic services, or extra cash. Some were able to do this, either because they were more efficiently managed than the average, or because they were extra careful in choosing their clients. They could not, of course, demand a higher premium from someone who was a 'bad risk', since the premium was fixed by law, but they could refuse to accept him. The result was that there was a considerable variation in the benefits obtained by the insured, although the contributions were the same for all.

For the general medical service the natural thing to do, one would have thought, was to entrust the organization to the local government authorities which were already in charge of public health, but the doctors were strongly opposed to this. They considered it essential, in the interests both of efficiency and of confidentiality, that the real control of the service should be in the hands of medically qualified persons, and they did not trust the local authorities to allow this. Their attitude on this point has not changed. They were even more strongly against a full-time salaried service run by the government, and they insisted that the patient must be free to choose his doctor. In their anxiety about what Lloyd George might do they threatened for a time to refuse co-operation, but the friction was largely due to the cavalier way in which he treated them during the negotiations. In principle they were with him, once he had made it clear that he accepted the three points just mentioned. So the service was organized by special Insurance Committees set up for the purpose, the patients could choose their own doctor, and the doctors who wanted to come into the scheme built up a panel of registered patients and were paid a capitation fee of so much for each patient on their register. The service was free, but it was confined to what an average general practitioner could be expected to give. It did not include specialist services, hospitalization, or dental and ophthalmic treatment and it did nothing for the dependants of the insured, which was a grave omission.

Governments had been much concerned about unemployment ever since the bad days of the 1880s, but their thinking had at first been directed more to finding ways to prevent or terminate it than to measures for making up lost earnings by cash benefits; the trade unions were doing that. The attempt to cure unemployment by getting the local authorities to create work for the unemployed was admitted by everybody to have failed. And little so far had come of plans to fit the unemployed for new jobs by passing them through training centres, though this idea was not dead and was revived after the war. More hope was placed in the device of the labour bureau, which had been imported from the continent and was showing some promise. It was one of the aims of the Unemployed Workmen Act of 1905 to establish a network of these bureaux, or labour exchanges, throughout the country, but it had achieved the purpose only in the London area. Nevertheless the results were significant enough for the Majority Report of the Poor Law Commission, when drawing up recommendations on unemployment, to begin with the sentence, 'in the forefront of our proposals we place labour exchanges', and the Minority agreed. In this case there is direct evidence of the influence of the Commission, because Churchill quoted this sentence when introducing the Act of 1909 which established a national system of labour exchanges under the direct control of the Board of Trade.[17] By 1914 they were filling just over a million vacancies,[18] but looking back on their history in 1930 William Beveridge, who had done so much to bring them into existence, found it disappointing; only one in five of the engagements of insured workpeople was made through the exchange.[19] They were, however, key points in the administrative structure of unemployment insurance.

The system of compulsory insurance against unemployment introduced in England in 1911 was the first of its kind, apart from a disastrous experiment in a Swiss canton. Everybody knew about the 'Ghent System' by which the municipality gave annual subventions to private schemes in order to increase the benefits, and France had launched the first national system on these lines in 1905, with Norway and Denmark following suit in the next two years. But even

Germany, the originator of compulsory insurance, had left unemployment out. It was not that there was any exceptional difficulty about
applying the insurance principle to unemployment in normal times.
On the contrary, one objection to a comprehensive state scheme was
that the principle was already being applied extensively and with
considerable success by the trade unions, and a state scheme might
interfere with their business.

But each scheme as a rule covered only one industry or occupation,
within which the risk of unemployment was of much the same kind
and magnitude for all. So the principle of 'mutual benefit' could be
applied. But a national scheme would have to include industries in
which the risk of unemployment differed widely, and the question was
how far the principle of the 'pooling of risks' could be carried. The bad
risks were not, as in sickness, individual cases, but whole sections of
the population to be insured. If contributions and benefits were the
same for all, the stable industries would subsidize the unstable, and
the efficient firms the inefficient. So the Liberal government decided
to keep the inequality of risks to be covered within bounds and to start
with a limited scheme confined to seven selected industries. These, as
Churchill explained, were industries in which 'the unemployment is
due not to a permanent contraction but to temporary oscillation in
their range of business, and that is the class of business in which
unemployment insurance is marked out as the scientific remedy for
unemployment'.[20] Some inequality of risk did exist among these
industries, but its effects were kept to a minimum by limiting the
number of weeks in any one year in which benefits could be drawn,
and consequently also the extent to which the contributions of one
industry might be called on to pay for the unemployment in another.
The scheme which was eventually embodied in Part II of the National
Insurance Act of 1911 covered about 2.5 million workers and was
financed by contributions from employers, employees, and the state.
For those not covered there remained the voluntary agencies, and the
Act provided for a small subvention to be available to help these by
adding one-sixth to the benefits they paid out of their funds. Beyond
this there was only the Poor Law.

Such were the beginnings of compulsory social insurance, and to
many people, including Winston Churchill, it marked the dawn of a
new age of social policy. 'If I had to sum up the immediate future of
democratic politics in a single word', he said in 1909, 'I should say
"Insurance". If I had my way I would write the word "Insure" over
the door of every cottage, and upon the blotting book of every

public man, because I am convinced that by sacrifices which are inconceivably small, which are all within the power of the very poorest man in regular work, families can be secured against catastrophes which would otherwise smash them up for ever.'[21] And many years later, in similar vein, he spoke of the Beveridge Report as 'bringing the magic of averages nearer to the rescue of the millions'.[22] In the first of these passages Churchill seems to be attributing to private thrift a power that is found only in public schemes, and in the second he appears to have forgotten that averages have disadvantages as well as advantages. For, as Professor Eveline Burns has well said, 'social insurance deals with *presumptive* rather than demonstrated need, and is a social institution dominated by a concept of *average* rather than *individual* need'.[23] She was obviously thinking here, not of health insurance, which provides a personal service to meet an individual need, but of cash benefits. In their case it is true that, whatever the system, the insured is paid the sum to which he is entitled without reference to his financial condition at the time. The *presumption* is that this will be about right. If it is too little, some method other than insurance must be used to make up the difference – and, as we shall see, no problem has proved more intractable than that of finding the best way of doing this. We shall also see that, since Eveline Burns made that remark, ever more elaborate and ingenious systems have been devised or proposed for tailoring social insurance to the measure of the individual. Lloyd George may have sensed some of the troubles ahead when he jotted down on a piece of paper (in 1911, while preparing his Insurance Bill) 'Insurance necessarily temporary expedient. At no distant date hope State will acknowledge full responsibility in the matter of making provision for sickness, breakdown and unemployment.'[24]

5 The inter-war years

It is tempting to regard the twenty years that elapsed between the two world wars as an interlude dominated by desperate efforts to cope with an unprecedented depression, and to assume that when the depression ended the stream of events we have been describing resumed its course with nothing added to it but unhappy memories. But this view is untenable. It is true that the period was one not so much of great innovations as of the consolidation and expansion of measures already tested. It is true also that the guiding principles which defined the main areas of public responsibilty and the rights and legitimate expectations of the citizen remained substantially the same. Nevertheless important progress took place and the scene in 1939 was very different from what it had been in 1914.

The war itself had some effect by fostering a sense of social solidarity among those who had seen it through at home and by evoking a determination to offer a better life to the men returning from hellish experiences at the front. In Britain this expressed itself in the popular slogan about 'homes fit for heroes', but the mood was short-lived. The depression which followed, striking the coutries of the Western world at different moments and with differing force, also presented a challenge to which, in some cases, the response was similar. In France the minister introducing the comprehensive social security legislation of 1928 said that 'the essential point is that society as a whole should, in a spirit of national solidarity, assist the wage-earners to defend themselves against the dangers by which they are constantly threatened', and he repeated the word 'solidarity'.[1] In the United States the first major piece of social legislation to be passed at the Federal level went through Congress in 1935. It brought that country at one leap, not quite into line with Western Europe in the matter of social policy, but at least within talking distance. In Britain the major effect of the depression was the collapse of unemployment insurance. But in this case the response was not a great creative effort, but a series of attempts to patch up the system. Nevertheless it is clear that the experience of those years prepared the way for the reorganization of social security which was planned during the Second World War and put into effect immediately after it.

In the history of social policy wars and depressions are accidents, however important their consequences may be. But beneath the surface we can discover processes of growth which are the product of the evolutionary forces at work within social policy itself. Before the First World War social reform was a political adventure run by enthusiastic amateurs; in the inter-war years social administration became a science practised by professionals. The commissions and committees which sat in Britain before the war, having gathered such information as they could about the past and present (and it was often fragmentary and unreliable), had little but their imagination and *a priori* reasoning to guide them when they tried to peer into the future and gauge the merits of policies which had not yet been tried. And often, as in the case of those studying the problem of the aged poor, they failed to make any recommendation at all, except that another committee should be asked to undertake further investigations. Those which met after the war were set to examine the records of systems which had been working for several years and could base their conclusions on empirical research. Typical of the first phase are the crusading fervour of Lloyd George and the hit-or-miss efforts of the little band of neophytes which he installed, with Braithwaite at their head, to design a system of health insurance under his inspiring but erratic direction. Typical of the second period are the dry matter-of-fact tones of Neville Chamberlain who, three weeks after the general election of 1924 and his appointment as Minister of Health, presented the cabinet with a detailed plan of social legislation, to be spread over three or four years, and consisting of twenty-five proposed bills.[2] One of these became the highly important Widows, Orphans and Old Age Contributory Pensions Act of 1925 which, more than any other measure, established social insurance as *the* preferred way of dealing with questions of income maintenance. Typical too are the highly expert studies by William Beveridge, especially of unemployment, but also of what he called *Insurance for All and Everything*. What strikes one about that hastily written but brilliant pamphlet is the clarity and precision of the thought, and the implied assumption that the level of understanding of the subject was by then high enough to make this very compressed picture intelligible to the general reader.

This new sophistication was a scientific not a political pheno-menon. It was concerned with applying techniques, which were of universal validity, to problems that were an intrinsic part of modern industrial society wherever the income of the family was derived from the earnings of labour, and men and women fell victim to accidents and sickness. Consequently those engaged in this work used concepts and spoke a language that were not local to their home country, but international. And they could meet in conferences called by the International Labour Office (later 'Organization') and freely exchange views, pool experiences, and adopt resolutions.

The result of all this was a marked convergence of social policy in all countries where social policy could be said to exist, but we must be careful not to press this point too far. We can see in the 1920s and the 1930s an emergent consensus about the nature and extent of government responsibility for social welfare. There was also general agreement as to the sections of the population to which social security legislation should apply. In addition most countries had accumu-lated much the same equipment of techniques and administrative machinery for use in the execution of their social policy. But here the convergence begins to weaken and is succeeded by a certain divergence of practice in deciding which instrument should be used for each particular purpose.

In some cases international convergence was the natural result of consolidation at the national level. Britain and Germany afford an example of this. Germany's first programme of social insurance included pensions and sickness but excluded unemployment; Britain's included sickness and unemployment (on a limited scale) but excluded pensions. It was natural that both countries, as they gained in experience, should fill in the gaps. Britain made unemployment insurance general in 1920 and introduced contributory pensions (at 10s. a week) in 1925; Germany added unemployment insurance to her system in 1927. After that the two systems matched very closely.

Another symptom of convergence was the movement which took place in several countries to unify their social security programmes and enclose them in a single administrative framework. France launched a composite scheme of this kind in 1928, covering sickness, maternity, invalidity, old age, and death (but not unemployment) and thus advanced one step from a relatively backward to a quite advanced position on the social policy scale.[3] The American Social Security Act of 1935 was also a composite measure, and it has been said that Roosevelt had deliberately blocked earlier proposals of limited scope because of his 'desire to combine old-age pensions with a general program of social security and his belief that a unified program should be worked out'.[4] The act covered pensions and unemployment, but not sickness, and it also provided Federal aid for a wide range of welfare services. But perhaps the most celebrated unified scheme is that contained in the New Zealand legislation of 1938, described by Sir Arnold Wilson as 'the most far-reaching scheme of obligatory social insurance ever included in a single enactment'. It covered old age, medical care, sickness benefit, invalidity, maternity, widows, orphans, disabled miners, unemployment, and family endowment.[5] But only superannuation and family allowances were free of a means test. Schemes of 'all-in insurance' were proposed in Britain by Beveridge, J. L. Cohen, Sir John Marriott, and others and were carefully considered by the government and rejected as impracticable.[6]

A typical system of social insurance at this stage would be confined to employees and would cover practically all industrial wage-earners, possibly – but by no means always – agricultural workers, and salary-earners with incomes below a fixed maximum (except those otherwise provided for, like civil servants). This gave the impression that society was divided into two layers: the independent, self-sufficient tax-paying layer and the compulsorily insured, benefit-receiving layer. The acceptance of benefits from these public services did not carry the stigma of pauperism, but had become an index of social class. And, for the first time in its modern form, the issue was raised whether social services should be used as an instrument for the redistribution of income between one class and another. Poor relief had never raised this question, since it was a kind of public charity which had no effect on society at large. But the system of social security as it had developed was a quite different affair. It was, indeed, difficult to calculate in what proportions it was returning money to those who had contributed it, transferring income on the 'mutual benefit' principle between members of the same economic class, or redistributing income from the richer to the poorer sections of the community. But it was certain that this last operation was taking place to some extent, and the question was whether it should be treated simply as the natural and inevitable consequence of services designed to satisfy real needs wherever they were found, or regarded as being an end in itself. The full-blown controversy on this point belongs to the period after the Second World War, but the situation that gave rise to it took shape during the inter-war period.

So far we have been taking note of the international convergence of social policy. When we turn to look at the techniques used in dealing with particular problems we are struck by the differences we find. In the Beveridge Report there is an appendix that summarizes the position in 1938 in thirty countries, other than Britain, scattered over Europe, Asia, the two Americas, and Australasia. It shows that twenty had compulsory insurance against sickness, twenty-four had some form of contributary pensions, all more or less made provision for industrial injury and diseases, but only eight had compulsory unemployment insurance (not counting Germany, where it had been discontinued by the Nazis). Only three (again not counting Germany) covered all three risks of sickness, old age and unemployment, as Britain did, and they were, rather surprisingly, New Zealand, Bulgaria, and Poland.[7] It would be quite wrong to imagine that the absence of a contributory scheme meant refusal to accept any responsibility for meeting a particular need. It indicated rather a difference of method. The responsibility towards the unemployed, for example, was frequently met by subventions to voluntary insurance supplemented by a well-developed system of social assistance, as in France. In this way the private efforts of the trade unions were stimulated, compulsion was avoided, and the objection to pooling in one scheme risks that were very unequal was met by basing the insurance on individual industries or occupations.

But arguments about principles and theories were soon over-whelmed by the catastrophic impact of the great depression and the mass unemployment that accompanied it. In Britain hardly had the decision been taken in 1920 to extend unemployment insurance to all industrial and commercial workers, in spite of the inequality of incidence of risk, than the blow fell. By March 1921 the number of unemployed had nearly doubled, and in the 1930s the total rose perilously near to 3 million. In Germany the peak figure was about 5 million, and in the United States probably nearer ten.[8] Insurance benefits were soon exhausted, and the choice had to be made between abandoning the relationship between contributions and benefits altogether or passing the burden on to the Poor Law, that is to say on to the local rates. The latter was impossible, so the compromise was adopted of abandoning the principle of insurance but retaining the apparatus and as much as possible of the terminology. Relief was paid far beyond what contributions had earned by means of a succession of so-called 'transitional', 'extended', and 'uncovenanted' benefits, into the nature and fortunes of which it is not necessary to enter here. The result was summed up by Beveridge in 1930. Social insurance, he said, was originally contractual in character, in that it conferred a right that was conditional on the payment of contributions. Now the obligation to pay the contributions had lapsed, but the right to benefit was still acknowledged. Consequently 'the insurance scheme of 1911 has become a general system of outdoor relief to the able-bodied, administered by a national in place of a local authority, and financed mainly by a tax on employment'.[9] He was speaking in terms of the sharp antithesis between insurance and assistance, which events had so dramatically outstripped.

An heroic attempt was made in 1934 to restore the integrity of insurance. Benefits, in the true sense, were once more to be paid only in so far as contributions warranted, but a new Limbo was created between the Heaven of insurance benefits and the Hell of poor relief over which ruled a national authority called the Unemployment Assistance Board. No stigma was to be attached to the acceptance of aid from this body but, as its payments were subject to a 'means test', which took account of the income of family members living at home, it looked just like the Poor Law under another name. Nothing in the history of social policy, except perhaps the old mixed workhouse, has inspired such hatred and detestation as this household means test. This was due partly to the inquisition necessary to make the assessment, and partly to the humiliation it caused to a man who expected to support his family, and not to be supported by it. But the more fundamental cause of humiliation was the enforced idleness and the necessity to go, week after week, to draw money that had not been earned by labour. It is significant that all those in this position, whether the money they were drawing was insurance benefit or unemployment relief, were said to be 'on the dole'.

In the United States the storm broke more suddenly and was even more devastating. A vast programme of relief for the unemployed was developed, including the invention of tasks to be performed at public expense by all classes of person, including writers, scholars, and artists. But in the midst of this an attempt was made to build a permanent piece of machinery into the administrative systems of the Federal and State governments for the maintenance of the unemployed. By the Federal Act of 1935 a pay-roll tax was imposed on all industrial and commercial employers of more than seven persons, with the provision that any State which established an unemployment insurance scheme approved by the Federal government would receive the proceeds of this tax and assign them to the scheme. The practice of unemployment insurance spread gradually over the economy, but a quarter of a century later there were still 14 million jobs not covered.[10]

The survey of foreign policies attached to the Beveridge Report said nothing about family allowances, because he treated them as an 'underlying assumption' of his plan and not as an integral part of it. Their introduction in Europe was one of the most important innovations of the inter-war period. The pioneers in this adventure were France and Belgium. Voluntary systems by which wages were supplemented for the benefit of dependent children had existed for some time in both countries, and the practice was made general and compulsory by legislation in Belgium in 1930 and in France in 1932. At first this caused a divergence of policy between the countries that adopted them and those that did not. But this was a passing phase. A movement of convergence soon developed as the example set by the pioneers was generally followed, until family allowances became as common a feature of social programmes as pensions.

Family allowances differ from the other services we have so far examined in that their primary purpose is to supplement the earnings of those at work, not to maintain the income of those unable to earn. They are a means by which an individual wage is converted into a family wage by being adjusted to the number of persons who must live on it. It was natural, therefore, that these early schemes should place the whole burden of the cost on the employers. The allowances were treated as a sort of employer's liability, and the principle of insurance entered, as in the case of industrial injury, only because the employers covered their liability by sharing it among themselves. They paid a contribution proportionate to the number of their employees into an 'equalization fund' by which the allowances were financed. This destroyed any incentive there would otherwise have been to employ bachelors in preference to fathers of families.[11] One aim of the policy of family allowances was, of course, to check and if possible to reverse the fall in the birth rate. But another, and more permanent one, was to sustain the family, as the vital nucleus of the social order. The emphasis, therefore, was on the satisfaction of need, not on the sanctity of contractual rights won by insurance contributions. In Britain the campaign led by Eleanor Rathbone on behalf of what she called the 'disinherited family' had not yet succeeded, when war broke out, in convincing the government of the merits of family allowances. Payments adjusted to family needs were an accepted feature of public assistance. It was true that they had, of dire necessity, been extended in 1921 to the unemployed in receipt of insurance benefits, but there was opposition to introducing them as a permanent feature either of the wage system or of social insurance. And when they were eventually adopted after the war, they were not placed in either of these categories, but in a special one of their own.

Meanwhile the campaign for the break-up of the Poor Law continued, both in Britain and elsewhere. The crucial question faced in all countries was, as we saw earlier, to decide whether the transfer of functions from the Poor Law authorities to other agencies could be carried to the point where the Poor Law as such would cease to exist. As far as relief in cash was concerned, its functions were being transferred to social insurance but, as we have just seen, not quite completely in the case of old people and widows and very far from completely in the case of unemployment. This movement was general. But national practices differed with regard to the services, in the fields of health, education, and welfare, which Poor Law authorities everywhere had administered for the benefit of those dependent upon them. British policy, true to the spirit of the Minority Report, aimed at their progressive absorption into the appropriate general services provided for the population at large. But these processes of transfer and absorption could not proceed freely as long as the Poor Law was administered by special authorities outside the local government apparatus. So in 1929 the critical step was taken of abolishing the Guardians and handing over the residue of their functions to Public Assistance Committees set up by the county and county borough councils. The Poor Law was not abolished, but it was placed under new management with a view to its eventual disappearance.

The act provided for the transfer of the Poor Law hospitals to the Public Health Authorities, but this happened only to a limited extent and the Poor Law Medical Officers continued to visit and treat the poor.[12] The Public Assistance Committees also became responsible for the old people, children, feeble-minded, and others who needed institutional care, because there were no institutions to put them in except those handed over by the Guardians. We have here the germs of some of the more important modern welfare services. It was obvious that the Poor Law medical services should be taken over by specialized medical authorities of some kind, and the delay in making the transfer was due to the fact that there was, at the time, general dissatisfaction with the way the medical services were operating, but as yet no clear idea what their future structure should be. Once it was decided to set up a National Health Service, the residue of the Poor Law in this field created no problem. But there was no obvious specialized professional authority to take over the embryo welfare services, and they remained where they were until after the war. Other committees (Education or Public Health) might lend a hand, but the Public Assistance Committee was still responsible and it still operated under the Poor Laws. It is not easy for welfare services to shake off all association with pauperism, for they do in fact deal to a large extent with cases in which a particular misfortune is aggravated by poverty. And anybody obliged to live in a public institution at the public expense is likely to look, and to feel, like a pauper. British policy tried to achieve the transformation by means of a clean break with the past. But the replacement of the Guardians of the Public Assistance Committees was little more than the announcement of a break that could not yet be made, and British social policy suffered for some time the natural consequences of having given the dog a bad name and failed to hang it. The reputation of the Poor Law was blackened, but it was not killed, and it continued to leave its mark on everything it touched. Eventually, as we shall see, the policy succeeded in creating welfare services for citizens, not paupers; but it got there the hard way, by wiping out the past and starting afresh.

Other countries pursued a different course. They did not condemn the Poor Law to death by dismemberment, but tried to humanize and modernize it. In France and Germany, for instance, public assistance continued to function as a multi-purpose service meeting all the needs of the very poor, who were treated as a distinct category, but one which should become smaller as social security measures became more comprehensive. The French *aide sociale* and the German *Fürsorge* provided not only maintenance of all kinds, but help in paying rents, medical and maternity services at home or in hospital (with choice of doctor), education, and vocational training of the handicapped. Thus, while the destitute were set apart from the rest of the population, it was intended that they should be served in the same spirit as the others, an ideal that could not always be realized.[13] In Scandinavia a rather similar development took place, which has been described as 'the transformation of poor relief into modern social assistance'. The sharp separation of the category of the very poor from the rest of the community seems to have been absent, and it was possible to bring under one authority the idle and obstreperous poor, who needed to be subjected to deterrent discipline, those whose main trouble was extreme poverty, and those for whom poverty was only a subsidiary factor in a situation dominated by some misfortune or affliction.[14]

In the United States public assistance, which had been modelled on the English Poor Law, was indeed broken up, but mainly by a process of internal specialization rather than transfer to the general public services. In the nineteenth century the practice had grown up of giving 'preferential assistance' to specially deserving cases; such assistance was both more generous than the average and was supposed to carry no stigma of pauperism. Several states then started special programmes for selected classes of persons – mothers of young children, the aged, and the blind. This so-called 'categorical assistance' spread slowly and was attacked as unconstitutional on the grounds that it involved the 'payment of public funds to persons who were not in need'. In a sense this was true, and it did imply a radical departure from traditional Poor Law principles. The Social Security Act of 1935 standardized the system by offering Federal aid for schemes on behalf of the old, dependent children, the blind, and the permanently disabled, while recognizing, but not aiding, a fifth category of 'general assistance', which was the old Poor Law under a new name. Thus the area of public assistance was expanded, both as regards the needs provided for and the population covered, but it remained 'assistance', in that the services were non-contributory and the benefits were granted subject to a means test.[15] But these measures did much to change the harsh spirit of what Edith Abbott called 'our un-American American Poor Laws'.[16]

If family allowances were the most important practical innovation in social policy during the inter-war years, housing was the most important item to be added to the list of things with which social policy had to deal. Speaking of Britain before the First World War Marian Bowley says that at the time 'the housing problem was the slum problem, the problem of people living in insanitary conditions'.[17] It is true that the main emphasis had been on housing as a branch of public health, but the idea that government, both central and local, had some responsibility for what another writer on the subject calls 'house building as distinct from slum clearance' had been translated into legislation in 1890 and 1909, and the distinction was reflected in the regulations governing the two operations. But, although 'housing became a burning question of municipal politics', very little was done to provide houses outside the slum-clearance areas.[18]

The war gave to the housing question a new urgency. Building had been suspended, and rents had been frozen in order to prevent the exploitation of the housing shortage. And the men at the Front had been promised 'homes fit for heroes' on their return. It would hardly have been tactful to greet them with a big rise in rents, and yet, at the level at which they then stood, there was no incentive to private firms to build houses to let to working-class families. And people were beginning to regard their controlled rents as representing the true value of their houses. It was in these circumstances that British housing policy first appeared in the guise of a social service. The responsibility for coping with the crisis was placed firmly on the local authorities; they were to make surveys and prepare plans to meet the needs that they revealed. They were to let the houses they built at rents which bore no necessary relation to their cost, but were assessed in the first instance by reference to the controlled rents for similar accommodation in old houses, and then adjusted to the tenant's capacity to pay. Any loss suffered on the transaction in excess of the yield of a rate of one penny in the pound would be made good by the Exchequer. Under a scheme of this kind both the local authorities and their tenants would receive aid in proportion to their needs. But this policy, which set no limit to what the local authorities could spend, proved too costly, and also failed to deliver the goods, and was abandoned in 1923. Thereafter the subsidies paid by the Exchequer to the local authorities were limited to fixed amounts, and the trend, if we ignore the oscillations of policy associated with changes of government, was towards relying mainly on private enterprise for new building, while concentrating public expenditure on special tasks, such as slum-clearance and the reduction of overcrowding. At the same time attempts were made to bring rent restriction to an end by gradually lowering the maximum value of houses whose rents remained controlled, but the operation was never completed, and at the outbreak of the Second World War about one quarter of the rents were still controlled.[19]

The experience of the other European countries involved in the Second World War was very similar. Some of them had started to evolve a housing policy, and the machinery with which to implement it, even before the war. France in particular had, by 1906, developed the whole apparatus of public loans, cheap land, guaranteed interest, and tax relief to help housing societies to build houses and let them to working-class families at rents which they could afford.[20] Between the wars there was a convergence of policy in Europe, in the sense that all countries took steps to control rents and stimulate building, but they differed as to the extent to which they subsidized rents. In Scandinavia rents rose as much as the cost of food, but in France, Germany and Italy considerably less. European policy also differed in certain points from British. There was less inclination to adjust individual rents to incomes than to adjust incomes to rent; governments preferred, as Alva Myrdal says of Sweden, to subsidize families rather than houses.[21] More use, on the whole, was made of tax remission as an encouragement to build, perhaps because there were more taxes that could conveniently be remitted, especially taxes on land. But most significant was the multiplication of housing associations, co-operatives, and semi-official, autonomous institutions for financing the building of houses on a non-profit basis. The methods varied but the purpose was the same, namely to provide dwellings which could be let at a moderate rent to families with incomes below a certain fixed level, with the minimum of administrative intervention by the local authorities.[22]

The inter-war years saw, finally, two developments of lasting importance which affected the whole character of social policy. The depression, and above all its devastating effects in the areas most heavily hit by it, caused the whole picture of social problems to change. It was realized that social policy must be conceived as allied to general economic policy, and not as a separate area of political action governed by principles peculiar to itself. The vital necessity was to restore the volume of employment, and the relief of the unemployed was a subsidiary matter. In fact, care was prepared for the Beveridge doctrine that there could be no effective system of social security without a policy of full employment.

In what came to be known as the 'Special Areas' the task confronting the British authorities was nothing less than the rescue of community life in all its forms. Efforts were made to set up new industries, to organize emigration, to devise 'sub-economic' occupations and provide land for 'subsistence production' by which men could be given something to do and could earn a small profit without sacrificing their status as unemployed, and it was equally essential to offer entertainment, recreation, and ways of using leisure which might stimulate the faculties and engage the attention of men and youths condemned to idleness.[23]

The second important development was in the role of the voluntary societies. It was probably in the nineteenth century that the boldest and most imaginative pioneering work was done by private individuals, after which there came a period when some of the leading voluntary organizations were associated with reactionary and conservative views, while the public services embarked on new enterprises, often following a lead that had been given them by the most effective private individuals and agencies. In the inter-war period the pioneering role of voluntary societies was once more conspicuous, while new forces began to stir in some of the older and more conservative bodies. But this time the public and private sectors advanced together so closely and in such harmony that the characteristic feature of the age was partnership between the two. In the early years of the century, says Bourdillon, the question was whether a service should be voluntary or statutory, but by the end of the 1930s the answer clearly was that both were needed, and the problem was 'not whether to co-operate but how to co-operate it'.[24]

Many examples could be given. Public services for maternity and child welfare began to be systematically developed on the basis of two Acts of Parliament. The first, in 1915, made it compulsory for the doctor or midwife to notify every birth within thirty-six hours. This gave an infinitely better basis of information for health visitors than the obligation on parents to register the birth, which had existed since 1874. Second, the Maternity and Child Welfare Act of 1918 authorized and encouraged local authorities to develop services for expectant and nursing mothers and for children under five. In this large field, which included health visiting, maternity and child welfare clinics, children's homes, nursery schools, and day nurseries, the voluntary and statutory agencies went forward side by side and hand in hand. The Blind Persons Act of 1920 empowered local authorities to carry out the duties imposed upon them through the medium of voluntary agencies, and this was extensively done.[25] Voluntary youth organizations had existed since the middle of the last century, but it was only in 1916 that the government made its first attempt to set up central and local machinery to co-ordinate the whole range of voluntary and statutory activities, recreational and educational, that were concerned with youth.

One of the most significant developments in this period was the creation of the National Council of Social Service, and its supporting regional or local councils, with the task of smoothing the way to co-operation between voluntary bodies of all kinds, and between them and the public authorities. It was primarily, said G. D. H. Cole, 'not a charitable agency, but a fosterer and co-ordinator of communal activities among ordinary people, and not merely among the "poor" in any narrow sense'.[26] It was the moving spirit behind the drive to establish local community centres run on democratic principles by Community Associations which attracted so much attention and aroused such high hopes in the years immediately before the Second World War. It was felt that this represented the vital change from services offered and institutions created by benevolent outsiders, to reliance on self-help and mutual aid. And the National Council also dispensed about a million pounds of government money for the foundation and management of 'occupational clubs' for the unemployed in the depressed areas.

Little or nothing has been said in this chapter about the health services. Had the story been told here it would have consisted largely of growing evidence of dissatisfaction with the state of affairs and tentative proposals for reforms and additions, on which no action was taken. It is more convenient to discuss these matters in the next chapter.

6 The war and the welfare state

A modern total war has certain predictable effects on the social problems of the warring nations. It absorbs the unemployed, it stimulates health services in both their technical and their organizational aspects, and it creates a housing shortage, either by destroying houses or preventing them from being built, or both. In a more general sense total war obliges governments to assume new and heavier responsibilities for the welfare of their peoples, especially by controlling the production and distribution of scarce necessities, like food and fuel, and by looking after those who have been made homeless by invasion, evacuation, or aerial bombardment. The experience of total war is therefore bound to have an effect on both the principles of social policy and the methods of social administration. But the nature of this effect will depend to a considerable extent on the fortunes of war – on whether a country is invaded or not, on whether it is victorious or defeated, and on the amount of physical destruction and social disorganization it suffers.

Britain's experience in the war was unique. It was the only sovereign state that fought right through from the beginning to the end, enduring attacks on the homeland but not invasion, and finally emerged victorious, without having at any time suffered social or political disorganization. These circumstances help to explain why the concept of the welfare state first took shape in England. The magnitude of her war effort and her vulnerability to attack called for sacrifices from all and equally for help given ungrudgingly and without discrimination to all who were in need. 'The pooling of national resources', said Titmuss, 'and the sharing of risks were not always practicable nor always applied; but they were the guiding principles.'[1] And the political stability of the country, combined with its unshaken confidence in victory, account for the most remarkable feature of the story, namely the way in which the people and their government, in the middle of the war, set about drawing the designs of the new society which was to be born when the fighting stopped. It was to be a society governed by the same principles of pooling and sharing that governed the emergency measures of the war. So the idea of the welfare state came to be identified with the war aims of a nation fighting for its life. It is not surprising that, in England, it wore a halo which is not to be found in other countries when, in due course, they undertook the task of social reconstruction. And it is not surprising that, when it came to be examined in detail, with the cold eye of reason, its more fervent champions strapped on their armour and declared a holy war on its critics.

As early as 1941 the Ministry of Health announced as 'the objective of the Government, as soon as may be after the war', the creation of a comprehensive hospital service available to all.[2] In 1943 the Board of Education published a report of the Youth Advisory Council (set up for this purpose in 1942) on *The Youth Service after the War*. In 1944 Parliament passed an Education Act which was intended to give full equality of opportunity to all, regardless of family income, and the government published its plan for a National Health Service. But the boldest attempt to set down on paper the nation's peace aims in terms of a new social order was the Beveridge Report of 1942. The government had already committed itself, through the mouth of Anthony Eden, to the principle that 'social security must be the first object of our domestic policy after the war',[3] and had insisted on writing 'social security' into the Atlantic Charter. So Beveridge was fully justified in saying, at the end of his report, that 'statement of a reconstruction policy by a nation at war is statement of the uses to which that nation means to put victory, when victory is achieved'.[4] And it was as a blueprint of the social order for which the country was fighting that the report was received and acclaimed.

Yet, when one reads it, one finds that it was in the main, as the government had intended it to be, a technical analysis of the problems and methods of social insurance, with some drastic and often very ingenious proposals for unifying the whole system and making it simpler and more efficient. In these respects it is a remarkable document which had a deep effect on social policy not only in Britain but in other countries as well. But this alone cannot account for its immense popular appeal. There was, in fact, in the social insurance plan itself only one really arresting innovation, namely the extension of the compulsory insurance scheme to include the entire population. But the main cause of the enthusiastic reception of the report was no doubt the picture it drew – or in parts merely sketched – of the total social programme of which the Beveridge plan proper was only a part.

The report expressed a great idea and presented a grand design which seemed to proclaim a social revolution. In a famous and much-quoted passage Beveridge declared that social insurance was indeed 'an attack upon Want. But Want is only one of the five giants on the road of reconstruction and in some ways the easiest to attack. The others are Disease, Ignorance, Squalor and Idleness'.[5] His plan for social security was a plan to abolish Want, but it could only succeed if the other giants were attacked at the same time. So he listed three assumptions which underlay his proposals, namely that provision would be made for allowances for dependent children, for comprehensive health and rehabilitation services, and for the maintenance of employment.[6] And he might have added, with an eye to the two giants Ignorance and Squalor, education and houses for the people.

Did all this amount to a social revolution? Beveridge himself answered this question. 'The scheme proposed here', he wrote, 'is in some ways a revolution, but in more important ways it is a natural development from the past. It is a British revolution.'[7] This is true. For what we see here is the final phase in the process described in the second chapter of this book, by which the logical development and natural evolution of ideas and institutions led ultimately to a transformation of the system. The transformation, or revolution, consisted in the welding together of the measures of social policy into a whole which, for the first time, acquired thereby a personality of its own and a meaning that had hitherto been only vaguely glimpsed. We adopted the term 'welfare state' to denote this new entity composed of old elements. The total ultimate responsibility of the state for the welfare of its people was recognized more explicitly than ever before, and the choice between the three political philosophies described in Chapter 2 was clearly decided. The social services were not to be regarded as regrettable necessities to be retained only until the capitalist system had been reformed or socialized; they were a permanent and even a glorious part of the social system itself. They were something to be proud of, not to apologize for. But even here there were reservations. When the National government presented (in 1944) its version of the Beveridge plan of social insurance, it prefaced it with a statement which contained a tactful warning. National policy, it said must aim to secure 'the general prosperity and happiness of the citizens. To realize that aim two courses of action must be followed. The first is to foster the growth of the national power to produce and to earn, with its accompanying opportunities for increased well-being, leisure and recreation. The second is to plan for the prevention of individual poverty resulting from those hazards of personal fortune over which individuals have little or no control'.[8] The government was anxious not to spread the idea that social security was a substitute for productivity, but it was referring at this point to social insurance only, and not to the whole programme of the welfare state. Education and health may well be regarded as contributing more to the increase of productivity than to the prevention of poverty.

Beveridge set himself the task of consolidating the various social insurance schemes, standardizing the benefits where appropriate, and adding new benefits where necessary so as to cover all needs caused by loss of income, or the incidence of exceptional demands upon income, such as those arising from marriage and death. He proposed to bring Workmen's Compensation (or Industrial Injury) within the scope of social insurance so that compensation would be received as a benefit, instead of having to be claimed from the employer, if necessary in a court of law. This was done. He proposed to convert old-age pensions into retirement pensions, payable only when the claimant gave up regular work. Those who preferred to go on working, and contributing, beyond the minimum age of 65 for men and 60 for women would receive proportionately large pensions when they retired. This was also done. Next, he proposed to fill the two most serious gaps in the pre-war benefits. Allowances for dependants had so far been given only to widows (in respect of their children) and to the unemployed (in respect of their families). They were not given to the sick or to pensioners with 'dependent' wives under pensionable age. Beveridge insisted that all benefits should include all members of the family, unless they were otherwise provided for. And he wanted husband and wife to receive a 'joint benefit', so as not to insult a wife by calling her a 'dependant'. This typical touch was ignored. Second, unemployment benefit was limited to a maximum number of weeks in each year. He wished to pay it without time limit, subject to the condition that, after a certain period, the unemployed man must attend a training centre. This bold proposal, showing great confidence in the possibility of maintaining full employment, was rejected.

Of the new benefits proposed the most important was children's (or family) allowances, beginning with the second child. The case for these had long been unsuccessfully urged, and it had now become clear that one could not refuse to do for the employed what had already been done for the unemployed, or the latter might sometimes find themselves better off than the former. The allowances, though an essential element in the total plan, were not to be given as an insurance benefit, but financed out of taxes. Of the six other new benefits recommended by Beveridge, only two were eventually accepted, maternity and funeral grants. His idea of adding a grant for marriage, benefits for deserted wives, home helps for sick house-wives, and training grants for the self-employed were either too ingenious or too complicated to win political support. Home helps did indeed materialize, but as part of the local health service.

Our main concern here is not with the details but with the basic principles of the Beveridge Report, and on this subject its author was quite explicit. We can group them under three heads. First, the plan must be one of universal, compulsory, and contributory insurance. Second, contributions and benefits must be at the same flat rate for all, the benefits being fixed at subsistence level. And, third, statutory benefits should be supplemented by voluntary savings, which should be encouraged by positive measures. These three principles are interlocked and interdependent.

Universal coverage was the boldest innovation in the Beveridge plan. And yet he had little to say in defence of this departure from generally accepted practice. He seemed to assume that, given the spirit of the times, it was inevitable. And so, perhaps, it was but it had its critics, of whom one of the most vehement and effective was the economist H. D. Henderson. He declared that the extension of compulsory insurance to the middle classes could not possibly do anything to further Beveridge's 'proclaimed objective of abolishing want'. The logical way to do this was to locate and measure the want and to raise and dispense enough money to relieve it.[9]

But Beveridge could not consider this for a moment, because it was not insurance. It resembled the New Zealand scheme, which was later described by one of its administrators as one in which 'each citizen would contribute according to his means, and from which he could draw according to his need'.[10] And that was public assistance financed by a tax. The essence of insurance was the interdependence of contributions and benefits, and it was contributory insurance, so he believed, that the people of England wanted. They wanted it as the only alternative to the hated means test of the inter-war years. His aim, therefore, was 'to ensure at all times to all men a subsistence income for themselves and their families as of right; that is to say without any form of means test or enquiry about other means they had'.[11]

In stressing the idea that benefits must be granted 'as of right' he was, of course, expressing correctly the central aim of European social policy since the beginning of the century. It had been internationally endorsed in 1925 when an ILO Conference resolved that social security for the workers 'can best be attained by means of a system of social insurance granting clearly defined rights to the beneficiaries'.[12] But it did not follow that these rights could be established only by contributions. Beveridge had himself argued, in his book *Insurance for All and Everything*, that insurance is simply the 'collective bearing of risks', irrespective of the source from which the insurance fund derives its income. A scheme ceases to rank as social insurance only when 'the receipt of the benefit depends in any way upon the discretion of some authority'.[13] And a French deputy went still further and maintained that social differs from commercial insurance precisely because the worker 'is insured not by personal contribution but by society, which give him rights and guarantees them in the prevention, relief, and compensation against loss arising out of social risks'.[14] That is the point; it is society that gives the rights, and it may attach them to contributions or not, as it pleases.

But, although he insisted on the contractual character of contributory insurance, Beveridge recognized, and clearly explained, the differences between social and other forms of insurance. In social insurance, he said, there can be a 'pooling of risks'. We have already seen how this worked for sickness and unemployment, where in each case risks of the same kind but of different degree were covered by equal contributions. In devising a comprehensive plan in which a single contribution on one card covered all benefits, he extended the 'pooling' over the whole field and over risks of different kinds. Second, although contributions must be related to benefits, the relationship could, he said, be whatever seemed desirable on general grounds; it need not be based on actuarial calculations. The contributions should be 'high enough to give the insured person, because he has contributed substantially without reference to means, a justifiable claim to receive benefit without reference to means'.[15] But what level of contributions that indicates is anybody's guess.

There are also grounds for questioning, or amending, Beveridge's sharp distinction between a benefit received 'as of right' and one that is subject to a means test, or dependant 'upon the discretion of some authority'. For the means test, as used between the wars, was not really discretionary. The benefit was adjusted to the family income by a fixed scale; there was inquisition (which was resented), but not much scope for discretion. Discretion enters when one begins to assess needs. Means can be measured by rule of thumb and arranged along a scale, but needs cannot, because each case is unique. A means test is an appropriate instrument for assessing what somebody should pay for a service, like a university education, but not for assessing what somebody, who *ex hypothesi* is on the verge of destitution, ought to receive. In such cases it is liable to be used to check extravagance and to detect malingering. What is really required is a 'needs test', which, in the broadest sense of the term, is the foundation of every benevolent welfare service.

Beveridge's second principle, of the flat rate and the subsistence level, was also, as he well knew, one that few other governments favoured. 'In most countries', he wrote, 'the benefits are percentages of the wages, and vary, therefore, from one man to another.'[16] Here we see most clearly the influence of his political philosophy, the philosophy of early twentieth-century Liberalism. The state, he argued, was entitled to compel people to contribute to the cost of guaranteeing for themselves the absolute minimum income necessary for subsistence. There was no room here for individual preferences in expenditure. But 'to give by compulsory insurance more than is needed for subsistence is an unnecessary interference with individual responsibilities'. He called this 'the principle of a national minimum, above which all citizens shall spend their money freely'.[17] Subsistence benefits must be flat-rate benefits, for the subsistence level, however you calculate it, is the same for all citizens. And if the principle of contributory insurance is to be adhered to, flat-rate benefits imply flat-rate contributions. In so far as it was desirable to depart from this principle and transfer income from the richer to the poorer, this should be done through that part of the total cost which is met out of the proceeds of progressive taxation. That is why Beveridge favoured the tripartite system in which employers, employed, and taxpayers all contribute, and decided to increase the share of the taxpayers.

'Subsistence' was for Beveridge both an advance on the past and a limitation on the future. In the inter-war years benefits were not meant to provide a living, but merely a substantial supplement to other resources. Subsistence in Beveridge's plan meant an adequate income, even when there were no other resources at all. He envisaged a national assistance service, centrally administered, to take over the functions of the old Poor Law with respect to outdoor cash relief, but it was basic to his plan that nobody should have to ask for national assistance simply because his insurance benefits were inadequate. National assistance would be chiefly concerned with caring for the anomalies, including those who, whether by their own fault or not, were not qualified to receive benefit. It would give relief, subject to a means test, and it 'must be felt to be something less desirable than insurance benefit; otherwise the insured people get nothing out of their contributions'.[18]

Could such a scheme really work? The subsistence level of Beveridge looked suspiciously like the 'poverty line' of Rowntree, and the calculations on which the former was based owe much to those used for the latter. But whereas Rowntree's 'poverty line' was an instrument of social research which could, in accordance with the definition of a 'line', be without breadth, the subsistence level was an operational concept which must provide a margin of safety and some room for manoeuvre in a changing world. When the value of money steadily falls and prices rise erratically and unevenly from place to place and commodity to commodity, a universal subsistence benefit becomes unworkable. And if the benefit is raised for all above the danger point, the flat-rate contributions which correspond to the new level become higher than the poorest members of the society can afford. It was on these grounds that the National government, in its White Paper of September 1944, explicitly rejected Beveridge's proposal. It would, they said, mean tying the benefit to the cost of living, and either varying benefits according to individual needs (which is not insurance), or raising contributions to an impossibly high level.[19] The scheme later introduced by the Labour government did aim at subsistence but failed to achieve it, for the government was driven more and more to supplement the benefits of those who had no private means by allowances from national assistance. For this they were denounced by Beveridge in the House of Lords, who called on them either to raise the benefits or to state 'that they formally abandon security against want without a means test and declare that they drop the Beveridge Report and the policy of 1946'.[20]

On that occasion Beveridge was defending his beloved child, and he may be forgiven for passing lightly over its possible defects. But did he, when making subsistence the guiding principle of his plan, foresee the difficulties it would encounter? In one respect he certainly did, for he discussed it at some length. This was the matter of rents. Rents vary from place to place and may represent a large item of expenditure in small budgets. And it is not always possible to reduce the expenditure by moving to a cheaper home. Could a uniform subsistence benefit absorb this item? In the case of national assistance it was found that it could not, and the practice was followed of fixing the standard allowance exclusive of rent, and adding what was needed to pay the rent afterwards. Beveridge carefully considered arrangements of this kind and rejected them as inconsistent with his basic principles. His whole attitude to this question, and to the problem of rising prices, now seems to have been short-sighted. Perhaps he anticipated more effective measures to check inflation than were actually adopted. Undoubtedly he relied very much on his hope that most people would add to the statutory benefits by voluntary insurance.

And this brings us to the third of his major principles, the importance of leaving room for private saving. He wanted positive steps to be taken to encourage this. He had two suggestions to make, which he put forward, not as integral parts of the plan, but as 'eminently desirable'. He had decided against continuing to use 'approved societies' to operate sickness insurance as independent agents because of the inequality of benefits that resulted. But he wanted them to act as channels through which standard, statutory benefits were distributed, so as to give them an opportunity to persuade people to take out additional policies voluntarily. Second, he proposed that the industrial assurance, or 'collecting', societies, which were run for profit, should be replaced, and their business taken over, by a national board having a statutory monopoly in this kind of insurance. Neither of these proposals was adopted.

As a result, the balance of the plan was upset. Beveridge spoke of it as 'combining three distinct methods: social insurance for basic needs; national assistance for special cases; voluntary insurance for additions to the basic provision'.[21] The third of these methods was left to take care of itself, but action was taken to institute the second. The act of 1948, which set up the National Assistance Board, opened with the words (already quoted in an earlier chapter) 'the existing poor law shall cease to have effect'. The clean break with the past was made at last, and it involved two important innovations which distinguish the British from most other systems. First, relief in cash was shifted from the rates to the taxes, that is to say, from the local authorities to a national body. The ancient tradition of the western world that the relief of the poor is the affair of their neighbours was brought to an end. Second, assistance in cash was, as a result, separated from the welfare services, which remained a local responsibility. This meant that, as these developed, they had a better chance of avoiding the taint of pauperism which clung obstinately to the National Assistance Board. On the other hand it can be argued that, had the two not been separated, the humiliating character of cash assistance might have been neutralized by association with the more humane atmosphere of the personal services. This was the pattern adopted, apparently with some success, in the Scandanavian countries.

The second main supporting pillar of the welfare state was the National Health Service. When the Labour government introduced the bill which became the act of 1946, its spokesman stressed the fact that it was the 'outcome of a concerted effort extending over a long period of years', and achieved what responsible people had been advocating since before the war. Nor was it 'the preserve of any one party'.[22] This was perfectly true, but it cannot be too strongly emphasized that a national health service is something essentially different from a system of health insurance. The survey made for the Royal Commission of 1924–6 of fourteen foreign countries showed that medical care was treated in all of them as an insurance benefit, as it was in Britain. In some countries the schemes were still voluntary, but there were clear signs of a trend towards the introduction of compulsory schemes covering specified classes of the population, again as in Britain. Most of them were administered by local bodies – either 'approved societies' or semi-autonomous statutory bodies representing the locality. These negotiated with the local doctors and made arrangements with the local hospitals and clinics for the medical care of their clients, the insured families. They tried to cover as many types of treatment as possible, and they generally offered at least some of them to dependants. Patients usually had to pay part of the cost of the treatment they received. But, as we have seen, systems of this kind do not always function smoothly. Friction often develops between the local agencies and the medical profession. One way of reducing this, used extensively in Germany and as the general practice in France, was to leave the patient to pay the doctor and to reimburse him subsequently for the prescribed proportion of the amount. This, however, involved retaining that direct financial transaction between patient and doctor which it had been one of the main objects of national health insurance to eliminate. The other weakness of a locally based health insurance system is that it does not lead to, and may even hinder, the creation of overall plans for the distribution of medical resources and services throughout the country and for their systematic development.

The pre-war British system was a compromise. General practice by 'panel doctors' had something of the character of a national service, and it was claimed that the distribution of practitioners in relation to population had greatly improved, as well as the quality of the service provided.[23] But there was no local authority to co-ordinate the medical health services; hospitals, general practice and public health were separately administered. And, as in Europe, the operation of the whole machine was clogged by the paraphernalia of insurance. This can be illustrated by a few random quotations from a description written during the war. 'The inside of an Insurance Committee's building is a gigantic filing system. ... Every insured person is indexed both according to his doctor and according to his Approved Society. ... Changes of doctor give endless trouble to the staff. ... The scheme suffers because it is geared to the obsolescent organisation of general practice in this country. ... The trouble with the National Health Insurance is that it is not "national". Administrative emphasis is on the word "insurance". The sick are considered not as citizens but as insured persons.'[24]

The case for a planned national health service was foreshadowed by two reports published between the wars. The first, the so-called 'Dawson Report', was prepared by the Consultative Council set up to advise the government. It approached the subject from a strictly practical and professional angle, and not with any preconceived theories about the principles of social policy. 'The changes that we advise', it said, 'are rendered necessary because the organisation of medicine has become insufficient, and because it fails to bring the advantages of medical knowledge adequately within reach of the people.'[25] The general practitioner was cut off from modern facilities for diagnosis and treatment and from contact with specialists and consultants. To remedy this the report proposed to set up health centres at two levels, local ones as bases for the general practitioners, and regional ones for specialists. The latter, it seems, would in fact be miniature hospitals. The existing voluntary hospitals, which had 'fallen on evil days', were to be resuscitated and worked into a general service directed by local health authorities. The Royal Commission of 1924–6 saw things in much the same light, and had visions of a comprehensive medical service. 'The ultimate solution will lie', they said, 'in the direction of divorcing the medical service entirely from the insurance system and recognizing it along with all the other public health activities as a service to be supported from the general public funds.'[26] But the time, they thought, was not ripe. In view of the mounting burden of public expenditure, 'the State may justifiably turn from searching its conscience to exploring its purse'.[27] So nothing of importance was done.

The war conquered these inhibitions, and the Beveridge Report paved the way for action. It is interesting to compare the plan put forward by the National government with the act passed under the Labour government. The former left the hospitals much as they were, but created new Joint Authorities, formed by amalgamating contiguous local government areas, to run the rest of the services. The aim was to rehabilitate and reintegrate general practice, and make it the backbone of the service, which was what all the inter-war experts had recommended. But the doctors were alarmed. They saw this as the first step towards converting them into 'a service of technicians controlled by central bureaucrats and by local men and women entirely ignorant of medical matters'.[28]

Aneurin Bevan, for the Labour government, turned this plan upside down. He left the general practitioners much as they were, except that the old Insurance Committees were replaced by Executive Councils, half of whose members represented the professions, and new and more effective means were devised for controlling the distribution of practices. But he took the drastic step of nationalizing the voluntary hospitals and putting them, and the municipal hospitals, all under boards appointed by, and responsible to, himself. The teaching hospitals had each its own governing body directly under the minister, while the rest were grouped geographically under Regional Boards. And, in due course, it became clear that the hospitals had become the backbone of the service, while general practice struggled along in a state of intermittent dissatisfaction both with its remuneration and with the conditions under which it had to work. An optimistic general practitioner wrote in 1949, having described what was then wrong with the service: 'The new order of things may alter this. The liaison between health centres and hospitals, the idea of general practitioner hospitals, the growing feeling that it is absurd to train students in modern methods and then to deny them the use of these methods when they go into practice, are likely before long to ease the general practitioner's task in curative medicine enormously.'[29] People are still discussing how these hopes may be realized; but that belongs to Chapter 9.

But Bevan's great achievement consisted in the creation of a genuinely universal, free medical service, wholly detached in its administration from the contractual apparatus of insurance (though receiving a portion of the contributions) and aiming at a standard of performance as high as the medical resources of the country were capable of achieving. 'The field in which the claims of individual commercialism come into the most immediate conflict with reputable notions of social values', he wrote, 'is that of health.'[30] And he was determined that no trace of commercialism should creep in between doctor and patient in his service. He agreed later to a charge of 1 shilling for each prescription, but when the Labour government introduced further charges he resigned, saying that it was the 'beginning of the destruction of those social services in which Labour has taken a special pride and which were giving to Britain the moral leadership of the world'.[31]

The three pillars of the British welfare state were the Education Act, the National Insurance Act, and the National Health Service Act. They are associated with the names of Butler, Beveridge, and Bevan – a Conservative, a Liberal, and a Socialist. When one remembers the mixed origins of social policy at the beginning of the century it is not surprising to find that the welfare state, when it eventually saw the light, was of mixed parentage.

Part Two
Beyond the Welfare State?

7 Re-assessment of the welfare state 1950–70

The British welfare state, as we have suggested, belonged both to the past and the future. Those who looked at it critically in the 1950s against the background of British history were inclined to identify what belonged to the past in it with what it had derived from the Beveridge Report, while recognizing that the National Health Service, in spite of imperfections, represented a step forward into the future. But the picture as seen through European eyes was rather different. Many European observers regarded the National Health Service, with its strong centralized control over the medical services and the medical professions, as not necessarily the model to be copied by all progressive societies, while their attitude to Beveridge was coloured by their tendency to distinguish between the conceptions of social insurance – built up of contracts covering specified risks and covering only paid employees – and social security, which extends to all citizens. Insurance bases rights on contributions, but social security, in the words of a report of the European Economic Community (the Common Market), published in 1958, is based on 'a right directly accorded to the individual by virtue of the protection owed him by society'.[1] Now it is evident that the Beveridge plan, and the British policy which rested upon it, belonged to the era which emphasized the virtues of insurance and the distinction between it and assistance; an era which Pierre Laroque – who might appropriately be described as the French Beveridge – and some other European thinkers regarded as belonging to the past. On the other hand its bold insistence on universal coverage as a right of citizenship gave to it the character of 'social security' as they understood it, and on that account they honoured Beveridge as a great innovator.

However, when one turns to the first flush of home-grown British criticism levelled against the welfare state in the years after the war, it is useful to distinguish between its two principal parts, the social security system or Beveridge plan, with its guarantee of the minimum, and the National Health Service, with its promise of the optimum.

Both came under attack, but for different reasons. The social security system bore clearly upon it the marks of its origin and history. It had been constructed of measures designed to wage war against poverty, and it was in order to complete the victory over poverty, or want, and the other four giants in the path that Beveridge had elaborated his plan. When the laws that it inspired were being debated it seemed that the giants were still there; they had not vanished with the coming of peace. Times were still hard. The war had drained the country's resources, laid waste great areas in its cities, and its end was followed by a period of economic strain. The principal controls were kept in force, including the rationing of food and other consumer goods which was not finally abolished till 1954. The nation had chosen to submit to a regime of austerity in order to prevent the reappearance in large sections of the population of the extreme poverty that had befallen them in the worst of the inter-war years. It was not unnatural to assume that the principles on which the social security system had been built had lost nothing of their relevance in the post-war age. The methods that had been designed to conquer poverty should still be appropriate for holding poverty at bay.

Thus, in the early 1950s, it is perhaps not surprising that some influential commentators concluded that the welfare state was at fault, not because it was over-obsessed with poverty, but because it did not concentrate on it enough. The typical charge was one of extravagance – usually directed against the National Health Service – and the typical question: 'Can we afford it?' There was a good deal of despondency about demographic trends, best expressed in the 1954 *Report of the Committee on the Economic and Financial Problems of the Provision for Old Age* (the Phillips committee). This recommended a gradual rise in the pensionable age to 68 for men and 63 for women: its gloomy pages were bespattered with the word 'burden'.[2]

However the document most representative of this mood had appeared somewhat earlier, in 1952 – the pamphlet by two future Conservative ministers, Iain Macleod and Enoch Powell, entitled *The Social Services – Needs and Means*. Here the theme was that the welfare state had been trying to do too much, given the prevailing conditions of continuing economic stringency, and had failed accordingly. Benefits had fallen below subsistence level, and those without other sources had to apply for additional assistance to what was in effect the old Poor Law under another name – assistance given not as a right, but at discretion and subject to a means test. This is

what Beveridge himself denounced in the following year as abandonment of 'the policy of 1946'. The most economical way of abolishing
want was not to distribute standard cash benefits and free service to
all and sundry, whether they wanted them or not, but to concentrate
scarce resources at the points where they were most needed, with the
help of a test of means. 'The question therefore which poses itself',
they said, 'is not "should a means test be applied to a social service?"
but "why should any social service be provided without a test of
need?"'[3] This came near, as Titmuss asserted in his broadcast
commentary, to advocating 'a new version of the nineteenth-century
poor law' as far as cash benefits were concerned,[4] a return, one might
say, not to the pre-Beveridge but to the pre-Lloyd George situation. If
applied to the National Health Service it would mean, as *The Times*
rightly pointed out in the second of two articles on *Crisis in the
Welfare State*, 'a reversion from Bevanism to Fabianism'[5] for the
Fabians had held that everybody should pay as much as he could
afford for the public services. The scrapping of social insurance and
its replacement by national assistance and a means test, though this
seemed to be logically implied by the remarks of some of the critics,
was hardly ever explicitly proposed, and certainly not by the authors
of the pamphlet. But the idea of charging for services, including both
health and education, was definitely favoured by many Conservative
writers, and even more emphatically – for a time – by the
Liberals.

Many of the contributors to this debate of the early and mid 1950s
underestimated the differences between the situations before and
after the war, in both their economic and the social aspects. The most
obvious of these was the contrast between the persistent large-scale
unemployment of the 1920s and 1930s and the continuous state of
full, and at times 'overfull' employment of the 1950s. (It is salutary to
recall that in July 1955 there were 185,000 persons registered as
unemployed in Great Britain; at that time the number of vacancies
notified to Employment Exchanges and Youth Employment Offices
was 473,000). This sellers' market for labour was accompanied by a
rising standard of living for the bulk of the wage-earning class, and a
shift of interest – to which we have already referred indirectly – from
unemployment benefits to retirement pensions as the item in social
security which mattered most. A system obsessed with the ideas of
poverty and subsistence began to look out of place in a society
enjoying the first fruits of a new prosperity. The change in mood came
late, but when it came, it came abruptly; with remarkable speed the

conviction spread that the time had come to give the Austerity Society decent burial and to welcome the Affluent Society in its place. And an Affluent Society should not need to maintain a complicated and expensive apparatus for waging war on poverty. To apply the Beveridge principle in 1960, said a Conservative MP, 'is to swallow the drug after the disease has gone. For primary poverty has now almost disappeared. Full employment has lifted the mass of our working population to a level of affluence unprecedented in our social history'.[6] This estimate of the economic situation was over optimistic, and it seemed to overlook the fact that one factor in the reduction of primary poverty was precisely that system of social security of which Beveridge was the chief architect. Without the 'drug' the 'disease' would have been more widespread.

The proposal to which this line of thought generally led was strangely similar to that expressed by Macleod and Powell, working from different premises. People should be released from the system of compulsory insurance and given more freedom to exercise personal responsibility and provide for themselves. And when they used the public services they should be charged according to their means. For a time little attempt was made to discover what the effects of such a transfer would be, either on the public services which would still have to function, or on the private institutions which would in part replace them. The emphasis was still on the negative side, on how to get out of the false position in which the country had placed itself by carrying the legacy of the past into the present. The one thing that seemed to emerge clearly was that the critics wanted to cut down the public social services, though whether this was because the country could not afford to keep them up or because it could afford to do without them was not always obvious. What did appear certain was that, in some influential political circles, the tide was turning against the view, which had grown in strength from Lloyd George to Beveridge, that the public social services must be regarded as a permanent part of the national culture of which the people should be proud. Such statements as the following struck a different note: 'The true object of the Welfare State, for the Liberal, is to teach people how to do without it' (by a leading Liberal economist),[7] and: 'Conservatives must strive for a large reduction, in the long run, of the public social services' (by a member of the Conservative Bow Group).[8]

In the event, despite twists and turns in the current of opinion, the welfare state survived the attack, and the 1950s turned out to be a quiet period for the social services. This can be illustrated by developments, or by the lack of them, in the health services, and in social security. So far as the former was concerned, British policy had had an enthusiastic and adventurous phase when it established the NHS, but this was followed by a period of timidity. It was believed (not without cause) that the best system of popular medical care in the world had been created in Britain, but it seemed to have cost a good deal more than had been anticipated. For a decade or more little was done to expand the service. The Guillebaud Committee (1955–6) explained that the figures generally quoted were misleading. For, although the initial cost was more than double some preliminary estimates, and rose steeply thereafter, the proportion of the Gross National Product absorbed by the service had actually fallen slightly from 3.51 per cent to 3.24 per cent while the cost per head of the population (at 1948–9 prices) had risen only from £7. 13s. to £8. 12s.[9] However, caution continued to prevail. Expenditure increased slowly and for some time no major developments took place either in the building of hospitals or in the rehabilitation of general practice – two crying needs. Furthermore, administrative reform was quite out of fashion. Guillebaud documented many failings in the post-1948 structure of the NHS, but concluded that the time was far from ripe for any further upheaval.

There were, however, two important departures from Beveridge's principles. The first became apparent very early on. As pointed out in the previous chapter, it soon became clear that far greater use was being made of national assistance, as opposed to national insurance, than Beveridge had intended. This is often thought to have come about by default, but it was not really so. In 1946, the prospects for the British economy – and hence for the ambitious social programmes outlined in the Labour Party's 1945 election manifesto – were totally dependent on the successful negotiation of a loan from the United States, designed to ease the burden of wartime indebtedness. In the event, the terms obtained were somewhat less generous than either Keynes, who headed the delegation to Washington, or the British cabinet had hoped for, but it remains true, and paradoxical, that the post-1945 British welfare state arrived by courtesy of American politicians and bankers, many of whom had scant sympathy with 'socialistic' experiments. However, it was not surprising in such uncertain circumstances that a storey or two was shaved off Beveridge's edifice: the benefits provided under the 1946 National Insurance Act were, in key respects, not as generous as he had recommended. Thus was set in motion the dual system which has been a characteristic feature of British social security ever since, and under which national assistance, and its successors, have been, in cash terms, a superior form of benefit to national insurance, largely because the former have met housing costs and the latter has not. In all this, of course, doubts about Beveridge's concept of subsistence (see pp. 84–5) have played their part: the more deeply it became felt that subsistence was not an acceptable standard for total income, the more objection there was to giving the maximum to all. Hence the means testing.

The second departure occurred in 1959 with the erection, on top of the flat-rate pension, of a modest earning-related scheme for 'graduated' pensions. At first sight, this looked like a theft from Labour's hamper, for Labour had produced a plan for national superannuation in 1957, hoping, vainly, to sway the next election thereby. However, the government was explicit enough that its principal intention was to cure what a 1958 White Paper called 'the large emerging deficits' of the insurance fund.[10] These were only book-keeping entries in the national accounts – there had never been any pot of money under a Whitehall bed – but were nevertheless significant to a government anxious to secure the revenue to meet its current commitments. It would be wrong, ministers said, to put an additional burden on the taxpayer, and it was impossible to raise the level of the flat-rate contributions, because 'the speed of the convoy is that of the slowest ship', i.e. the contributions must be within the capacity to pay of the poorest contributor. So the answer to the financial pressure was to collect new contributions, graduated according to income from wages and salaries, in the belief that the health of the insurance fund would be transformed long before any payments out became due. The Conservative graduated pensions scheme had many critics, and few real friends, largely because the benefits promised were rather scanty and very long delayed. What mattered most for future planning was the introduction of a controlled co-operative relationship between the state pension scheme and the private, or 'occupational' schemes, run by business firms. Any firm which provided pensions on at least as good terms as the state did could contract out of the graduated part of the pension scheme on behalf of its employees. Ironically, such contracting out was on a scale greater than the government had envisaged and so, after one good year, the insurance fund swung once more into deficit.

Meanwhile elsewhere much greater and more positive improvements were taking place. It is true that in France the proposal, made in

1946, to extend insurance to cover all risks and all citizens met with so much opposition that the government was forced to modify its programme, while the reliance, for unemployment insurance, on private schemes and collective agreements continued unchanged. But there was no move to reduce the role of the state, and when de Gaulle tried to launch a campaign for economy, he had to bow to the protests of the champions of the public social services. In the United States, too, where Federal social policy always had to contend with stubborn individualists and defenders of States' rights, the trend was towards a shift in the balance between statutory and voluntary services in favour of the former. News was coming in of interesting developments in Sweden, in health, housing and pensions, but probably the strongest impact was made by reports of the German legislation of 1956 which replaced a wage-related pension scheme of standard pattern by a system of universal superannuation. The German scheme was announced with a great flourish of trumpets as a decisive step forward and away from traditional practices. Finally, when Britain began to negotiate for entry into the Common Market it was natural to compare the levels of social provision at home and in the six European member states. Some thought that Britain might be under pressure to lower her standards if she joined. But a survey of expenditure on social security and health services published by the ILO in 1961 showed that the proportion of the national income devoted by the United Kingdom to these purposes was lower than the lowest in the Community and not quite three-fifths that of the highest.[11] The authors admitted that the figures could not be entirely reliable and must be used with caution. But, when all allowances were made, the headline in *The Times*, 'Britain lagging behind in Social Security Spending', seemed to be justified.[12]

By the beginning of the 1960s the emphasis in discussions of British social policy had shifted from curtailment to expansion. In January 1962 the Conservative government announced a plan for spending £500 million in ten years (and eventually £700 million) on hospital building and improvement, while decisions were taken in rapid succession for the funding of seven new universities in England alone. This was not exactly parsimonious. As the prospect of a general election moved nearer, there began to emerge from the political parties, or from semi-official groups within them, blueprints for the social services bolder and more grandiose than anything which had gone before. The Conservatives' manifesto for 1964 – 'Prosperity with a Purpose' – was only a little less enthusiastic in its expansionary ambitions than Labour's 'The New Britain'. And Butler and Stokes's survey of the opinions of a large sample of the British electorate in 1963 showed how strong was popular support for increased outlays on the social services: as an issue of high impact, it ranked only below concerns about the functioning of the economy.[13] Such themes were most congenial to, and most readily associated with, the Labour Party, so Labour tended to win out in the electoral contests of the 1960s.

It would be tempting to assume that the feeling of affluence had put an end to the economy drive and restored the kind of consensus originally engendered by the Beveridge Report and then shaken by political and professional disputes over the measures to be taken to implement it and by the 'crisis' of 1952. Such a view, however, understates the importance of the growth of awareness that all was not well with the British mixed economy. In February 1963 the number of unemployed rose to 3.9 per cent of the labour force, the highest figure since the fuel crisis of 1947. This was quite largely owing to appalling weather, but there were plenty of other indications of torpor in the economy. The Conservative government was converted to a more expansionist and more interventionist stance. If something close to a renewed consensus did emerge in the early 1960s it was not so much born out of affluence *per se*, as out of a shared belief that an active government could do much to redress economic and social ills. The setbacks of 1962–3 were not grave enough to strike at the optimism that Britain's problems were susceptible to political solutions, but they were sufficient to dispel complacency.

Both before and after Labour was returned to power in 1964 there were social policy innovations which had their origins in the desire to streamline British industry, and to remove bottlenecks which were impeding the smooth running of the economy. The most important of these was the legislation of 1963 and 1965 governing redundancy. Henceforth, when economic, organizational or technological changes made certain workers superfluous or unemployable they were not to be 'sacked' but 'made redundant', to indicate that the causes of their dismissal were structural rather than personal. They therefore became entitled to receive compensation in the form of a lump sum assessed in relation to their length of service. Redundancy payments, and the procedures associated with them, are regulated by the acts, and payments are made from a fund fed by employers' contributions. Co-operation between government and industry has been very close here, perhaps because of the common interest in overcoming social obstacles to economic progress.

Another departure – not least from Beveridge's principles – during the period concerned the scheme for short-term unemployment, sickness, injuries and widows' allowances. All those for whom these risks were covered for flat-rate benefits, including those 'contracted out' for pensions, were obliged to participate in a state earnings-related insurance scheme through which they could draw a supplementary grant for a limited period, i.e. for six months following the first two weeks after the onset of the misfortune. The rates were calculated quite differently from those of graduated pensions, and the *total* amounts received could be very much greater, partly because the sick, unemployed and widows often have dependent children whereas pensioners do not. An unemployed father of a family of four would probably be getting *in toto* over 70 per cent of his average wage, and could get up to the statutory maximum of 85 per cent.

During the Second Reading debate on the National Insurance Bill in February 1966, the Opposition spokesman, Sir Keith Joseph, said that he understood that the measure had been given legislative priority because of the wish of the National Economic Development Council to encourage labour mobility, while the minister, Miss Margaret Herbison, referred to the National Plan, and declared that earnings-related unemployment benefit should be viewed as complementary to the Redundancy Payments Act.[14] The trouble was that the new benefits were intended to advance social, as well as economic ends. Only a quarter of the payments disbursed under the new act were to be in the form of earnings-related unemployment benefit, with which the economic arguments in favour were solely concerned. And since the new benefits were to last for a maximum of six months, nothing at all was being done to aid those subject to longer periods of dependency. The social case for the provisions of the act therefore boiled down to the argument that they might assist in relieving the pains of adjustment to new circumstances. As we shall see, this innovation failed to survive the return of large-scale unemployment in the early 1980s. Like some other measures of its time it depended on a perception of social and economic problems as serious, but at the same time tractable.

One characteristic belief of the 1960s was that there were great advantages to be gained from seizing hold of any potential economies of scale. This can be seen in governmental encouragement of industrial and commercial mergers. It can be seen, too, in the way in which local authorities (often Labour-controlled) went in for massive schemes of city centre redevelopment in partnership with private sector property developers, and in the interest in industrialized systems of house-building. The look of many urban and suburban localities was transformed by towers. In 1954 rather less than 5 per cent of all dwellings approved under tender for building by local authorities and New Town Corporations in England and Wales consisted of flats in blocks of five storeys or over: five years later the proportion had grown to 13 per cent, and in 1964 reached 24 per cent.[15]

One area which many thought was in urgent need of comprehensive redevelopment was public administration. In a fine flush of latter-day utilitarianism each set of institutions in turn was scrutinized and found wanting. The story here starts with the Royal (Herbert) Commission on Local Government in Greater London (1957–6); it goes on through the (Seebohm) Committee on Local Authority and Allied Personal Social Services (1965–8), the (Fulton) Committee on the Civil Service (1966–8) and the (Redcliffe-Maud) Royal Commission on Local Government in England (1966–9) and similar bodies for Wales and Scotland. Although the Todd Royal Commission (1965–8) reviewed Medical Education, and the Briggs Committee (1970–2) studied Nursing, the National Health Service had to wait until the late 1970s for its own comprehensive Royal Commission. This did not prevent the 1966–70 Labour government from producing two Green Papers on administrative reorganization, nor the incoming Conservatives from capping them with a Consultative Document. This example may serve as a reminder that schemes of reform were often implemented only when the 1970s were well under way (and are hence described in greater detail where necessary in the following chapters). However, this was according to a political agenda set several years earlier.

Certain shared assumptions animated the reformers. There was, first of all, the very general belief that rather a wide range of problems could be solved, or at least mitigated, through administrative restructuring. Second, the existing organizational frameworks, geographical boundaries, and distribution of functions within and between Whitehall and subordinate authorities were seen as having been suitable, doubtless, for the world of pony and trap, but as having been rendered inappropriate by technological and other changes. The answer was typically sought in fewer, larger units arranged in coherent hierarchies. Third, there was much emphasis on both professional and managerial expertise, and on educational and training programmes specifically designed to provide them. Fourth, considerable importance was attached to consumer involvement in decision-making. Some of this was doubtless lip-service, but assertions that the new local authorities would be remote and would flout community ties could be sincerely countered by the argument that there was little point in having democratic local government if it was too weak and disjointed to provide effective service delivery. A further line of defence against such charges – which were, of course, frequently made – was to plan for the introduction of new semi-formalized channels for a limited popular participation, standing outside, and in uneasy relation with, the line service allocating hierarchies. Planning forums, and, later, the Community Health Councils would be examples here.

The impression might have been given so far that the debate on social policy in the 1960s was fuelled, largely or solely, by a commonly-held desire to bring about modernization and greater administrative efficiency. Such a view would grossly underplay the significance of the reawakening of an explicitly humanitarian urge, seen most obviously in the phenomenon known as the 'rediscovery of poverty'. Yet this, too, was in many ways of a piece with the trends and developments which we have outlined. Keith Banting, in his recent discussion of family poverty and family policy, has shown that much was owed here to a small group of social scientists, especially Professor Richard Titmuss and his colleagues and protégés at LSE, Brian Abel-Smith and Peter Townsend, who set out 'to reshape policy makers' interpretation of their environment',[16] employing the classic Fabian (and Utilitarian) techniques of enquiry and report, and, later, of single-issue campaigning, directed essentially towards ministers, civil servants and other members of the political élite.

The sequence of events would follow a common pattern. First, the academic researchers would obtain the funds from one of the grant-giving foundations for a modest sample survey, or would scour government-collected data in order to re-analyse them. The resulting report – Cole and Utting's *The Economic Circumstances of Old People* (1962) or Abel-Smith and Townsend's *The Poor and the Poorest* (1965) – would produce evidence suggesting that the conventional wisdom had gravely underestimated the poverty likely to be encountered in the kind of population under review. *The Poor and the Poorest* was particularly influential because of its conclusion that there were, in 1960, approximately 2.5 million children locked into impoverished households. Findings like this would be received with interest, and with polite scepticism, in Whitehall. Some time later, however, the Government would publish the results of its own survey – *Financial and Other Circumstances of Retired Pensioners* (1965), *Circumstances of Families* (1967) – which would amply confirm the estimates of the freelance academics. This came about because the government's researchers had accepted the validity of the academics' most significant exploit in intellectual engineering – the setting of a new, and more generous, poverty-line, based on the government's own national assistance scales, but taking account of the additional regular weekly payments which many applicants at the time received. From this, says Banting, 'all else flowed'.[17]

It was, however, one thing to succeed in redefining the problem for social policy, and indeed, to have the ear of ministers. It was quite another to ensure effective action. The Labour government seemed slow to get off the mark. In order to drive some wind into the sails, the poverty researchers were instrumental in founding new pressure groups, most notably the Child Poverty Action Group in December 1965. Like the troops landing in France at the beginning of the First World War, they expected that they would be home and dry by the following Christmas.[18] It soon became apparent that the government had other preoccupations, like getting itself re-elected. But even after Labour's handsome victory in 1966, most of the government's energy was used up in the task of avoiding being crushed by the troubles of the economy. The attention which could be accorded to social policy was limited, and so were available resources, especially those needed to fulfil the more expensive electoral commitments. It is true that, in the favourable atmosphere generated by the revelation of the Rachman and other scandals in London, the contentious issues of private-sector rents and security of tenure could be grasped, and rather neatly defused, in the 'fair-rent' legislation of 1965 and 1968. However, the promised 'Income Guarantee' early sank without trace, and the new pensions plan, flagship of three election manifestos, only left port in 1969, just in time to be torpedoed by defeat in 1970. As for measures to relieve family poverty, there was a bitter and protracted battle in cabinet between November 1966 and February 1967: the outcome was a compromise, in which family allowances were raised (in three instalments between October 1967 and October 1968) but accompanied with the device of clawback, which meant that the benefit of the increase to the standard-rate income-tax payer was taken back through a reduction in child tax allowances. Thus for the first time the principle was accepted, even if timidly, that there should be a coherent relationship between the social security and income tax systems. It could also be argued that the government had shown some courage, in so far as the message picked up by Labour MPs in their constituencies was that these measures were not popular among many of the party's supporters. However, the poverty campaigners regarded them as rather a pallid result for all the effort of persuasion which had been put in, and relationships between the poverty lobby and the government were henceforth cool. They would have been even cooler had it been more widely known at the time that proposals for a much more thoroughgoing experiment in means-testing – similar to the family income supplement introduced by the Conservatives in 1970 – were only narrowly defeated in cabinet.[19]

In the circumstances it was not inappropriate that one of the most memorable ventures of the Labour government, in 1966, was intended to render means-testing more acceptable, to public and to party opinion. By that time Beveridge was dead, but he would doubtless have been gravely disquieted by the fact that nearly 30 per cent of those in receipt of social insurance benefits (excluding maternity and industrial injury) were also getting means-tested assistance supplements, and, looking at it from the other angle, 77 per cent of all weekly means-tested payments were being made to people already receiving insurance benefits.[20] The action taken in 1966 did not aim at reducing these proportions; on the contrary it was designed to encourage more of those entitled to assistance to claim it. The two systems of insurance and assistance were administratively merged in a new Ministry of Social Security and the invidious term 'national assistance' was abandoned in favour of the innocuous 'supplementary benefit' (or 'pension') which was used even in cases where there was no benefit to supplement. The significance which these changes were meant to have is indicated by the appearance in the pension books that 'people over pension age have a right ... to a guaranteed income' followed by instructions on how to claim it. This was in direct contradiction to the Beveridge principle that there can be no right where discretion enters into the making of an award.

The spirit of the 1960s evaporated slowly. The Conservative victory in 1970 appeared to mark a clear transition, and yet, as we have noted, some of the favoured nostrums of the previous decade, like the enthusiasm for bigger and (presumably) better units of administration, survived to motivate the incoming government. Even here, however, critics were becoming more insistent, and one incident heavy with symbolic value, the collapse of Ronan Point, a tower-block in East London, occurred as early as May 1968. Again, optimism about the economy outlasted the travails of the Labour administration, the sterling crisis and the enforced devaluation of November 1967. Brian Lapping, writing in 1970, correctly commented that the problem 'pressed down upon the Labour Cabinet as devastatingly as though it has been a great rock liable at any time to fall on the Cabinet room' but also disarmingly suggests that 'in retrospect, it looks so easy to solve'.[21] In the chapters to follow, we shall be looking at the consequence for the welfare state as hopefulness of this kind gradually leaked away. It remains a remarkable fact that for something more than twenty years after the passing of the welfare legislation of the Attlee government the consensus about fundamentals was sufficient to prevent changes of government from driving social policy along a zigzag course. Political conflict was, for the most part, about what might be called the technology of social policy (sometimes referred to as 'social engineering') or about priorities, levels of provision and the speed of advance towards goals which each party claimed to be pursuing in its own way.

8 Social security

The term 'social security' is used here in its narrower sense of arrangements for providing cash benefits, through social insurance, by means of tax-supported regular payments to meet particular dependencies, like family allowances for children or some benefits accruing to the disabled and those who look after them, and through the various grants made subject to means test which we can refer collectively as 'assistance'. Some of the purposes for which these benefits are provided can also be met by devices incorporated into the system of taxation and these must be brought into the picture. These purposes are varied, and are frequently difficult to disentangle. E. M. Murphy of the Department of National Health and Welfare in Canada has recently distinguished four 'roles' for, or 'concerns' of, social security programmes: protection against common risks, like sickness or unemployment; the generation of compulsory savings; the redistribution of income towards greater equality, and compensation.[1] We shall consider these briefly in turn.

The first purpose has traditionally been met through social insurance – social insurance differing from private insurance because premiums are not adjusted to risk, and because the compulsory coverage of large groups in the population allows chosen cross-subsidies to be built into the programme: as Murphy points out, the existence of these cross-subsidies betrays the presence of objectives other than protection against common risks. Social insurance does, however, share with private insurance the feature that there must be an explicit link between contributions and entitlement to benefit. This is a weak requirement. It leaves open the extent to which there should be actuarially calculated benefits for each individual, or whether social insurance is more like a compulsory club, where payments in and payments out are not closely related, but membership of which is an essential precondition for any benefit. In the British industrial injuries scheme, a person injured on his or her first day of work, before any contributions have been made, is eligible for benefit, so the rules of the club may be very loose indeed.

Social insurance programmes can usually best be viewed as a means of adjusting the flow through time of earnings of the working population, the transfers being either between generations or within a single working life and beyond. This brings us to a second possible purpose, that of compulsory savings. This is obviously most relevant to programmes which take a long time to mature, like many of those directed towards the elderly. Funded pension schemes are frequently advocated because they are held to advance aims which are outside the boundaries of social welfare as conventionally understood, especially the provision of resources for fixed capital investment in productive industry.

A third role for social security is to seek to alter the distribution of income in the direction of greater equality. This usually means in practice the establishment of officially approved minimum levels of income related to general levels of living in a society. One important aim of social security programmes has been the eradication, or at least the diminution, of poverty. However, since the relationship between the lessening of poverty and the increase in equality is a vexed question, and since poverty, however defined, is not a matter only of cash income, we shall look at the whole topic in a separate chapter, confining what is said about it here to an explanation of how grants specifically designed to help the poor fit into the structure of the cash benefits system.

Compensation, Murphy's fourth purpose, usually appears particularly clearly in the areas of personal injury at work and employment-generated diseases. However, as we have seen, Britain no longer has a workmen's compensation scheme, by which the employer pays for these risks either through experience-related, state-imposed premiums, or through private insurance. Nevertheless the concept of compensation continues to inform certain aspects of the current scheme for industrial injuries – industrial injury disablement benefits are non-taxable, may continue after retirement, and are treated especially favourably in the assessments for means-tested benefits. Similar considerations apply to war pensions. In recent years the rationale of compensation has been extended to certain benefits for the 'civilian disabled'. Attendance allowances and mobility allowance, for instance, are exempt from income tax and do not count as resources under the supplementary benefit scheme.

Social security programmes, then, are designed to further a number of objectives which it may be difficult to ensure are compatible one with another. Yet it is clear that developed industrial nations have not plumped for a single role for social security, with its particular logic and implied system of financing: instead they have chosen to follow a middle course, which picks its way among the alternatives. Pierre Laroque, some of whose views are described in the last chapter, believed that one of the most important features of social security was its treatment of the problem 'as one to be solved for the whole population by a general policy and under a general scheme'.[2] In such a general scheme, he said, one may expect to 'see the disappearance of all connection between contributions and benefits'. Yet this has not happened. As we have seen, there are countries, like New Zealand, which never developed proper contributory benefits. Elsewhere, however, the link between contributions and benefits, far from disappearing as Laroque foretold, has been elaborated and built more firmly into systems of benefits than ever before. Governments do aim at solving the problem 'for a whole population by a general policy' but it is a policy which uses a combination of different methods, one of which – and increasingly the central one – is a system of earnings-related contributions and benefits.

This is, in itself, not new, as we can illustrate in relation to pensions. As we have seen, the original practice in most countries other than Britain was to relate both the contributions and the pensions to earnings. However, the new type of pension which was introduced in most countries in Northern and Western Europe in the 1950s and the 1960s is also related to earnings, but in a quite different way. Pensions of the older kind were small in amount and designed only to soften the blow of retirement. The grading of contributions and therefore of benefits was little more than a financial device for increasing the revenue of the pension fund and reducing the burden to be borne by taxes. With pensions of the new type the starting point of the calculation is the idea of a decent provision for old age, and 'decent provision' is not, like subsistence, an absolute quantity, but is relative to the standard of living enjoyed by a man and his wife before retirement. It will be less than what they had then, but will not imply any catastrophic change in their manner of life. An ILO convention of 1967 set the minimum 'replacement ratio' of pension to earnings at 45 per cent for a man and his wife, but since then many countries have adopted a *target* of 70 to 75 per cent of a man's average earnings in the last few years of his working life.[3] The effect of such schemes, broadly speaking, is to apply to the working population in general the principle which has long governed the pensions of public servants, civil and military, and which we may call 'superannuation'. The policy cannot be given any political label, for it is found in both 'capitalist' and 'socialist' countries. It contains in itself elements of both socialism and individualism, because it recognizes a universal social right in a manner which takes account of individual differences. For each beneficiary (or insured person) has, as it were, a personal account which determines the size of the pension to which he or she is entitled.

We must now turn to the way in which these generalities were made into actualities in the Britain of the past decade. During the space of six years (1969–75) three schemes were hammered out in the backrooms of Whitehall and of Westminster. It was in January 1969 that Richard Crossman published a White Paper on *National Superannuation and Social Insurance* (Cmnd 3883) but the Bill based upon it foundered in the general election of 1970. In September 1971 Sir Keith Joseph presented the Conservative proposals in a White Paper entitled *Strategy for Pensions* (Cmnd 4775). The act to turn its recommendations into law was passed in 1973, but it was not due to come into effect until 1975, by which time the government had fallen. The incoming Labour government was pledged to start afresh, and in the late summer of 1974 Mrs Barbara Castle produced yet another White Paper, *Better Pensions* (Cmnd 5713). The Social Security Pensions Bill was introduced into Parliament early in 1975, and by the summer of that year had obtained the Royal Assent. The scheme started three years later, in April 1978.

It is tempting to concentrate on the eventually successful 'Castle Plan' and to consign the 'Crossman Plan' and the 'Joseph Plan' to the status of historical footnotes. Certainly most of the detail will not concern us: even at the time it was only of interest to those involved in the technical aspects of social security planning. However, the similarities and differences among the three schemes are instructive, in that they show how a generation of politicians of the major parties viewed an important area of social policy. The schemes were similar in that they all had the wide aim of regulating the income structure of the whole working population in such a way as to provide an income when earnings cease, or are interrupted, bearing an acceptable relationship to income earned before this happened. They were not, like the Beveridge plan, only an 'attack on Want'. But they set about their task in different ways. We must now examine the issues of principle which were at stake.

To begin with, the basic structure of the three schemes needs to be considered. Here the contrast between the Crossman and Joseph schemes was stark: many politicians and commentators argued that the differences were clear evidence of a fundamental ideological divide. The Crossman Plan aimed to abolish the two-tier structure which had existed since 1959, in which a structure of graduated insurance for earners only was superimposed on flat-rate insurance for everybody. It wanted to put in its place a single one-tier system of earnings-related insurance to cover all social insurance, both long-term (pensions) and short-term (health, unemployment etc.). 'Contracting-out' by occupational pension schemes which satisfied certain conditions was to be permitted, as under the 1959 scheme, but was to be on a limited and closely circumscribed basis: there was no intention to hand over total responsibility for the social insurance of sections of the public. The Joseph Plan, on the other hand, went a long way towards this objective. It retained the then existing two-tier structure, but with the difference that the upper, earnings-related tier was designed to be manned chiefly by independent occupational schemes: the state was to provide at this level only a Reserve Scheme to serve as a model, or standard, and to accommodate those who were not otherwise catered for. The Castle scheme, in this respect, resembled Joseph rather more than Crossman. It retained the ideas of a personal flat-rate pension (called the basic level) and of an additional state earnings-related pensions scheme (SERPS) for those who are not members of occupational schemes. Contracted-out schemes were to take over responsibility for paying the whole of the additional pension for a contributor on retirement and half the additional pension payable to a widow. However, there was a very important difference between Joseph and Castle, in that the latter plan did not break with the traditional British practice that state-provided pensions should be 'pay as you go', current beneficiaries being paid out of current receipts, whereas contributions to Sir Keith's State Reserve Scheme would have been funded and invested in the ordinary commercial way.

This brings us on to a vexed set of questions. There is a very long gap between the time when a new entrant to the labour force begins to pay contributions and the time when he or she becomes eligible to claim a pension. Pension schemes have to take account, during this period, of changes in the general level of prosperity, changes in the value of money, and variations in the patterns of employment of members. The Crossman Plan aimed to base the amount of pension to be paid on a calculation of earnings throughout life revalued in tune with average earnings at the time that the benefit fell due. Sir Keith

Joseph promised that his flat-rate pension would be annually reviewed and adjusted to the cost of living, while the dynamic character of the State Reserve Scheme would rest, like that of occupational schemes, on the fortunes of its investments: it was expected that 'bonus additions' would 'offset, or offset to a substantial extent, the effect of rising prices on the purchasing power of the pension' (App. 3, para. 17). Mrs Castle followed her Labour predecessor, Richard Crossman, in laying down that all pension rights earned before retirement would be revalued to keep pace with the general rise in earnings: her scheme also introduced the interesting feature of calculating the amount of pension on the best twenty years of earnings in a contributor's working life. This is fairer than calculations based on final salary for those, like many manual workers, whose earnings peak relatively early in their careers.

So far we have only described in broad outline the schemes which scudded across the political landscape in the late 1960s and early 1970s. We have said enough, however, of the differences among them to make it worth asking the question at this point – how did it come about that, after all the fiery speeches which had been made, the issue was settled quietly, almost amicably, in 1974–5? The Opposition did not divide the House of Commons against the Second Reading of the Social Security Pensions Bill in March 1975. Conservative spokesmen criticized some of the details of the bill, but otherwise contented themselves with regretting the three years delay or so which had arisen because of the government's refusal to build on the Joseph Plan, and with observations that the new measure would do nothing to help existing pensioners, and little to help those who were shortly about to retire.[4] (The latter was perfectly true – the Exchequer's liability for the payment of earnings-related pensions will not have fully built up until practically the end of the century – but it was a criticism which could have been levelled against *all* the plans which had followed on each other in such swift succession in the previous few years). Sheer exhaustion must have played its part, distaste at the prospect of more guerilla action along the byways of pensioneering. So, most definitely, did the unprecedented inflation rates of 1974–5, which put a big question mark over the feasibility of relying on occupational provision to the extent contemplated in the Joseph Plan. A further point is that the Conservatives had become rather defensive about the levels of pension offered by the State Reserve Scheme. They had had to be kept low, in order to provide an inducement for employers to set up their own schemes: in terms of the replacement of previous earnings, Mrs Castle's additional pensions were more generous, but not so much more generous that charges of profligacy or hostility towards occupational schemes could hope to stick.

But Labour had moved too. Mrs Castle's willingness to compromise was important, and the party had implicitly recognized that a one-tier graduated scheme for earners on the Crossman model was unlikely ever to be able to provide for all who retire with an adequate pension as of right. Yet the two parties had never been so far apart as some supposed. Much of the argument over the Crossman Bill had been concerned with the precise amount of 'abatement' to be offered to those employers who contracted their employees out of the state scheme. Crossman himself undoubtedly hoped that in due course, after ten years or so 'more and more firms would be finding it convenient to take the State scheme and merely add a little on top of it'.[5] However, even in the late 1960s, when Labour was preparing its plan for national superannuation, there were 65,000 occupational schemes in operation covering 12 million workers, of which 70 per cent in the public sector and 30 per cent in the private had contracted out.[6] Thus already a big body of investment and of accumulated rights had built up which had to be taken into account; and the Labour government had no intention of killing the goose which was thought to be laying the golden eggs of future industrial prosperity. That being said, the significance of the acceptance in the Castle Plan of 'partnership' between the state and occupational schemes should not be underrated.

There was one other reason for the atmosphere of benign agreement which surrounded the Social Security Pensions Act of 1975. This was the tacit understanding between the political parties that some especially knotty problems would be reserved for later resolution. Two of these concerned this very reliance upon occupational provision. The first was how to preserve pension rights when people change their jobs. In a state scheme (like the Crossman Plan) there is no problem, and neither is there one in a sufficiently broadly based occupational scheme which provides enough room to accommodate such mobility as normally occurs. The French have evolved a system of this kind for providing supplements to their rather low state pensions. It has been done by collective agreement between firms and between whole industries to create broad schemes which are then federated into a national association and supervised by a national institution.[7] But there was nothing like this in the Joseph Plan which could only guarantee that a man's accumulated rights should be preserved as 'deferred' fractions of a pension, to be collected and pieced together by him on retirement. And the current scheme offers little improvement in this regard, only giving employers the additional option of buying a member back into the state scheme (which had indeed been provided for under the Joseph Plan for those who left a job after fewer than five years service). Thus, in effect, those who stay put with one employer for forty years are heavily subsidized by job-changers, including those who experience redundancy. A man working in the private sector – public sector schemes have their own 'transfer club' – who changes his job three times during his working lifetime may end up with a pension of only one-third of his final salary, instead of the two-thirds (including state flat-rate pension) typically promised by the schemes of which he will have been a member. It seems indisputable that the very large number of separate and uncoordinated occupational schemes in Britain – by now around 100,000 of them – acts as a substantial deterrent to labour mobility, especially among older employees.

The body charged with consideration of this matter was the Occupational Pensions Board, a creation of the Heath government. In 1981 it published a report,[8] which recommended that pension entitlements 'frozen' when employees changed jobs should be up-rated each year in line with wage inflation, but subject to an annual maximum of 5 per cent. These proposals were modest ones – they would erode only some of the advantage enjoyed by stayers over leavers – but the government nevertheless left the report on the shelf for three years before announcing that it accepted the substance of the recommendations. Without complete indexation or complete transferability the inequity will remain. And any attempt to give a better deal to early leavers will raise pension costs.

The second problem concerns protection against inflation after a pension has been put into payment. A man of 65 can expect to live on average for a further twelve years, a woman of 60 for another twenty years, and occupational pensioners have slightly more favourable life-chances than others. These are quite large slices of time, particularly in the case of women – which is one reason why occupational schemes have met the needs of women less adequately than those of men. The Castle compromise, like the Joseph Plan before it, has made no promises in this area: the leaflet of general guidance on the Social Security Pensions Act, 1975, says that 'whether there is any inflation-proofing of an occupational pension above the levels of the guaranteed minimum will be a matter for the scheme itself'.[9] Most private sector pensions are up-rated periodically, but according to the latest (1983) survey of the National Association of Pension Funds only on average to the extent of about half the increase necessary to take account of inflation.[10] So these occupational pensioners have to face a gradual whittling down of their standard of living as they grow older. In this respect, as in others, those who formerly worked for a public sector employer are more fortunate. This is especially true of ex-civil servants. In 1981 the Scott Committee, which had been set up in the confident expectation that it would conclude that civil servants were getting their inflation-proofed pensions on unfairly favourable terms, went beyond its terms of reference and recommended that full indexation should apply in the private sector, too.[11] This was not a welcome message, and was duly ignored, but the proposal went to the heart of the problem.

The question has its wider aspects. A state-run funded scheme, like the Joseph State Reserve Scheme, obviously runs into the same difficulty. And even pay as you go arrangements, like those for the present basic and additional pensions, depend upon the willingness of future generations of contributors to permit sufficient transfers to provide promised levels of pension for their cohort of old people, and on the willingness of future governments to see that this comes about. This situation offends the moral susceptibilities of some commentators: Dilnot, Kay and Morris, in a recent publication from the Institute of Fiscal Studies, have declared that 'the device of meeting yesterday's claims from today's premiums has been familiar to fraudulent and foolish financiers for millennia, and the gaols and workhouses of the world are filled with those private individuals who did not realize that reality breaks through eventually'.[12] The question is thus: are those who are now in the prime of life promising themselves greatly improved pensions at the expense both of those who came before them and those who will follow them?

Present arrangements certainly raise acute problems of inter-generational fairness. This can be illustrated by the calculation of Altmann and Atkinson that those who retire with full additional pension in 2001 (state benefits only) will be receiving, on average, 40 to 50 per cent more than those in their 80s at the same time.[13] However, there seems to be no reason for panicking, at least on demographic grounds. The pensioner dependency ratio (the ratio of pensioners per person of economically active age) is actually set to decline marginally, from 0.29 in 1978 and 1988 to 0.27 in 2008, before rising again to reach its previous level in 2018.[14]

Certainly there is a question mark over the proportion of those in the economically active age groups who will, in fact, be economically active. But, although unemployment erodes the pool of contributors, at the same time it plays havoc with pension entitlements, thus reducing the eventual commitment for both SERPS and occupational schemes.

This raises the point that governments, anxious about the present or future call upon resources, can, in a pay as you go system, do one of two things – they can increase the amount they take in from the working population, or they can decrease the current or eventual amount which they pay out to pensioners (and other beneficiaries). Indeed, they have already done both. An important departure from previous arrangements in the current scheme – one borrowed from the Joseph Plan – is that *flat-rate* benefits are financed by *earnings-related* contributions. This was designed to solve the problem posed by such benefits in a period of inflation, which is, put simply, to ensure that enough is gathered in to cover the 'dynamization' promised in the annual review. These graduated contributions for financing flat-rate benefits carry no equivalent differential rights, graduated pensions being a quite separate affair. What is being done, in fact, as Sir John Walley has argued, is to impose a progressive tax to finance a welfare service, with nothing of the true character of insurance remaining. That being so, he continues, would it not be both fairer and more effective to levy the tax on all forms of income, not only on earnings (and even on them only proportionately up to a certain level), and to make everyone, not only earners, eligible to receive the service?[15]

The prime example of the second strategy is the decision, under the Social Security Act of 1980, to index pensions henceforth by prices alone, instead of by either prices or earnings, whichever was the greater. In most years the former works out cheaper for governments, but this was more than a matter of an administration snipping away at some short-term commitments it found troublesome. The debates over the issue revealed a substantial disagreement about the purposes of social security. Up-rating benefits according to the retail price index may make sense if the aim is to guard against some fixed standard of poverty, but it is not so appropriate if the intention is that dependent populations should share in any rising levels of living enjoyed by those in work. This is a matter to which we return in Chapter 12.

Earnings-related schemes (in relation to contributions *and* benefits) are in some respects less comprehensive than the system advocated by Beveridge. They are tailor-made for a modern industrial society in which the vast majority of the population works for money, and the great majority gets its money from an employer, public or private. Some would put this differently, and say that they *were* tailor-made for the sort of society which appeared to be emerging in the 1960s and early 1970s. However, the norm has not changed, even if the great tail of the unemployed, projectable apparently into the distant future, rubs in the truth that there are large groups in the population which earnings-related systems suit considerably less well. Those who do not earn at all, but live on unearned income or are supported by others, will be totally excluded, unless they are allowed to join voluntarily. There are difficulties with the self-employed, too, particularly in calculating their pensionable earnings. These can be overcome, although this has not happened in Britain: an inter-departmental committee examining how this group could be brought fully into the new state pension scheme was abruptly disbanded in 1976, apparently because the then government was unprepared to countenance the increased number of civil servants which would be necessitated by such an extension of the scheme. As things stand, the self-employed have been required since 1975 to pay what are termed Class Four contributions on a percentage of their gains or profits between a lower and an upper limit,[16] but they earn no additional benefits as a result – to the vociferously expressed disgust of their representatives.

Again, it is hard to cater adequately for those whose employee status is intermittent. The special problems of women have been recognized, particularly in the Crossman and Castle Plans – in the latter case through the 'best twenty years' provisions already mentioned, and through such devices as 'home responsibility protection' which reduces the effect on entitlement to long-term benefits of not paying contributions while looking after children or invalids. These features of the scheme are not technically linked to the sex of contributors of beneficiaries, and they may assist categories of low and irregular earners other than married women, but they do no more than modify the picture of a system which is designed for employees who remain under continuous contract of service from a 'normal' age of leaving school until they reach the standard retirement age.

It is obvious that the state earnings-related pensions scheme will not be tried and tested until the early years of the next century. The same is true – in some respects truer – of private occupational schemes. Most schemes, especially those operating outside the public sector, have not yet had to realize significantly on their promises. And does *occupation*, at a time of high unemployment and record company bankruptcies, provide a stable and reliable basis for security in old age? Employees almost invariably have no choice about whether or not to join their employer's pension scheme, and, once in, they or their representatives usually have precious little say in its investment and other policies (although there is a trend towards the appointment of member trustees). Fund managers may make good decisions, or they may make bad ones, and the result will be that their members' prospects in retirement will differ between schemes in ways which may seem to the latter to be arbitrary. No comprehensive data are available about funding levels in UK schemes, and the seesaw in financial markets in recent years makes it difficult to assess either the risk of insolvency, or the prevalence of its opposite, overfunding (taking in more from contributors than would be warranted by the likely eventual obligations of the scheme). In 1975 the Occupational Pensions Board presented a detailed list of disclosure requirements which they said should be mandatory on all schemes; in 1982 they repeated their plea, noting that in the interim virtually nothing had been done to implement any of their recommendations.[17]

Some critics on the radical right have responded to the deficiencies of the present system with the rather startling suggestion that compulsory pension contributions should be eliminated completely. Nigel Vinson and his colleagues at the Centre for Policy Studies have advocated 'portable pensions', meaning that people should be able to shop around with the money which would otherwise have gone in contributions, and purchase the pension arrangements of their choice from the financial institution of their choice.[18] Such proposals, like others fired by the desire to dispose of 'paternalism', would, if implemented, thrust an enormous load on to the individual. It remains to be seen what headway they will make in the present climate.

Pensions are not the only area where state and occupational provision has grown up separately, and where the two fit together somewhat uncomfortably. Sick pay provides a further example. A survey of occupational sick pay schemes, conducted by the DHSS as far back as 1974, showed that well over 90 per cent of both male and female employees in non-manual occupations were included in such schemes.[19] Coverage of those in manual jobs was significantly lower, but still amounted to nearly 75 per cent of men, and between 50 and 60 per cent of women. The overlap in the late 1970s and early 1980s was considerable: most of those who took more than three days off work drew their replacement income from two sources, with a consequent duplication of administration machinery. Some of them, those employees who received the equivalent of full pay during sickness, were actually better off than when they were working, since national insurance sickness benefit was not (and still is not) subject to income tax. In 1980, the Thatcher government decided that the time was ripe for an exercise in rationalization, with a welcome bonus in the shape of reductions in public expenditure. It therefore published a Green Paper which signalled its intention to hand over to employers responsibility for sick pay for periods of less than eight weeks.[20]

The proposals were not well received, either by the poverty lobby or by employers and their organizations. The latter were opposed because they were expected to incur additional costs, for which they would be only partly compensated by the government through reduced employers' national insurance contributions. The events which followed demonstrated some of the perils of plans for privatization, at least when powerful interests are abroad. The government produced, in rapid succession, five separate detailed sets of proposals, each of which made further concessions to the employers' point of view. Employers' statutory sick pay, as finally implemented, allows employers to deduct the actual amounts they pay out in benefits from their national insurance contribution payments. The result was that the government 'saved' on only about half of the 5000 civil servants it had anticipated, because of the need to check on employers' sick pay returns in order to prevent abuse. And the projected cut in public expenditure on £400 million was more than offset by compensation to employers worth £565 million.[21]

Representations by bodies like the Child Poverty Action Group did not succeed in altering the elements in the scheme to which they particularly objected. Statutory sick pay is flat-rate, without increases for dependants: it therefore redistributes away from those with family commitments and towards single people and childless working couples. It also discriminates against the low paid, who receive lower payments than the statutory amount, because of the fear that otherwise what they would be obtaining might approach their wages while at work.

The new scheme has done little to reduce administrative complexity. Only around 3 per cent of spells of sickness last for six months or more (over 90 per cent last for less than the eight weeks of ESSP). However, those who are ill for such a long period of time, start with statutory sick pay, then transfer to national insurance sickness benefit, and finally, when the six months is up, go on to invalidity benefit. The Specialist Advisor to the House of Commons Select Committee which considered the Government's proposals wrote in a memorandum that they appeared likely 'to continue the "dog's breakfast" which is social security provision in the United Kingdom'.[22] Perhaps an opportunity was missed in statutory sick pay of fashioning a coherent scheme which had the welfare of the sick as its primary objective, but it should be noted, in fairness, that the arrangements which it replaced were a good deal more jagged and inequitable, and also that this major departure in social security as it had developed over seventy years was implemented with little fuss and no serious bugs in the system – certainly when compared with the coming of housing benefit a little later (see Chapter 12).

It is noteworthy that, whereas a great deal of ink and time was devoted to the question of fairness to employers in the new scheme, little attention was given to the parallel possibility of compensating employees for the reduced benefits which *their* contributions would entitle them to. National insurance has traditionally rested on precise links between contributions and benefits, as we noted at the beginning of the chapter. These links provide entitlements, which, if not sacrosanct, could not, it was thought, lightly be altered to the detriment of one of the parties involved. Many trade unionists were deeply suspicious of Lloyd George's schemes in 1911, but over the years the unions (and notably the TUC) became doughty champions of the principle of social insurance, to a considerable extent because they believed that it brought with it built-in obstacles to abrupt changes by government fiat. This now looks more and more questionable. We have already cited Sir John Walley's views on the way in which Britain moved over to financing flat-rate benefits out of graduated contributions. An even clearer example of unilateral action without compensation was the abolition in 1982 of earnings-related short-term benefits, the introduction of which we saw earlier was widely regarded in the mid 1960s as an important advance.

Rights to benefits have always been only part of the story. This is because entitlement to a benefit is attached to a status, and a status, although it may be an objective fact, is also undeniably shaped by the political decision which creates it. National insurance is a method of grouping beneficiaries into large, crude categories without test of means and without further test of need, other than that established by ensuring that the individual has been correctly slotted into the appropriate category – hence the low administrative costs for the sums paid out and the number of people assisted. Frequently a process of accreditation may be required – for example, by doctors (mostly general practitioners, but also those directly employed by DHSS) in the case of sickness benefits, and by doctors and lawyers for industrial injuries benefits. However, even where such professionals are not needed to man the gates, there are problems. Age may seem easy to establish (although it was not in the Ireland of 1908–9, because compulsory registration of births had been embarked on less than seventy years previously). Pensions are usually paid unconditionally in old age, but this can mean anything from 55 to 70, and it may be the same for men and women or different. Very often the pension may be drawn at an earlier date, conditionally or at a lower rate, for instance by those in poor health or who have for a long time been unable to obtain employment. In the British system, since Beveridge, old age begins at 65 for women and 70 for men, but the pension can be drawn at 60 and 65 respectively on condition of retirement. This also has to be defined. To retire is to give up regular work, but the so-called 'earnings rule' allows a man to continue to earn up to a prescribed limit by casual work, above which the pension tapers away as the earnings increase. This concession has come to be regarded as an imposition, but if there were no limits placed on earnings, the retirement pension would become an old age pension, which in some countries it is. The tendency elsewhere, in so far as there is one, seems to be lower the age where it was over 70, as Canada and Norway have done, and to have the same age for men and women, as is now the case in about half the industrial countries. In 1982, a report of the House of Commons Select Committee on the Social Services recommended a common retirement age in Britain for both men and women, with full state pension at the age of 63.[23] The government has formally rejected these proposals, but they and similar ideas remain under discussion.

Another complication is the rule that those who postpone retirement and continue both to work and pay their contributions eventually receive an increased pension. Beveridge thought that this would induce many people to extend their working life, but in fact the proportion of men over pensionable age continuing to work full-time has fallen markedly since the late 1940s. The bait has not been sufficiently attractive, and what matters most is how the employer organizes his workforce. Recently, with higher unemployment among older workers, the trend has been even more the other way:

governments would like to encourage earlier retirement, if they could find sufficiently cheap ways of doing so.

Certain other conditions are now treated as the equivalent of retirement and therefore pensionable in advance of the normal age. Invalidity, or permanent incapacity to work owing to ill-health, is a pensionable status which was well established abroad for some time before it was introduced into this country in 1971. Once it is separated from sickness benefit, which is essentially short-term, it can be shaped and expanded to fit the special needs of this distinctive category of persons. Special consideration is given, for instance, to young mothers with dependent children, and the 1974 Labour government began the practice of paying invalidity benefit (and other long-term benefits) at a higher rate than sickness benefit (and other short-term benefits).

The case of widows is rather different, since what they have lost is not the capacity to work but the support of a husband. But it is assumed that, if widowed in middle age, they might be unable to find employment. So they are granted what is in effect a premature pension if widowed at 50 or later. Currently the responsibilities attached to the status of married women are being redefined, not least in feminist circles, and it may well be that in the future such special treatment accorded to a particular category of middle-aged women will be regarded as inappropriate, inegalitarian, or unnecessary. However, the most recent developments have been in the opposite direction: the harshness of the fixed cut-off point was softened in 1970, when the age of entitlement was lowered to 40, but with a much reduced pension rising year by year to the full amount at 50. A widow also receives an allowance (since 1966) for the first six months of her widowhood to allow her to settle her affairs, and a widowed mother's allowance if she has dependent children. The pension used to be subject to an 'earnings rule', but this was dropped in 1954.

The rights assigned to widows have recently been extended to the divorced, and in some countries separated and deserted wives are given the same status. An Australian Act of 1942 referred to such people as '*de facto* widows', and Norway enlarged the category to include the 'family widow', the woman prevented from either marrying or earning by having to look after her parents. The closest Britain has come to these Norwegian provisions – and it is not very close – is the invalid care allowance, another invention of the mid 1970s. This is a non-contributory benefit which can be claimed by any person (not necessarily a woman) who does not have full-time paid employment but instead looks after a severely disabled relative. A woman living with, and caring for, a severely disabled husband or cohabitee is barred from receiving this benefit: the social security system thus continues to sustain a view of a married woman's role – as contrasted with that of a married man – which many would see as increasingly old-fashioned.

Unemployment is another status which is hard to define precisely, more so indeed than retirement. Registration at the Unemployment Benefit Office (formerly the Labour Exchange) is an essential precondition for obtaining this status, and there are groups – women with dependent children under 16, for instance – who are not obliged to register in order to get social security benefits. Others, such as married women continuing to pay the 'small stamp', do not bother to register because there are no benefits which they can claim, even though they may well be actively seeking work: employers are not required in Britain to notify vacancies to the Department of Employment. Yet others, perhaps older men and women with poorish health or employment records who are in no real sense in the job market, are nevertheless required by the DHSS to sign on (although this no longer applies to men over 60). All this has led to a long running and highly politically charged argument concerning whether the regular official figures on unemployment understate or overstate the true extent of the problem. However, now that the number of those registered unemployed has passed the 3 million mark some of the heat has flowed out of this controversy since the discrepancies are likely to be of marginal significance in relation to such a total.

The melancholy thing about unemployment benefit is that so many of the unemployed do not receive it. If we take men alone, who are more likely to qualify and to register than women, we find that fewer than a third of unemployed claimants are obtaining the benefit, while more than 60 per cent are in receipt of means-tested supplementary allowances. As unemployment has risen, the role of unemployment benefit has declined relatively (although not of course absolutely). Showler and Sinfield complain with some justice that 'the general failure of the original "pillar of security" for the unemployed – national insurance unemployment benefit – has never been fully acknowledged'.[24] There are many reasons for this low coverage. The most important is that unemployment benefits only last a year, so that the long-term unemployed are automatically excluded. So are school-leavers who have never had a job – they fail to satisfy the contribution conditions, as may those whose employment has been intermittent.

Disqualifications from unemployment benefit, normally for periods of six weeks, also play their part. These are put into effect where a man or woman leaves a job voluntarily without just cause, or has been dismissed for what is known as 'industrial misconduct', or does not use the opportunities offered to find a new job, or fails to take up an offer of 'suitable' employment i.e. similar and at the prevailing rates. Supplementary benefit may be obtained during a period of disqualification, but subject to a penalty of 40 per cent of the allowance for the claimant's own needs.

The major forms of social security which are not provided by social insurance are supplementary benefit, family income supplement, and child benefit. The two former are selective measures devoted wholly to the relief of poverty and will be further considered in the chapter concerned with this topic. Before discussing the relatively new child benefit system, however, it might be sensible to consider briefly a few minor non-contributory benefits, a small shrubbery of which has grown up over the past decade or so. The various benefits for the severely disabled and those who look after them have already been noted in appropriate places in this chapter. All that requires to be added is that the amounts in question are usually quite low (lower than supplementary allowance, for instance), and that the fact that they are not means-tested certainly does not signify that they are easy to obtain. The qualifying conditions are often restrictively drawn and hard to satisfy, and there may be, as with attendance allowances and the housewife's non-contributory invalidity pension, some pretty tough medical and bureaucratic policing. (While this edition is in the press, non-contributory invalidity pensions for housewives and for others are being gradually merged into a new severe disablement allowance, so married women will no longer have to undergo the rather fearsome task of proving that they are incapable of normal household duties; a small victory for administrative simplicity, common humanity and the anti-sexist cause.)

Then there is the Christmas bonus (currently of £10): this started life as a politician's occasional gimmick, but seems to have become an established feature of the social security scene. It goes to almost everybody in receipt of contributory and non-contributory benefits, with the significant exception of nearly all those obtaining a supplementary allowance. This means that the long-term unemployed and most single-parent families, whose need for a little extra cash is as great as any, and more than some, are excluded.

Next, there is the maternity grant (at present £25): this has recently been moved from the contributory category into the non-contributory one, which at least now ensures that those mothers most in need of the money, such as teenagers who have never worked, are able to claim it. However, the most important point to be made about the maternity grant, and about the £30 death grant (which remains, for the present, a contributory benefit), is that they cover a small and ever-diminishing proportion of the costs of having a baby or of a funeral. Successive governments have been strangely and stubbornly reluctant to raise the amounts in the annual up-ratings – the death grant has remained fixed since 1967. This must be a good indication of the low value which they have attached to these benefits.

In 1982, the DHSS published *The Death Grant: a Consultative Document*, which showed that the current administration wishes to jettison this part of the national insurance system. The principal suggestion was that the grant should be greatly increased, but that it should in future be means-tested, so that the relatives of most of those who had paid contributions towards it, among other benefits, would no longer be able to claim it. At the time of writing no action has been taken on these proposals, but their adoption would be bound to be resented as another example of a government rewriting a contract in the middle of its term. The alternative, however, appears to be that the grant slips into complete insignificance; already administrative costs amount to nearly half the sums paid out.

Family allowance was another benefit which was increased infrequently and which usually lagged well behind inflation and the growth in general levels of prosperity. When child benefit was introduced in 1977 (after yet more dissension in the Labour cabinet)[25] it was widely believed that henceforward all would be different. This was because child benefit replaced child tax allowance (although the two coexisted between 1977 and 1979) and income tax allowances had been raised regularly to keep in line with changes in income generally. Child benefit is non-taxable, and goes to all those looking after children under 16 or still at school. It is paid to mothers rather than to fathers, and hence differs from the old tax allowances which usually disappeared into the man's general income. Single people (not only parents but also grandmothers or aunts) can obtain an additional amount, called the child benefit increase, in respect of one of the children they are caring for.

The record so far has been patchy. Child benefit fell quite sharply in real terms after 1979, but since 1982 this decline has been arrested, and to some extent reversed. Nevertheless, the amounts have not been raised sufficiently to replace any of the sums paid through social insurance or supplementary benefits in respect of dependent children. In fact, the present government has tended to try to help families by the clumsy and expensive means of raising the tax allowances for married men, so relatively benefiting couples without dependant children, in general a notably well-off group. This is rather surprising, since Conservative spokesmen in opposition concurred with the then Labour government in regarding the cost of higher child benefits as equivalent to a reduction in direct personal taxation, and not as an increase in public expenditure. However, this always made more sense in social and economic terms than in political ones – Conservative and floating voters would need a lot of persuasion to be convinced that paying out large sums of money is the same as cutting taxes. But there may be further reasons for the ambivalence of the present administration concerning child benefit, and a clue to their nature is given in a speech made in 1977 by Patrick Jenkin, later Secretary of State for Social Services. He explained why his party was committed to child benefit thus:–

First, because that is the way to restore the position of families. Secondly, it is the best way to ease the poverty trap. Thirdly, it is the best way to help poor families in work – those who earn their poverty. Fourthly, it is the best way to reduce the nonsense of people being much better off out of work. Fifthly, it is the best way of reducing the dependence of families on means-tested benefits.[26]

Now all these reasons except the first are concerned with meeting the needs of the poor, and it is at least arguable – as the government has sometimes appeared to be arguing – that increases in selective benefits like family income supplement would be a more cost-effective means of advancing this aim. Recently an argument has gained ground which is quite contrary to that put forward in this book, namely that the relief of poverty is the sole reputable function of social security. We have already mentioned Dilnot, Kay and Morris' *The Reform of Social Security*, a work which promises to be very influential: in it, all other claimed purposes for social security are described both as 'subsidiary' and 'controversial'.[27] Child benefit provides an excellent illustration of an alternative proposition. It is not primarily a means of coping with family poverty. It is a way of effecting horizontal equity between two people with the same original income (whether they be two directors of major companies, or two street cleaners) one of whom is responsible for dependent children, and the other is not. It is therefore, in the absence of tax allowances, the principal mechanism for aligning the financial circumstances of families with those of other kinds of household unit.

As this book goes to press, social security is in the melting pot. In April 1984, Norman Fowler, the Secretary of State for Social Services, announced a series of reviews which he described as 'the most substantial examination of the social security system since the Beveridge Report forty years ago'.[28] There are four separate reviews – into provision for retirement, benefits for children and young people, supplementary benefit and housing benefit – all except the last being chaired by ministers. The structure of the exercise rather depresses hopes of the outcome: it is impossible to weave a coherent pattern if the threads required are set up on separate looms. It is anyhow apparent that there is a heavy emphasis on conserving public expenditure, so that calls of a strategy of 'back to Beveridge', which have been made and ignored for so long, are unlikely to be heeded.

9 Health care

All modern governments recognize a responsibility for the health of their people. However, even if they are all moving towards the same objective, they differ vastly in the distance they have travelled along the way, and very significantly as to the route they have chosen. In a country like India, with a vast population and limited resources, a high priority has been given to preventive measures and the fight against epidemic and endemic diseases like malaria, smallpox, cholera and leprosy. These, and the provision of hospitals, are, under the Constitution, a 'State Subject'. There is health insurance, but in the early 1980s it covered only 7.2 million workers, or 28 million people including dependants, out of a population of 680 million.[1] In the USSR, too, health care is a state service, but a comprehensive one, with a salaried staff and a ratio of doctors to population which is one of the highest in the world.

The dominant features of health care in Western Europe are national health insurance and an independent medical profession, although the United Kingdom, as we have seen, replaced national insurance with a national service after the Second World War. The United States government persistently rejected all forms of 'socialized medicine' until 1965, when it introduced public insurance for the old (Medicare) followed by public insurance for the poor (Medicaid). Before this only one-quarter of the total expenditure on health came from public funds, and the prevalent national philosophy continues to favour reliance on voluntary private insurance. The doctors have wanted it so, just as British and European doctors have clung to their form of independence. The fact that a policy for health care must operate through members of one of the proudest of the ancient professions accounts for many of its characteristic problems. It is not easy to harmonize political with professional authority, nor bureaucratic with professional procedures, yet this is what has to be done.

There are other ways in which the planning of a policy for health care is peculiarly difficult. It is important when resources are scarce to use them in the most effective way, and it is relatively easy to see that, for India, this points to a high priority for epidemiology and hospitals. Where a health care system is already well developed, the allocation of resources to it and within it presents subtler problems. It is generally agreed that medical services are costly, that the level of service achieved always falls short of that which, with unlimited expenditure, could be realized through the application of current knowledge and skills, and that advances in medical science and technology are continuously improving and adding to the means for treating sickness and promoting health. This constant striving for something that is just out of reach engenders both strong demands for a general expansion of the service and a complex of pressures on behalf of various sectors of it for priority treatment.

There is still very little to go on when assessing the merits of competing claims except the confident assertions of those who make them, that is to say of senior members of the medical professions. And they are not accustomed to having their authority challenged in professional matters. Practitioners are well aware that medicine is not an exact science, but in some respects an art. They are inclined to be suspicious of quantitative measurement, and to prefer to rely on the subjective assessment of their personal experience. When faced with an inveterate quantifier, a cost-conscious economist, perhaps, they are apt to murmur that one cannot put a value on human health and human life – even though, in those extreme instances where a professional decision may confirm life, or confer death, a few of them will be doing precisely that. The best evidence of such covert rationing relates to renal failure.[2] Those who are accepted for dialysis are likely to be under 45 years of age, not subject to other disease, and probably married and with children. Those without such desirable characteristics will generally be refused treatment and will not live long.[3] Such examples make it easy to understand why there is so much pressure, from members of the general public and of the medical profession alike, for continual expansion of costly facilities which may benefit relatively few people, and also why, in conditions of grave shortage, there is reliance on a decentralized form of decision-making without the codified and publicized rules which would accompany more explicit planning.

Thomas McKeown has written that 'medicine is the only enterprise, private or public, in which it has not been considered essential to equate effectiveness and cost'.[4] The first step towards such an equation would be a more serious attempt to establish with scientific accuracy to what extent, and under what conditions, the treatment used produces the results aimed at. One well-known technique for effecting this is the randomized controlled trial (RCT), in which, in its simplest form, a population of patients is divided at random into two groups, one of which receives the treatment to be tested, and the other is given no treatment or a placebo. Professor A. L. Cochrane, the most eloquent advocate of the RCT, gives many examples of their potential utility as an aid to policy-makers: for instance, he cites a trial which casts considerable doubt on the superiority, for sufferers from ischaemic heart disease, of treatment in expensive coronary care units over treatment at home.[5] The technique, with appropriate modifications, can also be of use where the question posed is of a more complicated nature, as when it is desired to relate benefit to cost, or output to input, and to compare the benefit in one case with what could have been achieved by an alternative use of the same resources. This is the kind of information which planning ideally requires. For example, the success of mass X-ray examinations in detecting incipient turberculosis encouraged the idea that 'screening' would be equally successful for other diseases. But this depends on the accuracy of the test, the severity of the disease and the effectiveness of its treatment at a later stage. All this can be, and has been, measured, showing in some cases that the results obtained by screening would not justify the cost. Thus, it is by no means clear that the diagnostic impact of CT (computerized tomograph) scanning for clinical situations other than brain disorders is sufficiently great to justify the heavy investment involved. There are, however, obvious ethical problems about the establishment of RCT experiments wherever, as here, diseases have the gravest of prognoses, since they would entail a denial of surgery in some cases where a smear result was positive.

During the first twenty-five years of the NHS, planning remained rather a hit and miss affair. 'At present', said an official of the Department of Health and Social Security in 1972 'there are no means of arriving at scientific assessments of priorities, and decisions are taken mainly on political judgements or on grounds of expediency or in relation to known public pressures.'[6] Planning was hampered by the unforeseen and rapid change in the nature of the task with which health services had to grapple. Beveridge had believed that, although costs would certainly rise, total expenditure in 1965 would be about the same as in 1945, because a national health service must surely improve the national health, and so reduce the volume of work to be done. The truth was almost exactly the opposite. For one thing, technical progress creates work (and additional expense) by making it possible to do what was previously impossible. Surgery offers many examples of this. Second, if a service is efficiently organized, it should increase the proportion of those in need of treatment who actually get it. Third, there is the obvious fact that those saved from death in early or middle life must still face a terminal illness, often after a long period of continuous invalidity. The National Health Service, said Rudolf Klein, 'from being conceived primarily as a service for dealing with disease, is becoming a service for maintaining those who it cannot cure'.[7]

One interesting study of the earlier years of the NHS is Christopher Ham's account of the making of policy in the old Leeds Regional Hospital Board.[8] In this he showed how much the policy-making and planning processes revolved around inputs, of buildings, plant, equipment and staff, rather than around outputs, such as improvements in health status – the former, indeed, were widely held to entail the latter, just as bumper crops can be secured through irrigation schemes and a generous accretion of fertilizers. Second, he documented the extent to which outcomes were determined by the dominant position of certain members of the medical profession, especially consultants in the acute specialties; even in the years of the Hospital Plan of the 1960s, when the going was good for expansionists, resources could be shifted into the 'Cinderella' areas of geriatrics, mental illness and mental handicap only when special, and additional, funding was made available by Whitehall.

Of course, the Leeds RHB, together with its sisterhood of RHBs and HMCs, was only responsible for the hospital service, and that, in the eyes of many commentators, was just the trouble. The tripartite structure, of separate hospital, general practice, and local authority health services, given to the service at its birth, had been something of a makeshift, but the obstacles to its unification seemed for a long time to be insuperable, and such official committees as studied the matter advised against it (see p. 97). When in 1962 the Porritt Committee, representing the medical profession, produced a plan for a kind of unification, or at least federation, this showed which way the wind was blowing.[9] By 1970 certain decisions had been taken, or were being taken, which greatly simplified the problem. If the local authority *health* services were to be absorbed into the NHS, it was essential to know where the division lay between these and the local *welfare* services, and this was a highly controversial subject. However, the Seebohm Committee (1965–8) had drawn a firm line between them, and this had been accepted (see p. 166). The second important development was the reshaping of local government, which created in the counties and metropolitan boroughs, areas which it was thought would be substantial and uniform enough to serve also as the key geographical units in the administration of the NHS.

The hierarchy of power in the new structure which came into existence in England in 1974 was meant to be composed of three tiers: the Minister at the top, Regional Health Authorities (RHAs) below him and Area Health Authorities (AHAs) below these. The RHAs were responsible for strategic planning, for the deployment of certain top-level specialist services, and for liaison with university medical schools. They were also charged with the allocation of resources among the AHAs. The latter were to be the key executive authority. Their areas coincided – although rather approximately in places – with the counties and metropolitan boroughs, and they were to be responsible for co-ordination with local government services. Most of the areas were divided into districts, which were not meant to be an additional tier in the hierarchy, but the operational arms of the AHAs. The district, said one official document, was expected to become 'the basic operational unit of the integrated Health Service'.[10] Whatever the intentions of the responsible minister, Sir Keith Joseph, the districts were from the start widely referred to as 'a tier', and thus the NHS was seen as having been furnished with a four-tier structure.

The government made it quite clear that the whole service was to be run, so far as decisions were concerned, by the minister and his officers. Members of the Regional and Area Authorities, largely nominated from above like those of the former Hospital Boards, were expected to see that the right questions were asked and that there was full awareness of health needs. 'They are not there to do the work that their officers are trained to do.'[11] There was to be, however, no nominated board with a majority of lay members for the districts: instead, the public's voice could be heard through a Community Health Council representing local government and relevant local organizations. This arrangement, said the government, was designed to avoid the 'dangerous confusion between management on the one hand and the community's reaction to management on the other'.[12] It is clear that the administrative plan was based on the belief that a service of this kind cannot be efficiently run unless control is in the hands of professionals. Consequently, in spite of the emphasis on 'community health', the scope given for community participation was small. The 1974 reorganization was much criticized at the time for being 'undemocratic', perhaps particularly in Labour Party circles, but the incoming Secretary of State, Barbara Castle, contented herself with an increase in the proportion of the membership of RHAs and AHAs which was directly nominated by local authorities.

Proposals for the top level internal organization of the new authorities were contained in a document which became known as the 'Grey Book';[13] some professed to believe that the adjective referred, not to the dour livery in which the Stationery Office thought fit to dress it, but to the bureaucratic managerialism of its contents, which they found repellent. Actually, the proposals in the Grey Book were intended to be subject to local variation after consultation, but the deadline for reorganization was pressing, and it is not surprising if it was widely seen as an edict from on high.[14] The arrangements recommended were that at each level there should be a small group of chief officers, in nursing, 'community medicine', finance, administration, and in the case of the Region 'works', who would form the Regional Team of Officers (RTO), the Area Team of Officers (ATO) or the District Management Team (DMT). In addition, the DMT, as the operational level in the hierarchy, would include two officers chosen by their professional colleagues, a specialist and a GP. Each team would be a consensus-forming group of equals.[15] 'Consensus management' was not new in the NHS; it predated reorganization. These arrangements did, however, formalize, and to some extent enhance, the position of professionals other than doctors, and, although it would be going too far to say that either the intention or the effect of the new structure was 'to get a grip on the consultants', the involvement of some of their number in resource allocation has surely served to modify their attitudes to the very considerable sums of public money which they deploy each year. The point to note, however, is that this was a consequence of an *increase*, rather than a reduction, in the amount of say accorded to members of the medical profession in matters of NHS management, especially at district level. This is not solely a question of team membership: one innovation of the 1974 reorganization was the establishment of District Medical Committees, which brought together into one body hospital doctors, GPs and community physicians, and was intended to serve as a focus for medical opinion and for its transmission to the DMT. Thus the old charge of 'medical corporatism', so frequently levelled against the post-1948 NHS, was certainly as applicable to its post-1974 successor, and in some respects more so.

The 1974 reorganization was an exhausting experience for many of those who took part in it. Established loyalties were fractured, and there was a good deal of short-term dislocation of work. Some officers had to fight, against competition, to retain what was in essence their previous job. This 'turbulence', as it came to be called, convinced many that it would be impossible to contemplate a further upheaval for at least a generation. And yet this 'reorganization to end all reorganizations' lasted in England for a mere eight years. How did this come about? One reason may be sought in the 'turbulence' itself. 'Before 1972', says Nick Bosanquet in the first words of one of the first books on the subject, 'industrial relations in the National Health Service were a matter of sentences lost in fine print.'[16] 1968 may have been an exciting year in the universities of Europe, but the NHS, Britain's largest employer, experienced just one dispute, involving eighty workers, and with the loss of eighty days work in total.[17] When in 1972 the ancillary workers embarked on industrial action after having been caught by the pay freeze, this was not taken as a portent – the Grey Book was insistent on the importance of the personnel function, but failed to mention industrial relations at all. Since then they have frequently made the headlines, although the matter must be kept in perspective – in terms of days lost, the record of the NHS in the 1970s was a great deal better than that of British employers generally. Still, the number and frequency of disputes made a striking contrast with the quiet of earlier decades. And this was not just a matter of the entry, centre stage, of the ancillary workers and their unions. Unexpected groups discovered the attractions of industrial action: for example, both the consultants and the junior hospital doctors 'worked to contract' in 1975. Many commentators thought that such conflicts were clear evidence of an unprecedented decline in morale.

Another reason why the NHS came in for renewed scrutiny in the later 1970s was the frequently expressed belief that the service was over-administered. Such criticisms often rested on the further implicit belief that administrators were at best a necessary evil, and that at worst a growth in their numbers diverted resources which should have been devoted directly to patient care. Thus, doctors were wont to allege that the best and most experienced practical nurses had been siphoned off into management as a result of the enhanced career opportunities offered by the acceptance in 1968 of the Salmon Report on the nursing staffing structure, and, subsequently, through reorganization. The figures on this were, however, decidedly ambiguous, since the proportion of all NHS nursing staff employed in the grades above ward sister actually *fell* between 1966 and 1977 (from 4.7 per cent to 3.6 per cent),[18] even though there was a small increase in their absolute numbers. Nevertheless, there can be no doubt that in the period which spanned reorganization there was a very sharp increase in NHS administrators generally: between 1971 and 1975 the numbers of staff employed in administrative work other than secretarial, clerical and support services grew by no less than 73 per cent.[19] What should be made of this is open to question in the absence of criteria which would allow us to determine the amount of administration which would be appropriate. It might, for instance, be plausibly maintained that the old tripartite NHS, with its scissors and paste attitude to management, was woefully *under*-administered, and the time of professionals had been misspent on tasks which could have been more sensibly and economically performed by others.

The Labour government proceeded cautiously. It instituted some new checks on administrative costs, but otherwise decided to put the NHS under the microscope of a wide-ranging independent inquiry of a kind which many thought should have been carried out before the exercise of reorganization had ever been embarked upon. The terms of reference of the Royal Commission on the National Health Service, which was chaired by Sir Alec Merrison, a university vice-chancellor, were 'to consider in the interests both of the patients and of those who work in the National Health Service the best use and management of the financial and manpower resources of the National Health Service and the parallel services in Northern Ireland'. Thus the remit of the Royal Commission covered much more than the administrative structure of the service, and, as we shall see, many of its recommendations on other subjects fell on stony ground: it reported late in 1979, by which time the Labour administration which appointed it had been replaced by the Conservatives. On one thing, however, the Labour government, the Conservative government, the members of the Royal Commission, and virtually everyone who gave evidence to it, were agreed – that the NHS was burdened with one tier too many.

But which tier should go? As nobody seriously suggested getting rid of the districts, and the Royal Commission firmly rejected the idea of vesting the functions of the DHSS in a National Health Service Corporation analogous to those in nationalized industries, there were only two candidates, the RHAs or the AHAs. Here there was more disagreement, but the balance of opinion was in favour of excising the areas. So the Royal Commission recommended, and so the government decreed. In place of the AHAs there were to be, from April 1982, new District Health Authorities (DHAs), appointed in the same way, and with essentially the same functions, as their predecessors.

There were a number of reasons why the regions were spared. One was the existence of a number of important responsibilities which were held to require authorities covering larger populations or of greater geographical size than the areas – functions such as strategic planning or the provision of specialized clinical services like blood transfusion. Then there was a span of control argument – the DHSS could relate satisfactorily to fourteen English regional authorities, but would find it impossible to supervise the activities of ninety areas. A third point is that the relationship between the ATO and the DMTs was not in all respects clear: in some areas the former assumed what was essentially line management control over the latter, while in others the district officers gained much more autonomy. The new NHS planning system, which was adumbrated in big handbooks published in 1975 and 1976, was complicated, and communications had to trundle their way between authorities, guidelines down from region, annual plans up from district, all the time through intermediaries. The possibilities for confusion and bad blood were considerable. Things seemed to work much more smoothly in the minority of single-district areas.

One might have thought that the poor National Health Service had enough to digest with the 1982 reorganization. Less than a year later, however, the first steps were taken towards a re-reorganization, with the appointment in February 1983, of the National Health Service Management Enquiry, under the chairmanship of Roy Griffiths, of the grocery firm, Sainsbury's. In some respects, the Enquiry was a modest exercise, which took little more than six months to complete. Its Report neither was, nor looked like, one of those hefty blueprints of the 1960s – indeed, it took the form of a 'letter of advice' to the Secretary of State. Some of its critics insinuated that it was a matter of a few ideas written on the back of an envelope, but it had a coherent, if sketchily worked out, philosophy.

Griffiths' principal themes were summed up in the two most sparkling sentences in the report, namely: 'If Florence Nightingale were carrying her lamp through the corridors of the NHS today she would almost certainly be searching for the people in charge', and:

'To the outsider, it appears that when change of any kind is required, the NHS is so structured as to resemble a "mobile": designed to move with any breath of air, but which in fact never changes its position and gives no clear indication of direction.'[20] The diagnosis was thus one of headlessness and aimlessness; the remedy, it was suggested, was to be found in the 'general management function'.

This signifies that management structures, from the top to the bottom of the NHS, should be so altered as to create at each level a single focus of authority. The recommendation was that each region, district and unit (meaning a single hospital, or a grouping of hospital and other linked health facilities) should have its own general manager, who might be any of the professionals in the management team, or, possibly, an appointee from outside. Perhaps the most far-reaching changes proposed, however, concerned the oversight of the NHS at a national level – the establishment of a Health Services Supervisory Board, chaired by the Secretary of State, and, immediately below this, the insertion of a new body into the hierarchy, the NHS Management Board. The Chairman of the latter would perform the function of 'general manager, chief officer or director general' of the NHS as a whole. The idea is that the Management Board should have no separate corporate status, but in conception it nevertheless takes the NHS closer to the nationalized industry model than ever before.

The Griffiths proposals are open to attack from opposite ends. On the one hand, the case against consensus management is far from proved. As the tasks to be performed in the NHS require the willing co-operation of several separate professions, a multi-peaked management structure may well be appropriate. Most of the academic commentators who have considered the consensus system have given it a fairly clean bill of health: Professor Kogan and his associates found that support for it was wide-ranging, and that 'only a small minority of respondents thought that it could never be successful'.[21] On the other hand, it can be argued that Griffiths was less full-blooded in his managerialism than he ought to have been for the eventual success of his scheme, since the creation of a cadre of professional NHS general managers would require permanent career posts and probably rigorous training on staff college lines. Instead, the Secretary of State has laid down that appointees should take up their posts for initial periods of three, four or five years, with annual renewal thereafter. This raises an obvious problem about how ex-general managers can be slotted back into a working role in the NHS when their periods of office have expired.

The position at the time of writing is that the Secretary of State has accepted the Griffiths' recommendations, and the first steps have been taken to implement them. Most estimates of the outcome so far as appointments are concerned suggest that administrators are well placed to take advantage of the opportunities offered, doctors will do less well, and nurses will, in general, lose out.

This discussion of the 1982 reorganization and of Griffiths has concentrated on issues of internal organization. But as we noted earlier, when considering pre-1974 development, the NHS is not vacuum-sealed; its structures have to be related to those of other services. Here the surprise was that by the time of the Royal Commission there were few who spoke with any conviction about the advantages to be gained from health authorities having the same boundaries as their local authority counterparts – and yet this had been perhaps the clinching argument in favour of inserting an area tier into the structure of the NHS. One reason for this was that co-terminosity was so very incomplete, with district, area and even regional boundary lines crossing into the next county where hospital catchment areas dictated it. Another was that, at the operational level, the relationships which counted were between members of the DMT and their counterparts in other bodies directly concerned with the management of service delivery. And here one finds an intricate mosaic of small territories and overlapping jurisdictions – social services and LEA areas or divisions, the District Councils, DHSS area offices and so on – where coterminosity seems quite unattainable, and practitioners have to rely on Joint Committees and more *ad hoc* arrangements, including personal contacts. Any integrating operation closes some gaps but opens, or widens, others across which bridges must then be built. This is very obvious in the case we are considering. There were good reasons for incorporating, in 1974, the personal health services hitherto run by the local council in the reorganized NHS. These include domiciliary nursing, health visitors, midwifery, ambulances, maternity and child welfare and, as a new responsibility, family planning. On the other side of the dividing line are all the personal social services for the aged, for children and for the mentally disordered, including their non-hospital residential accommodation. It is clear than an integrated health service and integrated social service departments must work very closely together: often they are dealing with the same individuals or families, and in some areas, such as child guidance and health education, the responsibility is shared. This is a matter which will preoccupy us both in this chapter and the next, although some important recent developments in the relationship, such as the establishment and growth of joint funding, will be discussed alongside other aspects of the personal social services, since the flow of funds has been mainly towards them.

A particularly important role in the co-ordination of services to the individual is performed by the general practitioner. However, the position of general practice in the service has remained virtually unchanged through all reorganizations. In the early 1980s, as in the early 1970s, and as always, the family doctors were determined not to surrender their independence, and they prevailed. The 1964 to 1970 Labour government's first Green Paper had proposed to bring them directly under the general health authority in each area, but the reaction was such that the proposal was dropped. The 1971 Conservative plan was quite explicit. The family practitioners were assured that their status would not be affected by the reorganization. 'They now provide services as independent contractors, and they will continue to do so.'[22] The Family Practitioner Committees (FPCs), with which they negotiate their contracts, and of which together with the dentists, the opticians and the pharmacists they nominate half the members, are the old Executive Councils under a new name – and, since the latter in their turn were, both in function and the general outlines of their composition, the lineal descendants of the post-1911 local Insurance Committees, these are truly historic monuments of social administration. In the early 1980s, with the impending abolition of the AHAs, the Conservatives had to decide again what to do with the FPCs. There were two possible logical courses they could have taken. One would have been to do what the Royal Commission recommended, and to have abolished them, subsuming them in the general administration of the NHS. As before, this turned out to be a non-starter for medico-political reasons. The second possibility was to set up a separate FPC for each district. This would have meant the creation of a large number of new administrative bodies, and was thought to be an expensive answer to the problem. So the government left them undisturbed, and hence anchored to no part of the revised NHS structure. Floating free, the FPCs are a constant reminder of the incompleteness of reorganization, and of the survival of an important element in the old tripartite system.

Another problem which was unavoidably raised by the 1982 reorganization was the future of the Community Health Councils. As we have already implied, the main impetus behind the invention of CHCs in the early 1970s had been presentational: the vacuum left by the mass slaughter of the largest element of lay representation in the old NHS structure, the members of the HMCs, had to be filled, in an era when popular participation was seen as a touchstone of political virtue. Now, however, there were to be DHAs with a majority of lay members. Should the CHCs continue in the new circumstances? Answers to this question were made difficult by the rather patchy results of the experiment of setting them up. Some of the CHCs had turned out to be largely decorative – they were truly, to adopt a picturesque image of Klein and Lewis's, Gothic follies in the grounds of a Palladian mansion.[23] Others, however, had conceived of their role in much more active terms. And here they encountered a familiar dilemma: should they reject Sir Keith Joseph's sharp antithesis between management and community representation, and get as involved as possible in the decision-making processes of the DMT, on the grounds that only thus could they fulfil their function of representing the consumer adequately? Or should they spurn 'co-optation', because their independence might be compromised? Either way, conflict could ensue, especially if the DMT was suspicious or unwilling.

In practice, it seems that there were fewer conflicts than might have been expected, partly because of the sleepiness of some CHCs, but more because producer interests and consumer interests in the NHS run parallel for much of the course. Even where the CHCs had genuine powers of delay, in matters affecting the closure of hospitals or wards, they generally went along with their DMT.[24] This example, however, merely points up the ambiguities inherent in trying to assess the performance of the CHCs, and there were certainly arguments for saying that they were no longer required in the new structure. The government decided to duck the issue for the time being, and put the CHCs, so to speak, on probation. It should be added that there are two functions which must be performed and which the CHC can perform. The first is to act as a pool, and a kind of induction training, for future members of DHAs and RHAs. The second is to help complainants to prepare and present their cases. This was a matter on which DHSS circulars were hesitant, but someone needs to undertake the job, and the paid secretaries of CHCs are in a good position to do it.

'Community' is a word which has featured prominently in discussions of national health problems in recent years, in such compound phrases as 'community health', 'community medicine' and 'community physician'. These are conglomerates of several ideas current for some little time past and, although rather nebulous, they have practical implications. Community medicine is in effect an expansion of 'social medicine', which was first in vogue during and immediately after the Second World War, as an offshoot of public health. For the Royal Commission on Medical Education (1968) community medicine was the 'speciality practised by epidemiologists and by administrators of medical services', and was concerned, not with individual patients, but 'with the broad questions of health and disease in, for example, particular geographical and occupational sections of the community and in the community at large'. This left sanitation, pollution and the physical environment to the Medical Officer of Health, or to the new types of lay specialist whom the Commission rightly thought might gradually supersede him. Of particular interest are the 'core subjects' recommended for the training of community physicians: epidemiology, biostatistics, medical sociology, operational research and management.[25] Clearly, one task of community medicine was conceived as being to monitor continuously the health of the community by assembling and analysing statistical and other data. This view was endorsed by a Scottish working party which said that 'a community medicine must in our view provide the basic skills to make reliable assessments of the problems and to evaluate the results of different courses of action'.[26] Taken in this sense community medicine is an invaluable aid to the rational planning of medical services.

For others community health is a blanket term which includes all this and pretty well everything else needed to give a global view of the health of a local community and of the activities engaged in promoting and maintaining it. The key concept is that of seeing, and treating, each individual or family case as a whole and in the context of its social and environmental setting. With so broad a view, it is impossible, and would be self-contradictory, to draw a clear line between health and welfare. This is particularly true when we come to consider the most popular of all the linkings between 'community' and another noun – 'community care'. This phrase, be it noted, does not refer, as do the others we have been discussing, to care for the health *of* the community, but to care for the health and welfare of individuals given *in* and *by* the community. The 'patients' live in families, or in hostels, or in sheltered housing, or just alone, and are cared for by relatives and friends and social workers, both public and voluntary, with the help of various establishments such as clinics, day hospitals, clubs and workshops. The burden of providing this care and these services lies heavily on the local population, which must be prepared and equipped to meet them. Otherwise, 'community care' is merely a rather crude method of shifting costs on to anyone who may be available to meet them, which will nearly always mean family members.

The major problems arise in the cases of the old, the mentally ill and the mentally handicapped. Since the services for all three groups display many common features, in their historical development, in the difficulties they face at present, and in the outlines of current policy towards them, it would seem sensible to discuss them together. However, it might be as well to start by emphasizing some differences between them. First, although there is a very blurred frontier between geriatrics and psychiatry, most of those who come under the care of a consultant geriatrician do not show any significant degree of mental confusion. Second, those concerned with the mentally ill and the mentally handicapped have often, and rightly, expressed resentment about the way in which these two groups have been wrapped up together in the general category of 'mental disorder'. Mental handicap is a state or condition rather than an illness, and some doubt whether the medically qualified have anything particular to contribute to its treatment, except in cases of multiple handicap: the Jay Committee on Mental Handicap Nursing and Care (1979) recommended 'interdisciplinary teams', and stressed the role of other professionals, such as educational and clinical psychologists.[27] By contrast, the trend in both mental illness and geriatrics has been to anchor them as firmly as possible in the mainstream of medicine. Thus those geriatric departments which have pursued active policies of rehabilitation have achieved a much brisker turnover of beds and a sharp reduction in the number of old people for whom life outside hospital is impossible. It is estimated that about 60 per cent of those admitted to hospital under the care of a geriatrician could be made fit for life outside. For the community and its services this is more of a threat than a promise.

Geriatrics, psychiatry and mental handicap are all specialties beset by shortages of medical personnel. A majority of those recently appointed to both consultant and registrar positions in geriatrics have been doctors from overseas.[28] Having noted that, the Merrison Royal Commission went on to observe, in a very similar wording for both psychiatry and mental handicap, that junior hospital doctor recruitment in these specialisms has been 'deficient in both quantity and quality'. Mental nurses have traditionally been recruited and trained separate from other nurses, which has added to isolation, and in all three areas of provision there is high turnover among nursing staff, and much reliance upon the unqualified. One reason for these personnel problems is that much of the work is concerned with what is sometimes termed, in an unpleasant but evocative phrase, as 'warehousing' or 'storage' of old people deteriorated through senile dementia, or of the severely mentally handicapped able to do little to help themselves with their bodily functions. The 'back wards' are to be found in establishments remote from the bustling power-house of the district general hospital: in the huge Victorian asylums with their sentinel water-towers; in the agglomerations of villas, commonly named after trees, which were erected in the first forty years of this century for the containment of the 'mentally deficient'; in the usually much smaller out-hospitals, still sometimes former workhouses, where the frailest of the elderly sit out their last days, In spite of the dedication of much of the nursing and other staff, the NHS has here a grave problem of quality control, to which witness is borne by the roll-call of scandals and major inquiries in the late 1960s and the 1970s – Ely, Farleigh, Whittingham, South Ockendon, Normansfield, to mention only a few of the more prominent of them. Most of these institutions have been mental handicap hospitals – Whittingham, as a general psychiatric hospital, was an odd man out – and it has been in this area that much of the effort of the new bodies set up from 1970 as a result of public disquiet has been concentrated: first of the Hospital Advisory Service (now the Health Advisory Service) and latterly of the Development Team for the Mentally Handicapped. In spite of this rediscovery of the virtues of inspection, and especially of the support from outside which it can bring, the problem of the quality of care in the long-stay hospitals is a deep-seated one, and there will surely be occasional fresh scandals for as long as the hospitals last.[29]

The main thrust of government policy towards the big mental hospitals was established as long ago as the 1959 Mental Health Act and the 1962 Hospital Plan. New guidelines were laid down to the effect that first priority in the care of mental patients should be given to treatment at home, second priority to residential hostels, and only third priority to hospital in-patient treatment. In the 1960s the local authorities were quite unready to assume the responsibilities thus placed upon them; the necessary provision of hostels and community facilities would require heavy capital investment, stretching over years. The policy – which was a bipartisan one – was not relaxed on that account; it was reaffirmed, in a series of White Papers relating to all three areas of patient care, and starting with *Better Services for the Mentally Handicapped* (1971).[30] The boldest plans related to the mentally ill: here the aim was to phase out the big psychiatric hospitals, to reduce the number of hospital beds by half, and to accommodate those that remained inside general hospitals. Policies for the mentally handicapped were a little less far-reaching: mental handicap hospitals were to be retained and improved, but not expanded, and there was to be a vigorous programme of construction of locally based units, or hostels, for both adults and children, and run by either the NHS or social service departments, the degree of dependence determining which authority took responsibility for which patients.

In recent years there has been some progress towards these goals, perhaps particularly in the provision of hostel places for mentally handicapped children, and of places in training centres for mentally handicapped adults, but everyone agrees that there is a very long way to go indeed (see Chapter 10). The specialist mental illness hospitals have been run down considerably in terms of numbers of beds, but so far just one of the old county asylums has been closed. It is possible to argue that the survival of the specialist psychiatric institution may be no bad thing on therapeutic grounds. Drug therapy can restore many seriously disturbed patients to apparent health, but their condition is precarious, and relapses, with which only a hospital can cope, may be frequent. A policy of speedy discharge can be distressing both for them and their families. They need a refuge and security, not only when they are acutely ill. It may be that this function of providing a retreat can be better performed in the old psychiatric hospitals, which at least have space and air, rather than some storeys up in a new block of a city general hospital, where the problems or the temptations which necessitated admission may be all too close at hand. However, the contrary view is also strongly held, and, as in any dual system, there is a danger that the old mental hospital will be used as a depository for the less interesting or the less easily treatable cases. Only experience, and experimentation, can establish the respective roles of the specialist hospital, the unit in a general hospital, the hostel and the day services provided for people at home.

At the same time as opinion regarding the long-stay hospitals was moving in favour of smaller units, policy relating to the acute hospitals was going in the opposite direction. The NHS, as reorganized in 1974, revolved around the concept of the district general hospital: these were to be establishments of 600 to 800 beds, covering populations of 100,000 to 150,000, and providing both in-patient and out-patient treatment in all the principal specialties. At the end of the 1960s the Bonham Carter Committee, fearful of the dangers of isolation among consultants in the less common specialisms, advocated even larger hospitals. However, the growing unfashion-ableness of bigness led to a renewed interest in 'community hospitals' (which had, indeed, been recommended by Bonham Carter), and, more important, the arrival of the first sharp financial frosts led to doubts whether the basic programme of covering the country with around 250 DGHs, one for each district, would prove attainable, while any idea of a network of still more expensive versions was knocked out of court. During the 1970s, ways of providing hospitals more cheaply were developed, such as standard, or 'off-the-peg' designs, and 'nucleus hospitals' which can be expanded to become full-sized DGHs as resources allow. The capital costs of a new district general hospital amounted, at 1984 prices, to some £40 million.

The National Health Service is inevitably dominated by the hospitals. First, they are immensely costly, both, as we have seen, to build, and to run. Hospital services account for nearly 70 per cent of NHS current expenditure, and for over 50 per cent of all revenue spending on health and the personal social services taken together.[31] Second, just as the focal point of the district is or is to be a district general hospital, so the focal point of each region is a teaching hospital and medical school. This is where the top levels of medical science and technology are concentrated; from these centres of excellence the stream of progress in medical knowledge and skills flows to and through the rest of the hospital system. Third, and as a consequence of this, hospital consultants are the elite of the profession, in terms of both pay and prestige. Unfortunately they have not been prone to conceal their sense of superiority from their colleagues in general practice. There has been some improvement of late, but a committee of the Royal Colleges reporting in 1972 could say no more than that 'the causes of mutual frustration and irritations between hospital doctors and general practitioners are slowly being removed'.[32]

In the early days of the NHS it was assumed, rather than decided, that general practice would retain its traditional place, but the issues involved in this assumption were not squarely faced. Then in 1961 the

Gillie Committee was set up 'to advise on the field of work which it would be reasonable to expect the family doctor to undertake in the foreseeable future'.[33] The basic question was whether, in this age of specialization, a 'generalist' could still give a service of the quality his patients were entitled to expect. The family doctor is the purveyor of 'primary care'. This denotes two things. First, provision of an easy and familiar point of entry into the health care system, from which the patient can, if necessary, be directed to any other part of it. Second, treatment – at home or in the surgery – of such ailments as do not need the services of a specialist or the facilities of a hospital, and supervision of the continuing treatment prescribed by the consultant. These two are interdependent and mutually supportive, but in one sense the former determines the latter, since if the general practitioner is seen as merely a go-between with the doctor in the hospital who really knows best he will find it difficult to build the relationship of trust and mutual understanding between himself and the patient on which a solid basis of personal service must rest.

The 1968 Report of the Royal Commission on Medical Education told the family doctor, rather unkindly, that he must learn to rely less on 'charismatic authority' and the 'mystique of his calling' and more on proven expertise, which the better educated patients of today are well able to appreciate. But does the generalist have any expertise, or is his work only, as has sometimes been said, the 'sum of a number of specialities practised at a lower level of competence'? As a counter to such sceptical thoughts, the Gillie Report endorsed the view that general practice was a specialism in its own right. This idea had gained support from the foundation of the Royal College of General Practitioners in 1952, but it has not been a particularly easy one to sell. The gravest problem for a doctor, even more than for most other professional people, is that the training by which he qualified becomes rapidly out of date; continuing education, theoretical and practical, is essential. For the GPs there were refresher courses in graduate medical schools, and some part-time clinical posts in hospitals. These were very valuable, but not enough, unless the conditions under which they worked allowed them the time and the opportunity to keep in constant touch with current medical progress.

In the early days of the NHS this was far from being the case. The family doctors, in their determination to retain their independent professional status, had accepted an arrangement which, in the words of Enoch Powell (ex-Minister of Health), 'combines private enterprise and state service without the characteristic advantages of either'.[34] This was particularly galling because hospital specialists enjoyed the characteristic advantages of both: security, salary with increments, premises, equipment and assistance provided at public expense, holidays with pay, and freedom to continue their private practice, even within the walls of the hospital. The family doctor, by contrast, had to provide, equip and staff his surgery, and be on duty (in person, or through a locum) round the clock throughout the year: for this he received a fixed income in proportion to the number of patients he enrolled, not to the amount of work he did. Conscientious doctors complained that they could not make a living without excessively enlarging their practices. It is not surprising that when the crisis broke in 1965 over a pay award the British Medical Association presented, not a pay claim, but a 'Charter for the Family Doctor Service'. The most important innovations which followed, and restored the peace, were the recognition of the doctor's right to annual and weekend holidays, the provision of funds to meet the cost of these, and the taking over by the government of the major part of the surgery overheads.

But even under these improved conditions a single-handed practice would only exceptionally be able to give an up-to-date service. Here, however, there has been substantial change since 1950; the proportion of principals in general practice who work single-handed has fallen in thirty years from around 45 per cent to around 15 per cent. A greater percentage (23 per cent in 1979) works from health centres. It will be remembered that in 1920 the Dawson Committee had recommended the establishment of a system of health centres, local and regional (see p. 88). The regional centre in the Dawson plan was intended to contain a group of specialists, and centres of this kind are a basic unit in the Soviet Union. They are sometimes called polyclinics, and resemble hospital out-patient departments brought nearer to the public. Something similar has been tried from time to time in the United States, where the generalist has almost disappeared in the face of the advance of the specialist. However, they have never found favour in this country, and so what we have instead is an up-dated version of Dawson's local health centre. Hesitancy among doctors and shortage of money meant that they failed to catch on in the first decade and a half of the NHS: in 1965 there were only twenty-eight health centres in England and Wales, from which 215 GPs worked. Thereafter, however, their development was extremely rapid, and by 1979 there were 953 in operation, with 5191 family doctors; a further 120 centres were added in England in the two years to the end of 1981.[35] In addition there are now many group practices of four principals or more, sometimes working from premises purpose built through private money.

In the public authority health centre – and in some group practice premises – will be found not only general practitioners, with secretarial and other support, but also health visitors, other community nurses, paramedicals like chiropodists, and sometimes social workers, dentists and others. Thus, in such establishments the Gillie Report's notion of the primary health care team finds expression, and the isolation of the family doctor is very much reduced. However, as with other attempts to invest the personal social services with a rational approach to organization, there may be losses to temper the gains: there is some research evidence that health centres are not universally popular among the doctors who work in them or the patients who use them.[36] Certainly the establishment of them tends to cut down the amount of real choice of family doctor which patients in a locality have, and this may make for some hardship when practitioners exercise their right to remove from their lists, or to refuse admission to their lists to, patients who for one reason or another they find unappealing.

We turn now from the organization of the services to the principles on which they are based, and which determine the relation between the service and the citizens. When the National Health Service was established, Aneurin Bevan made it perfectly clear what these principles were, and in 1970 the then Labour government recalled them in its Green Paper of that year. The first two, in this recapitulation (in reverse order to that in which they appeared) were: 'The service should be national in the sense that the same high quality of service, but not a standardized service, should be provided in every part of the country.' Second: 'The health service should be financed by taxes and contributions paid by people when they are well rather than by charges levied on them when they are sick; the financial burden of sickness should be spread over the whole community.'[37]

The first principle refers to well-known differences in life expectancy and other measures of health status among people living in the various regions of the United Kingdom. It has always been good advice to an embryo to get itself born, if at all possible, in Surrey rather than in, say, Manchester. This was true in 1848, true in 1948, and remains true today. There are also substantial variations according to social class, which have similar long historical roots – the rates of infant mortality, adult mortality, and morbidity, in so far as it can be accurately measured, all rise as one descends the gradient from the professional and managerial classes to the unskilled and their families. These differences, which have been exhaustively documented by the Black Report on Inequalities in Health (1980), overlap with, but are not reducible to, the geographical factor mentioned above: the health and life chances of all classes are better if they live in the more favoured regions rather than the less favoured ones.[38]

It is generally agreed that the NHS has done little to remove these geographical and social class inequalities (whatever improvements there may have been in absolute levels of health, even though there too the record could have been better, as is indicated by the league tables for infant mortality rates among Western countries). Indeed, in some respects the position has worsened in recent years. It is now very rare to find a cause of mortality which has a negative class gradient, with social classes I and II faring worse than social classes IV and V. There has been a striking reversal of pattern in what are now rather erroneously called the 'diseases of affluence', like coronary heart disease.[39]

The NHS is often criticized for its failure to rectify health inequalities. This may be rather unfair, in so far as some of the most important factors, like housing conditions, low incomes, the prevalence of micro-organisms, water-supply, and industrial pollution, are largely outside the remit and the control of the NHS. The same applies to variations in personal habits and patterns of behaviour – the incidence of cigarette smoking, for instance, is much higher among the unskilled than among professional people – even though here the NHS has an important, if under-funded and not always very effective, role in health education.

When one turns to matters for which the NHS is directly responsible, like the distribution of staff, buildings and other facilities, the picture becomes no less complicated. Some variations run on the lines posited by Julian Tudor Hart's 'inverse care law' by which the areas of greatest need are provided with the poorest resources.[40] Thus, in 1973, overall average general practitioner list size was 14.5 per cent below the national average in Bournemouth, 23 per cent above the average in Hartlepool. However, some of the less economically favoured regions are notably well provided with health facilities: Merseyside, for instance, has a relative abundance of general hospital beds, and spends way above the national average per head on them, while Scotland is exceptionally rich in doctors of all kinds – the production of medical personnel has long been a Scottish speciality, both for export and for home consumption. Utilization of services varies, too, in ways which are hard to interpret. For example, general practitioners are relatively thick on the ground, compared with other industrial areas, in both West Central Scotland and South Wales (where Tudor Hart himself practises). However, on Clydeside, with some of the poorest living conditions and the worst health indices in Western Europe, working-class adults appear to be relatively reluctant to report illness and seek treatment. Welsh adults, on the other hand, consult their GPs unusually often, and acquire, and presumably consume, prescribed drugs on a scale unparalleled elsewhere.

Although some of the evidence is ambiguous, and certain disparities persist, there is no doubt that the distribution of general practitioners in Great Britain is more even than in countries which have retained a system for covering medical costs by national health insurance. This was one of the great advantages foreseen for a national service in 1948. It was thought that, even if family doctors were independent contractors, they could be prevented from setting up practices in over-doctored areas and induced to set them up where they were most needed. The improvement was at first considerable, but it has not been wholly maintained. This is the price paid – and paid quite deliberately – for preserving the independence of the doctors. In a country in which, as in France, the general practitioner service is organized by negotiation between the local insurance funds (Caisses) and the doctors in the area, controls cannot be exercised in this way. A comparative survey published in 1973 showed that there were six times as many doctors per thousand of the population in and around Paris as in some rural areas, which is only marginally better than in America, where private enterprise prevails.[41]

In a national service the hospital system can be planned totally, and manned, as in the NHS, by a salaried staff. The first concern of an insurance system, by contrast, is not to build hospitals, but to cover the cost of the treatment given inside them. However, so vital is the role of a well-developed hospital system in modern health care that countries retaining the insurance system have increasingly evolved ways in which the funds, the local authorities or the central government can engage in hospital planning and production. In France, for instance, a Hospital Reform Act of 1970 established what is in effect a public hospital service, embracing both public and private hospitals, supervised by representative councils.[42] In this respect, therefore, there seems to be a convergence between the health insurance and health service alternatives.

After all this, it comes as a surprise to realize that the distribution of hospital medical staff and hospital service expenditure is actually *more* uneven in Britain than the distribution of GPs and family practitioner service expenditure, in spite of the greater degree of control that the NHS has, on paper, over the former than over the latter. The redress of geographical imbalances in hospital services was really only taken seriously as a major policy aim with the publication and acceptance of the report of the Resource Allocation Working Party (RAWP) in 1976. This came up with a formula to guide the shifting of resources from regions classed as over-provided, like the four Thames regions, which fan out from Central London, and the already-mentioned Merseyside region, to less well-off regions, such as Trent, East Anglia and Wessex. The formula has run into some criticism on technical grounds – for instance, for using mortality figures as surrogates for morbidity – but health service experts and professionals have mostly welcomed its general thrust. This does not mean, however, that the task set is easy of accomplishment, particularly now that the financial climate ensures that there will be absolute losers, instead of merely relative ones. The essence of the problem in the Thames regions, for instance, is the existence of a constellation of famous teaching hospitals, which have both a national role, in education, in research, and in the development of new, and often very expensive medical techniques, and a more local role of providing treatment and care for the declining population of Inner London. And for the latter function there are simply too many of them, set too close together. They coexist with general practitioner services in the inner areas which are often poor, with a high proportion of very elderly doctors working single-handed from lock-up surgeries, and with unprestigious and often hard-pressed general hospitals in the outer suburbs. As they are very well defended by influential friends and alumni, it is not surprising that the 'rationalization' of the London teaching hospitals has so far not proceeded very far or very fast, and it seems probable that the less glamorous care services will be the losers in the overall transfer of funds out of the Thames regions.

The post-1979 Conservative government endorsed RAWP, even though the financial stringency it has imposed may have eroded the consensus on which it depends for success. Its attitude to the evening up of class differences has been quite different. Here the story of the Black Report is instructive. The government did not clothe this in the panoply of a Great State Paper: instead, it was produced in a severely limited edition, obtainable only from an obscure room in DHSS headquarters. The Secretary of State contributed an icy little preface, which included the following: 'I must make it clear that additional expenditure on the scale which could result from the report's recommendations – the amount involved could be upwards of £2 billion a year – is quite unrealistic in present or any foreseeable economic circumstances, quite apart from any judgement that may be formed of the effectiveness of such expenditure in dealing with the problems identified.'[43]

This perceived shortage of resources also forms an essential backcloth to any contemporary discussion of the second of the basic principles of the NHS which we noted earlier. This asserts that there must be total pooling of risks among the citizens. Collectively, they pay for the system as a whole; individually, what they pay is unaffected by the cost of what they receive, and what they have a right to receive is unaffected by what (if anything) they may have contributed, whether as insurance premiums or as taxes. No money passes between patient and doctor, and no sum is mentioned; the service is not even costed. It makes no difference, either to the doctor or to the patient, whether the treatment prescribed is cheap or expensive. Even in those cases for which charges have been imposed, for medicines, dentures, and NHS spectacle frames, the charge is at a flat rate and is remitted for those to whom it might cause hardship. This was also the system for dental treatment until in 1971 the flat-rate charge was replaced by a proportion of cost. Another recent change is that spectacle lenses are now costed according to the dioptric power of the lens: this is perhaps an even more surprising breach of the basic principle, because although patients may themselves be held responsible for their failure to keep their teeth in good condition, they can scarcely be blamed for the extent of the myopia they have inherited.

In the continental health insurance systems doctors are paid on a fee for item of service basis: i.e. the rate for the job. The patient pays and claims reimbursement from the fund, exactly as happens with a private contract of insurance. The service, therefore, is costed, and the doctor's earnings are affected by the character of the treatments he prescribes. That he might be tempted to go above and beyond what was really necessary was recognized in Germany when it was laid down that the treatment must be no more than 'adequate and appropriate' and carried out 'with reasonable economy as to the means used'.[44] An example closer to home relates to British dentistry, in which remuneration is also structured on a fee for service basis, and in which clearance has to be secured from the Dental Estimates Board before the more elaborate works of reconstruction on the teeth or palate are carried out: many dentists chaff at procedures they regard as cumbersome, and this is often given as one reason why it has become rather hard to obtain NHS dental treatment in some areas of the country. The point is that fee for service methods of payment increase the need for detailed monitoring in defence of public money – although it may also be true that capitation systems of remuneration have the opposite risk built in, that of encouraging under provision of service.

However, the effect on the patient of fee for service is perhaps more important, because the practice is to make the patient himself bear a proportion of the cost. This is called in France the *ticket moderateur*, and it was increased in 1967 from 20 per cent (a common rate at that time in Europe) to 30 per cent. So the more expensive the treatment, the more the patient has to pay. The fee for service charged to the patient, in addition to the prepayment of his insurance contribution, is explicitly designed to act as a deterrent against frivolous and unnecessary demands on the doctor's time. In 1971 Germany tried the experiment of substituting the carrot for the stick, by paying a bonus to those who had not consulted their doctor during the year, but the principle is the same and it is totally at variance with the spirit of British policy. It is true that some calls made on the doctor are unnecessary, and this has given rise to quite a volume of complaints; but it would be inconsistent with the principle of a free service to use a financial deterrent, and illogical to discourage the reporting of minor symptoms while stressing the importance of early diagnosis.

It has, however, been suggested from time to time in this country that patients ought to be obliged to pay something, in addition to what they contribute through taxes and national insurance, for the service they receive. What this means is that the charges already in existence – which are, as we have seen, limited to scope, and now bring in only about 3 per cent of the income of the NHS – should be increased and added to systematically: proposals for new charges include fees for out-patient and GP consultations, and for GP home visits, although probably the most widely canvassed suggestion is that patients should be billed for all or a proportion of their board and lodging costs while in hospital. Such charges are advocated on various grounds – that they increase the income of the service without increasing the incidence of taxes, that they make patients recognize the value of what they are getting, that they strengthen their position *vis-à-vis* the medical profession. However, they would be expensive to collect, and all charges, old and new alike, move some way towards treating sickness as a personal liability and medical care as a consumer good, instead of treating sickness as a misfortune and medical care as a community service. The Royal Commission not only rejected the introduction of consultation and hotel charges, but also recommended the 'gradual but complete extinction' of all existing charges.[45] The present government spurned this suggestion without hesitation – prescription charges, 20p per item when they assumed office in 1979, were hoisted up in a series of jumps each far above the rate of inflation, until they stood at £1.60 per item in April 1984. The Chancellor of the Exchequer has also announced the intention that the proportion of NHS revenue raised by charges should be increased to 5 per cent. Even so they would remain very much a minority source of financing, and the government has disappointed some of its most vociferous supporters by its rejection of the various proposals for fresh charges, with the exception of those levied on foreigners who avail themselves of NHS treatment while in Britain.

The government has also been cautious – conservative, indeed – over the finance of the NHS more generally. Spokesmen have vehemently denied that they have any intention of moving over to an insurance method of financing. This is in spite of the fact that such a system might be thought to have certain clear ideological attractions for a government led by Mrs Thatcher. Continental health insurance systems, at the expense of introducing a 'commercial' element into the relationship between doctor and patient, allow a greater freedom of choice than the British NHS. For instance, a patient can pay extra and can obtain the services of a specialist of particular eminence in his profession, without going outside the system into an area of 'private' medicine. In fact, there is no sharp division between the public and the private health services, unlike in Britain, where the line has become stark, and the subject of bitter political controversy.

In the 1970s a protracted battle was fought over the relatively narrow issue of whether private (paying) beds should be permitted to continue to exist in NHS hospitals. Since the beginning of the health service the hospitals had been organized in such a way that the public and private elements were not merely interdependent but were interlocked. In the early years 75 per cent, by the mid 1970s around

45 per cent, of consultants were engaged part time and ran private practices, sometimes substantial ones. The 1974–9 Labour government resolved to disentangle the knot. It did not aim to bar NHS consultants from engaging in private practice, but wanted to ensure that it was conducted outside the curtilage of the public hospital. A new body, the Health Services Board, was set up to supervise the removal of private beds. The Labour government fell – and the Board was disbanded – long before this exercise was complete. Indeed, the number of pay beds only fell between 1976 and 1979 from 4800 to 3500: there had actually been as great a decline in their number in the ten years before the Health Services Board had started work, when governments had been benevolently disposed towards private medicine, or had other things on their minds.

What the Labour government did succeed in doing was to give a considerable fillip to private medicine, and in particular to the erection of private hospitals and nursing homes. It is this development which has become a burning political issue. The largest provider of private hospitals in Britain is the non profit-making Nuffield Nursing Homes Trust (NNHT) which by the end of 1982 was running thirty-two hospitals, mostly small ones, containing over a thousand beds.[46] Behind the NNHT lie the private health insurers, of which by far the most significant is the British United Provident Association (BUPA). These have grown rapidly, too – by the end of 1981 they were covering 4.1 million people, not far short of double the number five years previously. However, the momentum may not be maintained: in times of recession even so-called growth industries feel the draught. There is now, say some commentators, a real likelihood of a saturated market and an over-supply of private hospital facilities. In 1982 BUPA had only a 6 per cent increase in new subscribers, compared with an average of 18.5 per cent in the years from 1979 to 1981. To that one may add the observation that the number of short-stay private beds (6000) in 1982 was less than the total of pay beds in NHS hospitals twenty years earlier. It may therefore be that the Royal Commission was right in its refusal to be mesmerized by the potentialities of private medicine in Britain, and in its down-playing of any 'threat' to the NHS as a consequence.

Others, however, think, or fear, otherwise. They totally reject the idea that wealth should be able to buy superior health care: in this, they say, all should be equal. They also believe that the net effect of private insurance is to divert resources into the less essential areas of medicine, since conditions requiring long-term hospitalization are rarely completely covered, and may be completely uncovered, under the terms of the contract. They note with trepidation the arrival on the British scene of the two large US profit-making private hospital concerns, the Hospital Corporation of America and American Medical International. The spectre which looms, they fear, is that of an institutionalized dual standard of service. In the United States the private market dominates the scene, and it is generally admitted that, since the coverage the insurance companies give varies according to the amount subscribed, the result is a very unequal distribution of medical care. And the bills incurred by those not qualified to use Medicaid or Medicare, and not rich enough to pay the maximum subscriptions to Blue Cross and Blue Shield, can be quite crippling.

On the other side are those who welcome the expansion of private medicine on the grounds that the citizens should have the right to spend their money on buying the health care they prefer, if they wish to do so. They also argue that the existence of private practice has a stimulating effect on the medical services as a whole, and that in particular it benefits the hospitals to have part-time consultants working in their outpatients departments and treating patients in the private wards. They deny that the existence of private beds, inside or outside the public hospital, lengthens the queues for NHS treatment, for 'cold surgery' or for anything else: on the contrary, they say, private facilities help to relieve the pressure on the NHS. And when in a point-scoring mood they will doubtless add that what really puts months on to the period of waiting for an NHS admission is prolonged industrial action such as occurred in the latter half of 1982.

This argument turns on the answer to the following question: does the expansion of private medicine bring into existence new resources for medical care, or does it merely redistribute the scarce resources which are already there to the benefit of those who are able to pay? On the one hand, a new source of finance for health care is tapped through the insurance premiums of the employed, and the building and equipping of private hospitals produces additions to the national stock. On the other hand, private medical concerns do not educate doctors, nurses or paramedical staff, and have not so far played any noticeable role in their continuing training. Furthermore, they can offer better pay or conditions of service than are contained in the national agreements which constrain the NHS, so there is a real danger of the 'poaching' of those with skills and experience, especially nurses. Arguments concerning doctors' time are more difficult to place in this context: what consultants do over and above the terms of their contract is in one sense their own affair, and if they choose to neglect the golf-course and devote their time to their private patients then they are contributing a good which otherwise would be unavailable for health care. However, it is in the interests of their private and NHS patients alike that they do not work themselves into the ground, although this is one aspect of a wider question, since those who work the most punishing hours are junior hospital doctors wholly employed within the NHS. Perhaps there needs to be some equivalent of the tachographs affixed to long distance lorries to monitor the hours worked by their drivers.

The posing of questions such as these has recently led to the emergence of a middle position in the battle between the proponents of private medicine and those who would wish to destroy it, given the opportunity. Those who are distressed by what they regard as the polarized and dogmatic views of convinced advocates on either side, argue instead that 'the mixed economy of health' – a phrase currently in vogue – should be 'managed' in the interests of patients as a whole. Such commentators deplore the *uncontrolled* nature of the expansion in private medicine, rather than the expansion as such. The answer, they say, lies in employing the powers of the DHSS and the DHAs, most of which they already possess, to register and to regulate. Their aim would be to try to ensure that the private sector does not simply cream the market, but 'should shoulder its share of the total burden . . . so that the difficult patient load does not fall entirely on the public sector'.[47] This quotation comes from a paper produced by a group of academics and health service professionals from Birmingham. Whether the government will listen to their plea remains to be seen, but the auguries do not seem good.

Indeed, the government has opened up its heavy guns on another front. In September 1983 it issued a circular (HC(83)18) requiring health authorities to put out to tender contacts for their domestic, cleaning and laundry services. As previous requests to consider this course of action had evoked almost no response, the exercise has been closely controlled from Whitehall, including a tight timetable. It represents a form of privatization different from those we discussed earlier, since health authorities have to pay for these essential services whether they are supplied by commercial contractors, or are kept 'in house'. The problems of monitoring are, if anything, even more complex than those involved in an expansion of private medicine, and (at the time of writing) it is uncertain whether sufficient outside firms will be found who will be able and willing to measure up to the detailed operational and financial specifications which have been laid down. These doubts apply especially to hospital catering, only a minute proportion of which has hitherto been contracted out. It is interesting that the government has regarded the winds of competition as necessary to shake up the relatively low paid and mostly female workers who staff the support services, but has not so far applied the same philosophy to other areas of the NHS. The possibility of buying in managerial services might have been considered to be congruent with the Griffiths approach, for example. The trade unions (and especially the National Union of Public Employees, to which many ancillary workers belong) believe that the support services have been singled out for special attention because of what the government sees as past misdemeanours, and it seems certain that a bruising and highly politicized argument will continue, in this and other aspects of privatization. In this the current state of health care politics mirrors the situation in social policy more generally.

10 The personal social services

The phrase 'the personal social services' is fairly new. Phoebe Hall, in her book on the establishment of social service departments, notes her failure to find examples of its use in the literature before 1965, and suggests that it was coined for the Seebohm Committee which was appointed in that year.[1] The word 'welfare' did not appear in Seebohm's terms of reference, even though 'the welfare services' had been the usual form of description up to the mid 1960s (and was used in earlier editions of this book). For denoting an administrative area it was too narrow, for at that time welfare departments did not even include work with children, let alone other more peripheral relevant services. For definition of services by their objectives it was thought to be too vague. However, the imprecision of both of the adjectives in 'the personal social services' has not impeded that phrase's rise to popularity – indeed, it has doubtless contributed to it. 'Personal' should here be taken not to mean merely that there is a face to face meeting between client and agent, since this occurs even when pension are paid out at a post office. Rather it indicates that the two meet and communicate as persons, that the agent seeks to understand and interpret the needs of the client and is prepared to exercise some measure of personal judgement, based on his knowledge, skill and experience, in rendering his – or more usually her – service. This relationship is characteristic, however, also of such professions as medicine, law and teaching, and the rather arbitrary function of the word 'social' is to exclude them. Thus the Seebohm Committee interpreted its task as one which was given shape and coherence by a mode of operation – essentially the methods of professional social work – common to four of the five principal components of the new local authority departments which it wished to see established. These were the then existing children's and welfare departments of local authorities, medical and psychiatric social work within hospitals, and the community mental health services. (The fifth major component, the home help service, which was in almost all areas of the country part of the empire of the Medical Officer of Health, had never before been run by social workers, and was in certain respects different in kind from the others, a point to which we shall return).

This scattered heritage had diverse origins. Domestic help was a newish area of endeavour for local authorities: the service had developed during the Second World War, initially to provide assistance for mothers during confinements, but it was very soon catering almost entirely for the frail elderly living at home. Social work in hospitals had grown out of the efforts of the Charity Organization Society and others to ensure that the financial circumstances of patients in voluntary hospitals were correctly assessed; the term 'almoner', largely shorn of its original connotation of guardian of the charitable purse, continued in official use during the 1940s and 1950s, and in popular use far longer.

The other three services all had their roots in the Poor Law, and were carved out from the public assistance departments of local authorities (see Chapter 5) in the years after 1945. The break with the past was more complete than in many European countries, where the trend was towards the developing of the welfare element within the social assistance services. In Britain, however, the reputation of the Poor Law was such that a clean separation between financial support and other kinds of help was regarded as quite essential. Of the three, the mental health services underwent the least immediate change: mental welfare officers, provided with what seemed an obvious home in the health departments of local authorities, were the old Poor Law duly authorized officers under a new name. Children's departments represented a more classic example of a functional service deliberately and bodily removed from the Poor Law on the lines advocated by the Minority Report of the Royal Commission on the Poor Laws as long ago as 1909. The Curtis Committee, reporting in 1946, had been insistent that the whole responsibility for 'children deprived of normal home life with their own parents and relatives' should be entrusted to a single committee of the local authority, with a children's officer of senior rank as its executive agent. Opinions differed, they said, as to which committee should assume the responsibility, but 'the one point of agreement is that it should not be the Public Assistance Committee under another name' (para. 439). And, finally, all the bits and pieces which could not be assigned to specialized agencies when the Poor Law was broken up were lumped together into welfare services departments: Rodgers and Dixon aptly described the one they studied in a Northern town as 'the residuary legatee of the old public assistance department'.[2]

These bits and pieces were not even handed over as going concerns; the charge given to the welfare authorities was virtually to create services of a quite new kind, partly to replace those which were marked with the stamp of pauperism, and partly to supplement them. In its report for 1944 the Assistance Board, which had been instructed to perform its task 'in such manner as may best promote the welfare of pensioners' observed that in doing this it was breaking new ground, and that 'there was no common body of doctrine or practice indicating the kind of services required'.[3] After 1948 it became necessary to evolve one, and as the shadow of the Poor Law and the workhouse receded, the features of a modern welfare service gradually emerged, together with its characteristic problems. These arose chiefly from the change in the relationship between the provider and the receiver of the service, as the latter, once classed as a pauper, came to be treated, and in due course to be generally referred to, as a client. The sphere of operation of the service was to be extended in principle from 'the poor' to the public. It was to be available to all, without regard to means. Of course most of the clients would still in fact be poor, but they would no longer be classed as such. This was bound to affect both the content of the service and the way in which it was administered.

Services for children, thanks to gradual changes in emphasis in a series of measures spanning more than sixty years, and designed to deal with cruelty and gross neglect, had already taken the crucial step across the gap which lies between the punishment of crime and the promotion of welfare. The Children's Act of 1933 contained, in addition to a formidable array of penal clauses, a section providing that children 'in need of care and protection' could be brought before a juvenile court (without being charged with an offence) and placed in care of a 'fit person', who might be, and generally was, the local authority. Thus judicial procedure could be used, not only to punish parents for cruelty, but also to take their children away if they could not be trusted to look after them properly.

In 1946 there were 13,000 children (in England and Wales) 'in care' under this law, in addition to over 32,000 necessitous children maintained by the public assistance authorities.[4] But there was evidence to show that the new welfare approach had not fully prevailed over the old penal one. A voluntary committee under Mrs Hubback, which investigated the situation at that time, reported that in practice it proved difficult to do anything for the child until steps had been taken to prosecute the offending parent or guardian, and this was possible only if it could be shown that the neglect or ill-treatment of the child was 'wilful'.[5] This was equally true of the work of the National Society for the Prevention of Cruelty to Children, whose officers also operated by prosecuting or by threatening to prosecute.

The first requirement of the new regime, before it could explore the possibilities of striking out in fresh directions for service provision, was for a redefinition of the powers and responsibilities of the new authorities, designed to fit the status of their intended clients. This was provided by legislation for the three major categories of beneficiaries, the children, the aged, and the physically and mentally handicapped. The initial regulations were embodied in the Children Act of 1948 and in Part III of the National Assistance Act of the same year. When a blanket clause (such as had once fitted relations between guardians and poor) is replaced by a specification of rights and duties, inevitably there are gaps. The authorities responsible for the care of old people, for example, were authorized to provide residential accommodation for them, but not to do anything else for their general welfare. Thus local authorities were not empowered to provide meals on wheels directly, and this service, so essential for enabling frail elderly people to remain in their own homes, started as a very uneven patchwork of grant-aided voluntary initiatives – three-quarters of the people receiving meals in 1959 were served by the Women's Voluntary Service.[6] This particular deficiency was made good by the National Assistance (Amendment) Act of 1962, and was followed by more wide-ranging legislation in 1968.[7] The outlines of a community service were being established through trial and error.

The situation in respect of the physically handicapped was not dissimilar, although here there was an injunction very untypical of the Poor Law, that local authorities, as their first duty, should spread information widely about the new services. What these services were to be was not, however, very clear. Welfare authorities were required to submit to the minister their schemes for the blind, the partially sighted, the deaf, the hard of hearing, and 'the general classes of the handicapped' – the quaint phraseology indicates the prevailing doubts about what categories should appropriately be distinguished. The advantages gained by the disabled person through registering with the local authority were not, except in the case of the blind, in most instances significant, and here again voluntary organizations were accorded – and still retain – a major role as agents of the local authority. In this area, too, a new chapter had to await fresh legislation, the Chronically Sick and Disabled Persons Act of 1970.

In the case of children, there was both more relevant experience, and more certainty on the part of the experts and the providers about what the new post-war services should look like. In its recommendations the Curtis Committee followed the line of thought generally current at the time, namely that children taken from their homes should be put to live in conditions as much like a home as possible. Adoption and 'boarding out', or fostering, were probably the best solutions, provided the host families were well chosen. The Committee summed up its thoughts on this difficult issue by saying that, although there might be a greater risk of 'acute unhappiness' in a foster home, 'a happy foster home is happier than life as generally lived in a large community' (para. 422). This was no doubt true of the typical 'community' as it existed then, namely a big barrack-type institution, but the Committee looked with some favour on the intermediate solution of putting the children in smaller homes or groups of cottages where more of the atmosphere of family life could be created.

The main recommendations of the Curtis Committee were put into effect and the advance of policy from that point followed lines which the Committee itself had foreseen. Legislation in 1948 and 1952 gave local authorities the power, not only to accept children placed with them by the courts, but also to receive into care other children regarded as 'in need of care and protection'. Furthermore, the duty was laid upon them to seek out such children wherever they had cause to believe they might be found. But in these cases, where there was no court decision, the child could be taken from its home only with the consent of its parents, and this consent could be revoked at any time. In exceptional cases, however, the council could apply to the court for permission to 'assume parental rights' over the child, which meant that the parents could not take it back.

The next step was to develop welfare work in the home in two ways. First, to try to *prevent* a state of affairs from arising in which it would be necessary to take the child away, and, second, to try to *create* a state of affairs which would allow the child to return to its parents as soon as possible. The power to engage in preventative action was explicitly conferred by the Children and Young Persons Act of 1963 which authorized local authorities to give 'advice, guidance and assistance' with a view to 'diminishing the need to receive children into or keep them in care' – which in fact many of them were doing already. The assistance permitted included the grant or loan of money to obviate the danger of reception into care: the introduction of these

'Section One payments', as they have since come to be called, redrew the boundary between the income support and the welfare services. The rationale for this was simple: if social workers were to be able to offer effective help then they needed to have access to some limited material resources within the control of their own agency. However, some commentators, most notably Bill Jordan, have seen this development as betokening the re-entry of the Poor Law into the heart of social work.[8] Such criticisms may be exaggerated, but they illustrate the point that preventative action, although often rather simply recommended as the self-evidently logical final stage in the extension of welfare services, is usually more contentious than it seems. The intervention of a social worker in the affairs of a family before an acute need has become manifest can be regarded as – and may indeed become – interference.

Rather similar problems arise in the relationship between child welfare and the judicial apparatus. The two cannot be wholly detached because one of the things which may demonstrate a child's need for care and protection is its disorderly or delinquent behaviour, and the distinction between the two is a narrow one. There is general agreement that, from some points of view, it is best to avoid making the distinction for children below a certain age, and to treat all cases as 'children in trouble', presenting a question of welfare rather than of punishment. Belief in the appropriateness of a welfare philosophy in the treatment of children below school-leaving age, naughty or otherwise, reached it apogee in the mid 1960s, with the publication of the Labour Government's White Paper, *The Child, the Family and the Young Offender*.[9] This proposed the establishment of family councils, which were to be non-judicial bodies replacing the juvenile court for such children. The difficulty was that while this would have saved many delinquent children from the trauma of an appearance in court, it might have made some of the more law-abiding (and their parents) feel that they were being classed among the delinquents. Furthermore, many quite young children suffer a sense of injustice (as do their parents also) if, when charged with an offence, they cannot get the question of their guilt or innocence established by due process of law. Recognizing this, the White Paper took care to ensure that the child's right to protest its innocence should be preserved, but this concession did not deflect a storm of criticism. The government retreated smartly, and so the English system has remained mixed, with the judicial element in the mixture increasing as one moves from one age group up to the next. In Scotland, on the other hand, where the juvenile court had never struck deep roots, a system of children's hearings, presided over by lay panels, was instituted in 1968 (although with the right of access to the Sheriff's Court being retained if the facts were disputed).

The Child, the Family and the Young Offender, abortive though it was, played a significant part in quite another story, that of the tangled comings and goings which eventually resulted in the Seebohm reorganization of 1970. To understand this, we have to go back to the unofficial Longford Committee, whose 1964 Report provided the inspiration for the White Paper. As a preliminary to their proposals for decriminalization, Lord Longford and his colleagues recommended 'the establishment of a family service with the aim of helping every family to provide for its children the careful nurture and attention to individual social needs that the fortunate majority already enjoy'.[10] Support for the establishment of a family service soon began to gather momentum: members of the Longford Committee (including, of course, its chairman) were appointed to prominent positions in the newly elected Labour government. However, other influential people, mostly associated with the National Insitute for Social Work Training, and often also with strong Labour Party links, started to become alarmed at what they saw as the narrowness of the reorganization which was being contemplated. These fears were distilled in a speech made by Richard Titmuss at the Royal Society of Health Conference in April 1965: the proposal, he said, was 'too family-centred and child-centred. . . . I am doubtful whether a F.S.D. (Family Service Department) would effectively bring together within one administrative structure all social workers in the employ of a single local authority.[11] The first requirement, in the eyes of those who shared Professor Titmuss's views, was for a wide-ranging enquiry before government intentions had set hard, and a group started to meet together to press for this very soon after the RSH conference. The lobbying succeeded, and a committee under Lord Seebohm, a banker – and chairman of the National Institute for Social Work Training – was formed and announced before the end of 1965. Two of its members, Professor J. N. Morris and Robin Huws Jones, were also prominent members of the Titmuss group.[12]

The terms of reference of the Seebohm Committee were 'to review the organization and responsibilities of the local authority personal social services in England and Wales, and to consider what changes are desirable to secure an effective family service'. The last phrase, a reminder of the controversies which plagued the establishment of the

enquiry, was dealt with by the Committee in a decidedly cavalier
fashion. It quickly decided that 'family' must be taken to mean
'everybody', including the childless, single, widowed and divorced
(para. 32) – despite the fact that many of these would only come
within scent of a social worker precisely because of the non-existence
or looseness of their family ties. However, the Committee kept well
within its terms of reference in concentrating upon organizational
questions. We have already noted its central recommendation, which
was adopted, namely the unification into a single department of social
work and related activities. This unification was not in fact complete:
the probation service, indisputably the employer of a good number of
trained and professional social workers, being the most notable
absentee. To have included it in the remit of the Committee would
have incurred the enmity of the Home Office, although in Scotland,
with a different ministerial set-up, probation officers were in fact
absorbed into the departments of social work established there.
Welfare workers in education departments – the Education Welfare
Officers (EWOs) – and in housing departments also maintained a
separate identity outside the new social service departments.

Whether or not the Committee had decided on the outcome of its
deliberations before it started to hear evidence – as some commentators have suggested[13] – must remain a moot point. Phoebe Hall is
cautious, noting merely that committee members 'began their work
with the concept of unification well to the fore'.[14] In her view,
alternative forms of organization were 'unlikely candidates', because
of the Committee's identification of lack of resources, inadequate
knowledge and divided responsibility as the root causes of weaknesses
in the then existing structure of services. Thus the Committee
considered and rejected the idea of creating the 'effective family
service' by strengthening and enlarging the children's department,
while keeping the welfare department (for the old and handicapped)
separate. It also rejected suggestions for merging welfare with health,
and possibly with children's services and even education as well,
though here there was the qualification that the amalgamation of the
health and welfare services might come at some future date. Most of
these possibilities would almost certainly have meant that the medical
profession retained a stake in the direction of the personal social
services, but one of the Committee's less openly avowed aims was the
freeing of social work from medical suzerainty. Professor Morris, a
specialist in social medicine, was the only medically qualified
member of the Committee – there were no MOHs, general

practitioners, or consultants in the acute or chronic specialties. In the event, one of the big surprises was that the profession offered so little determined opposition to the Seebohm recommendations. However, doctors had other things on their minds at the time, especially the impending reorganization of the NHS.

Michael Brill, writing in the very early 1970s, described the Seebohm Report as 'a statement of faith by social workers and their friends about the nature of social work'.[15] An important part of this statement concerned the perceived necessity for the emergence of an integrated social work profession, with institutions and an ethos to match. Leading social workers were not slow to respond to this demand, and in 1970, after some years of planning and negotiation, eight specialized professional bodies joined together to create the British Association of Social Workers, and in the following year there was established a Central Council for Education and Training in Social Work (CCETSW), to cover all branches of the profession. The heady atmosphere of this period was well captured by the doyenne of social work education, Dame Eileen Younghusband, when she wrote 'something momentous happened between 1965 and 1968 which released energies still active by 1975, in spite of massive economy cuts. The social work profession had leapt from the margins to the centre and was faced with a challenge to do the job to which it had always laid claim'.[16] Furthermore, *pace* Dame Eileen's remark about 'massive economy cuts', the resources were made available during these years on a hitherto unprecedented scale. Current local authority expenditure on the personal social services constituted 0.9 per cent of total public expenditure in 1969/70, 1.9 per cent in 1975/6.[17] This was a faster rate of growth than that experienced by any other category of social service spending, although of course the call the personal social services make on the gross national product is tiny compared with that made by the NHS or by social security.

Since the mid 1970s the tide has ebbed. Although growth has not totally disappeared, the personal social services have had to run very fast to stay approximately where they were then. The view has been increasingly heard that social work, for optimal functioning, requires 'flatter' hierarchies than those supplied in the reorganized local government system, and that too much of the increase in expenditure after Seebohm went on enhancing the career earnings of those social workers who took on administrative posts. The Department of Health and Social Security seems to have become anxious about the quality of management in social service departments, and in 1980 the

Conservative government abolished the power enabling ministers to veto candidates for posts of director of social services in England and Wales who do not possess prescribed social work qualifications.

Social workers themselves have become less convinced of the virtues of professional status, and have increasingly adopted an alternative model, that of trade union organization. In 1979 social workers in several authorities withdrew their labour, to the unconcealed glee of some journalists and others who loudly proclaimed that the absence of cataclysmic consequences 'proved that social workers were not needed'. What research evidence there is suggests that the reality was a good deal more complicated than that,[18] but the episode was undoubtedly damaging to the reputation of social work. And, curiously, where there *were* cataclysmic consequences a similar lesson could be drawn, that social workers were useless. The melancholy succession of children who died while under the supervision of social service departments – Colwell, Menheniot, Meurs etc. – and whose deaths were followed by much publicized inquiries,[19] could be adduced as evidence of failure. Lastly, academics have added their mite to the criticism. For more than two decades there has been a skein of scholarly opinion which has linked together left-wingers like Baroness Wootton,[20] Adrian Sinfield,[21] and assorted Marxists,[22] with commentators of a much more right-wing persuasion such as Brewer and Lait,[23] the common thread being scepticism about the claims of a 'people-changing' profession.

In all this there is one major truth and a number of misapprehensions. The truth is that social workers have not generally been all that anxious to evaluate the results of their interventions, and that where such evaluation has been attempted its findings have not been especially reassuring. Here the Seebohm Committee is somewhat to blame. Although it took two and a half years to produce its report, it commissioned or conducted no research, into the efficacy of social work or anything else. As an example of evaluation research we may take the 'field experiment' carried out by Matilda Goldberg and her associates into the provision of social work support for the elderly.[24] In this, clients were randomly assigned to one of two groups, so that half of them received the services usually offered by the almost entirely unqualified staff of a London borough, while the other half obtained help from a team of highly trained caseworkers. The latter group was assessed as having benefited more, in terms of the relief of personal problems, involvement in activities and the meeting of practical needs, but then they had been accorded much more assistance than those who received the more routine service. Most of the differences in outcome between the two groups were small – very few were statistically significant – and all in all Goldberg's book would scarcely be a wise choice to offer a cost-conscious local authority treasurer in support of a plea for the employment of greater numbers of trained social workers.

In order to understand the misapprehensions – and to explore further the nature of some of the criticisms – one has to consider the history of social work in this country. Three phrases are relevant. The first takes us back to the closing years of the nineteenth century, and to the pioneering role played by the Charity Organization Society (COS) in the development of the methods of casework, and of training for the caseworkers, who were then part voluntary and part salaried. In due course, the COS promoted the establishment of a School of Sociology from which grew the Social Science Department of the London School of Economics, and thereafter similar departments in nearly all the universities in the country.[25] This may sound unexceptionable, but in spite of the emphasis on science, training and service, in practice (see p. 38) the focus tended to be on the moral failure and moral rehabilitation of the individual with, as the goal, his adaptation and willing submission to the conditions imposed on him by society and his place in it. Left-wingers frequently argue that the desire to impose the principles of middle-class morality still colours the present-day practice of social work.

The first half of the twentieth century saw a significant change. There began that development towards social democracy which has been described in Part One of this book, bringing new ideas about the status of the citizen in relation to his fellows and to the government. More directly, the academic atmosphere in which training took place favoured the objective scientific approach to the subject as against the traditional moral attitude, and the search for the social as against the purely individual causes of the trouble. Casework was still essential, but went arm in arm with social action. Contemporary right-wing critics are often suspicious of this association between social work and social reform, seeing in it the seeds of the politicization which has been advocated by the current generation of 'radical social workers'.

After the Second World War there was a further shift, largely under American influence, towards the conception of casework as the therapeutic treatment of the individual's psychological deficiencies and disorders. This trend has aroused the derision of both left and right. In her scathing criticism of it Baroness Wootton argued that a misdirected ambition to achieve a status equal to that of the higher professions, especially medicine, was leading social workers to attempt to render services beyond their competence. It was better that they should devote themselves to informing and advising clients about the social services and the benefit they could obtain from them rather than on 'counselling' them on how to conduct their personal lives.[26] June Lait goes further: since, in her view, social workers' 'only functions are to attempt to remedy the shortcomings of other services, and to refer clients to existing services', the solution lies in improving the operation and the publicity of these other services, thereby, apparently, abolishing the need for social work as a separate entity altogether.[27]

Such views grossly exaggerate the extent to which the feet of those who practise social work – or, indeed, teach and write about it – have left the ground. The 'psychiatric deluge' was always more like a rivulet in Britain, while the euphoria of the Seebohm years has given place to a sober recognition of the indeterminacy of much social work, a feature which it shares with psychiatry, and with much of the practice of medicine more generally. Martin Davies suggests, in a recent textbook, that the common elements in social work can best be sought in the unglamorous notion of 'maintenance' of persons 'in positions of severe weakness, stress and vulnerability'. 'There has emerged', he writes, 'almost wholly within the public sector, a large and still growing range of functions that comprise society's response to a variety of problems posed by marginal individuals of many kinds.'[28] Local authority social workers perform an astonishing variety of tasks, all of them with a strong practical component, and many of them statutory – social service departments currently exercise powers under some forty Acts of Parliament. Successive governments have certainly not piled on these responsibilities in order to advance the practice of 'luxurious casework', and the fact that the present administration is continuing to add to their number does not suggest that it shares Mrs Lait's view that social service departments could be dispensed with. There may still be a danger of encouraging in social workers an inclination to enter all their cases through a 'diagnostic doorway', looking for a personality disorder that can be treated, but there does not seem to be much substance in the accusation that they habitually discount presenting problems, many of which will be material.

Moreover, it is foolish to equate the practical with the simple and the unproblematic. Baroness Wootton and Brewer and Lait seem to underrate the complexity of the task of attempting to ensure that the services provided for the benefit of those in need are used to the best possible advantage. This is by no means a mechanical operation; it calls for investigation, interpretation and communication, all of which require the activation of personal skills. It is not enough to know what the services are and how they work (although this expertise is itself quite rare and difficult to acquire). Studies have recently been made which show how imperfect the communication between worker and client can often be because of differences of social class, education and ideas about the nature of cause and effect. But these barriers can be overcome, given the necessary skills and the right approach. It is interesting that in the Goldberg evaluation to which we have already referred one of the things which most clearly distinguished the trained caseworkers from their untrained confrères was their greater success in performing an 'enabling' role. This was defined as 'making needs explicit and helping clients to accept services which they need and to which they are entitled' and is rightly described as 'an important one among old people whose expectations are often low'.[29] There is in this an educational element which is even more explicit in some other kinds of case, as when a disabled person must be taught how to make the best use of gadgets and appliances, or 'self-care' in the routine of daily life is taught to someone who is mentally afflicted.

It is a short step from this to action the aim of which is to change a client's behaviour. This, sometimes referred to as 'assertive' casework, is held by many people to lie very near to the boundary between the permissible and the objectionable. Its acceptability in any particular situation must vary according to the degree of assurance or general consensus that exists about the kind of behaviour towards which the change is to be directed, the suitability of the methods used and the competence of the social worker to use them. The probation officer tries to induce, or to help, his charge to behave in a law-abiding manner; that is his function. But how far should he go in trying to change his personality or his attitude to society? Preventive casework in child care must often involve trying to persuade, or to help, a mother to manage her home and treat her child in a more orderly and understanding way. But does this mean that she is 'to encourage certain child-rearing practices and discourage others?' This is one example given by Olive Stevenson of what she had in mind when she said, in a talk to the Association of Social Workers, that: 'It seems unarguable that social workers are agents of social control, if by that is meant that they encourage individuals to adapt to certain ways of behaviour which society deems desirable and from which they have deviated.'[30]

This interpretation of the nature of social work contains a frank and salutary recognition of the power vested in its agents. And the powers in question here are certainly considerable: social workers decide whether a couple should be permitted to adopt or not; in cases of non-accidental injury they may recommend the removal of a child from its parents; they take part in decisions which can curtail the liberty of an adult, as when the question arises of sectioning (compulsorily detaining in a mental hospital) someone who is mentally ill. The most comprehensive study of local authority area teams (by Parsloe and Stevenson) found less anxiety about mental health emergency work than the authors had expected,[31] but this is an area, which, like the others mentioned, demands considerable experience and expertise.

The question of specialization was rather left dangling by the Seebohm report, and ever since has been a vexed one: there has been much argument about the extent to which Seebohm intended that social workers should be generic, that is, not only trained to perform the manifold tasks of social work with all the various categories of clients, but also actually performing them in the course of their everyday practice. The alternative possibility would be the generic *team*, composed of specialists of one kind or another. Parsloe and Stevenson encountered wide variations in the areas they studied, arranged on a continuum from the first to the second of these models. In some quarters 'genericism' has become a mild term of abuse, and there have been suggestions that recent trends have been away from it, but the authors maintain that nothing in their findings casts doubt on the desirability of a generic training or of mixed caseloads, although they recommend a degree of specialization, preferably on a planned basis in the course of career development. However, these specialists should be members of teams: the research clearly indicated that the services of specialists who acted as advisers or consultants without team membership were seldom utilized effectively.

The Parsloe/Stevenson research is also of interest because of the picture of local authority social work which it presents, a rather depressing one in many respects. The wearing pressures of trying to meet gross need with severely limited resources, the ever-present fear of 'another Maria Colwell', the resulting concentration on statutory duties often at the expense of other tasks, the almost universal backlog in the recording of cases, apparently caused, at least in part, by the niggardly provision of secretarial facilities by local authorities – all these are documented. Although the authors produce many examples of what they regard as good practice, and the general impression is that social workers are doing their best in difficult circumstances, the reality of what have been termed 'defensive social work' and 'subsistence social work' was evident.[32] The Barclay Report used the politer phrase 'the safety net approach' to describe not dissimilar phenomena.[33]

The Conservative government arranged for the appointment of the Barclay Committee in 1980, as a response to the varied expressions of disquiet which we have outlined. Its terms of reference were 'to review the role and tasks of social workers in local authority social service departments and make recommendations'. Some critics of social work hoped – and some practitioners feared – that this was to be the first prong of an assault on the profession as it currently operated. However, the report turned out to be generally sympathetic to social workers – cynics would say that this was because the job was turned over to the National Institute for Social Work.[34] Its keynote was struck in its first sentence: 'Too much is generally expected of social workers.'

The Barclay recommendations did not in the event make much of a public stir; their most notable feature was the strong advocacy of 'community social work'. The notion of community is a well-known conceptual swamp, but committees of inquiry always seem to find its fresh greenness fatally alluring. It was the Seebohm Report which said that 'a clear responsibility should be placed upon the social service department for developing conditions favourable to community identity and activity' – surely a most formidable undertaking. Barclay has gone even farther, and the community-oriented model of social work favoured by the Majority was backed by an even more thorough going note of reservation from Professor Hadley and others recommending the universal adoption of 'patch' or 'neighbourhood-based' systems of service delivery.

These various proposals can perhaps best be tackled indirectly, through the committee's views on social casework, which it tends to treat as an old-fashioned and slightly discredited activity, breaking it up into 'counselling' and what is termed 'social care planning'. It is not easy to know what is meant by this second concept, since it is intended to apply both to individual cases and to whole client groups. However, we learn that at the individual level it involves 'creating, with a client, a system or network of care, tailored to his particular situation',[35] and that more generally it includes a 'need to discover and bring into play the potential self-help, volunteer help, community organizations, voluntary and private facilities that exist'.[36] It therefore encompasses the community development advocated by Seebohm, although with questionable logic the Barclay majority envisage that community work would continue to exist as a separate activity.

The social services area office, covering a population of perhaps 60,000 to 80,000, served by one or more fieldwork teams, was one of the more successful innovations of the Seebohm period. It provided a single geographical focus for the delivery of services, thus making for greater ease of access on the part of clients, while at the same time it was not so decentralized as to render difficult the establishment and maintenance of the bureaucratic virtue of impartial administration, which has always depended on managerial controls as well as on self-ingested professional standards. Actually, social service departments have encountered difficulties in this respect, and one interpretation of 'social care planning' would be that it is a plea for the clarification of objectives and for the formulation of more overt and uniform policies within and between areas. As such, it is not only unobjectionable but is very necessary, although it would certainly demand both time and managerial skills, and hence would be expensive, as Barclay indeed recognizes. However, giving greater autonomy to more and smaller teams, whether geographically based or not, would deepen the problem of accountability, and probably worsen liaison with other agencies, which the various inquiries into cases of child abuse have repeatedly singled out as of crucial significance. In his Minority Report to Barclay, Professor Pinker makes many of these points. He also argues, disturbingly, that 'The most vulnerable, disadvantaged and stigmatized clients will be at greatest risk in community-based models of social work since they give greatest offence to local norms of behaviour and are often rejected by their communities.'[37] The evergreen popularity of participating local communities raises questions which go well beyond the personal social services, and we return to the matter in the last chapter.

So far – as with much of the literature on the personal social services – the impression may have been given that the staff of social service departments consists almost entirely of field social workers. This is very far from the truth. In 1980, out of a full-time equivalent of almost exactly 200,000 employees in England, only 23,000 or 11.5 per cent were fieldworkers – excluding senior managerial and professional advisory staff, but including trainees, welfare assistants and community workers.[38] By far the largest groups consisted of approximately 50,000 home helps and their managers, and another 50,000 members of staff of homes for the elderly (including mentally infirm old people) and for the younger physically handicapped. If one adds those employed in day centres for these groups, one can see what a large proportion of the manpower of social service departments is engaged in their support, mainly that of the elderly. Very few are social workers, trained or otherwise: four-fifths of the staff employed in homes are care assistants, or domestic, maintenance or clerical workers. Another substantial group, 22,000 in total, is made up of those working in community homes for children and young people. Smaller but still significant numbers are employed in hostels and day centres for the mentally ill, in hostels and training centres for the mentally handicapped, and in day nurseries.

Thus there are two principal forms of activity to be considered, residential services and services for those who remain in their homes. These two are often treated, at least in much popular-political debate, as being the antithesis of each other: the 'institution' is seen as bleak and rejecting, the 'community' as warm and receiving. Writers and practitioners in this field are often keen to break down this stereotype: day care could be regarded as a kind of buffer-state between them, while the Barclay Report argues that 'to think of children (or adults) living with families as receiving one form of residential care, diminishes the sharp differentiation often made between fostering and residential care and puts the relationship between them in what we believe to be a more helpful perspective'.[39] Both the regime in children's homes and the advocacy of fostering have long been dominated by the desire to provide a substitute family, although this concept may be a somewhat illusory one when there are so many short-term placements.

In any case, when people talk disparagingly of 'institutions' they have in mind the large establishments, the workhouse-descendent or the specialist hospital, especially for the mentally handicapped, rather than the smaller modern homes and hostels run by local authorities. Much evidence has accumulated over the years of the damage that the regimes of large institutions can inflict on the personalities of those who live in them, and one of the more cheering developments of the last twenty years has been the way in which the apparently eternally adaptable Poor Law buildings have at last been demolished, mothballed or turned over to non social service uses. However, there is a certain contradiction here. When government publications recommend 'Care in the community', like the recent

(1981) Consultative Document of that title, what they are suggesting is, at least in part, a move from one kind of institution to another. Homes containing perhaps sixty residents are not 'small' in many meanings of that word, and it is not a necessary truth that they have stronger local links or are able to attract more voluntary endeavour than the villas in mental handicap hospitals which they replace, or, in the case of old people, than the geriatric wards to which they may be an alternative.

In order to tease out some of the confusions which abound in this area, Philip Abrams makes a twofold distinction: first, between 'closed and open settings', or the institutional and the community-centred, and, second, between 'treatment' and 'care', the former being provided by professionals and specialists, the latter by lay persons.[40] He thus comes up with four boxes, only one of which can be filled with 'community care' using his terminology – he reserves the label for 'services provided in their locality by residents on a voluntary or quasi-organized basis'. Abrams argues, therefore, not only that 'community care' cannot be provided in an institution (however 'open' it may try to be) but also that what the paid servants of local authorities offer through their domiciliary services is not 'community care' but 'community treatment'. Furthermore, his classification does not exhaust the need for conceptual clarification, since 'community care' represents the yoking together of two shifty words, and it is not only the first of them which presents problems. Roy Parker concentrates his artillery on the second element: 'Care', he notes, is used 'on the one hand . . . to convey the idea of concern about people. It may find expression in a charitable donation, in lobbying, in prayer or in feelings of anxiety, sadness or pleasure at what happens to others. On the other hand, "care" also describes the actual work of looking after those who, temporarily or permanently, cannot do so for themselves. It comprises such things as feeding, washing, lifting, cleaning up for the incontinent, protecting and comforting'.[41] Parker suggests that we should employ the word 'tending' for this second, and considerably more active and demanding, manifestation of 'care'.

A comprehensive system of continuous neighbourly help may not be impossible – Abrams cites the Japanese *tsukiai* – but it is clearly very unlikely to develop in a society which vests all its stricter obligations in kin. As has often been pointed out, 'community care' all too often means in practice an unaided burden falling on close relatives – parents are expected to look after disabled children, children to look after aged parents. And the close relatives in question are almost invariably female. It is well attested that the domiciliary services retreat when there is a daughter or a daughter-in-law in the offing. This is especially so if they are sharing a household with the old person, even though the relinquishment of separate accommodation is usually a signal of major problems of coping. Another point is that, since the gravest cause for concern is the great growth in the numbers of the very old, there are now many women of over pensionable age themselves who are tending mothers or fathers aged 90 plus. Muriel Nissel and Lucy Bonnerjea, in their study of the costs of family care of handicapped elderly people, paint a very gloomy picture.

Although interviews were carefully designed to avoid stressing the burden of care, little or no mention was made by wives or husbands of any benefits which the family derived: they talked of the pain and the problems. The emphasis was on obligations, and it was the wife who mainly shouldered them, with the consequence that she was constrained in her work role, in her role as a wife and mother, in her status as a person who has no time for herself and in her very identity. She was caught in the situation and often her only means of escape seemed physical or mental breakdown.[42]

The taken for granted assumption that there will always be a supply of such women, able and willing to take on these heavy domestic and other tending duties when circumstances demand it, has become highly questionable both for demographic reasons and because of changes in expectations and styles of life. The smaller birth cohorts and smaller completed families of the years between the wars mean that there are fewer female relatives to go round than in the past, and owing to changes in employment patterns more of those that do exist are, and will be, in full-time work; their earnings and their career aspirations are now much more commonly thought to be as worthy of preservation as those of men. Furthermore, it should not be forgotten that many elderly people are childless; a survey in Mitcham found that 40 per cent of women aged 75 and over and living alone had no surviving children.[43]

The growing shortage of family tenders is already forcing something of a rethink of policy instruments. The obvious alternative is an increase in residential care, including the possibility of purchasing help in the private sector. This option has been opened up to a much wider section of the community by changes in supplementary benefit rules; since 1980 the DHSS has been prepared to meet reasonable weekly charges in private 'rest homes', which have mushroomed as a consequence, especially in retirement areas. More generally, it appears that filial and parental obligations are not seen as those which must invariably be discharged – in some cases the handicap is so gross or the senile dementia so advanced that it is felt that professional tenders should take over. This feature of popular perceptions may help to explain the all or nothing nature of the services which are frequently on offer: the choice is between, on the one hand, a place in an institution, without any requirement to continue to visit, or to contribute financially if the bed happens to be in a hospital, and, on the other hand, soldiering on largely without help from outside the family, in circumstances which may impose a very abnormal and limiting pattern of life on other members of the household.

The currently favoured formula for assisting those who wish to look after handicapped relatives at home, but without paying such a monstrous price, is summed up in the expression 'shared care' (or 'shared tending' in Parker's parlance), the sharing being primarily between family members and the statutory services. This is not so different from the Barclay prescription already cited, although without the same emphasis on volunteers and the 'community'. However, sharing sounds nice but is a great deal easier to talk about than to turn into a reality. There is some evidence that available domiciliary services are not always seen by the tending relatives as being helpful or appropriate: Michael Bayley documents this in relation to parents looking after severely mentally handicapped children.[44] Nevertheless, over the past twenty years, in both the health and the local authority sectors, there has been a very substantial growth in the services of most importance to relatives and those for whom they care – day hospitals, day centres, luncheon clubs, meals on wheels, home helps, training centres for the mentally handicapped, holiday admission schemes, warden-controlled accommodation, incontinence laundries. Some of these scarcely existed in the 1950s – and, it should be added, in many instances initiatives have owed much to voluntary organizations. The trouble is that the guidelines suggested by the central government for each service are hardly ever met anywhere, and although the current status of these relics of past planning exercises is doubtful – and they are all measuring inputs rather than outputs – it would be hard to deny that demand, and even more need, regularly outstrip supply. There are also some serious obstacles to the continuing expansion of these domiciliary services, even to the extent required to keep pace with growth in client populations. Some of these obstacles are organizational, some financial. We will first consider these separately (though they are very closely connected), and will then discuss certain policy developments of the past ten years which have been designed to try to surmount them.

Any large-scale reorganization of services facilitates the building of bridges in some directions, but digs new dividing ditches elsewhere or deepens existing ones. The Seebohm restructuring was based on the premise that a clear line could be drawn between medical and social services, but was there a similarly clear line between the medical and social needs of clients? In the case of the priority groupings – the mentally ill, the mentally handicapped, above all the handicapped elderly – it has always seemed to be hard to trace such distinct lines on the ground. And this problem has been aggravated as the old rationales for allocating responsibilities have crumbled in the face of demographic and other changes: for example, it has become widely, if reluctantly, accepted that Part III accommodation for the elderly is coming to consist of 'nursing homes without nurses'.[45] Similarly, frail and forgetful elderly persons are living in sheltered housing who twenty years ago would have been regarded as suitable only for admission to old people's homes, or, indeed, to geriatric wards – hence the current interest in 'very sheltered housing'. The frontier between housing and the personal social services is another ragged one – it should be recalled that since 1974 (except in the conurbations) they have been run by different tiers of local government. However, the problem here is less that it is difficult to delineate appropriate demarcations as that the criteria the two departments employ may sometimes point in different directions. Elderly owner-occupiers, or others who are judged as relatively well off in terms of accommodatiion, may be debarred from sheltered housing because they are 'not in housing need, which is harsh, and also pretty absurd from a social service point of view.

One possible answer to the problem of ensuring better co-ordination of services would be to assign administrative responsibility for particular client groups to either the NHS or to social service departments: thus, the local authority might be charged with running all the existing residential services for the mentally handicapped, while the District Health Authorities might take over 'community care' for the mentally ill. Either agency could then buy in assistance from the other as required. Of these two proposals, the first is easily the more feasible – it would fit in with the Jay Committee's recommendation of a social work model for the care of the mentally handicapped, and was one of the suggestions put out for discussion in the consultative document 'Care in the community', although the government did not pursue it. Local authorities have no recent experience of running institutions of the size of most of the mental handicap hospitals, and this would certainly have been seen as a major stumbling-block to such a transfer, even though the health authorities have not made a glorious success of the task (see Chapter 9). There seems, therefore, little immediate prospect of any bold experiments on these lines.

The most important of the financial obstacles to the improvement of domiciliary services is the general climate of economic stringency which has prevailed year after year since 1976, when cash limits were introduced. This is not, however, a simple story. The personal social services have continued to grow in real terms, in spite of the 'cuts'. This is partly because they have been protected by local authorities, who have persistently devoted more resources to this area of expenditure than Whitehall thinks they ought to have done. This response was especially important during the Conservative government's first year of office: the November 1979 Public Expenditure White Paper decreed a rate of cutback in personal social service expenditure which was actually greater than that demanded of local government as a whole.[46] Thereafter, however, government public expenditure plans resumed the practice of permitting social service departments modest levels of growth, because they became convinced that this made sense in financial terms: 'community care' has repeatedly been commended for its supposed cheapness compared with alternatives. This may only be true, from the standpoint of statutory authorities, because so much of the cost is borne by others, and obviously the more thoroughly the public sector undertakes its part of the task, the less favourable will the balance sheet be. In fact, the assembling of a mosaic of services, involving as it does the deployment of a number of skills, may be more expensive in total cost terms than reliance on institutional treatment, which is at least presumably able to draw on economies of scale. Nevertheless, the belief that a move away from residential care would eventually result in big savings for the Exchequer, fallacious though it may be, has undoubtedly helped the personal social services through a difficult period.

However, the 'cuts' have had their effects. Although almost everybody in local government has reacted adversely to the centralizing tendencies of the present administration, the government supporters who run the shire counties have responded differently to threats and sanctions than the Labour councillors who guard the battlements in the majority of metropolitan districts and Inner London boroughs. It has always been good advice to old people, if the range and quality of local authority services is of importance to them, to seek their retirement home in Coventry or Oldham, rather than on the south coast. Now disparities in service provision are widening. Furthermore, some of the most valuable services are especially susceptible to lopping. Domestic help will serve as an example. This is everybody's favourite social service, perhaps because consisting as it does of a body of relatively unorganized women, working part time, in isolation from one another, and with only intermittent supervision, it is one of the least bureaucratized; there is much evidence that home helps often develop strong relationships with 'their old people' and go well beyond their terms of service in discharging their responsibilities.[47] It is, however, a service which it is very easy to trim – an hour or two of help can be snipped off here or there, the vacancy rate can be deliberately maintained at a high level, and so on. The use of a lynch-pin service such as this as a short-term financial regulator is bound to cast a blight over the possibilities of developing a more adequate system of 'community care'.

In its annual rate support grant settlement, the government takes account of predicted changes in client populations – there is currently a 2 per cent increase each year in the personal social services component of the block grant to allow for the effects of demographic change. Only half of this sum is attributable to the growth in the number of the elderly, the other half being caused by other factors, such as the increase in children coming into care. The question is whether even this regular annual hoist in outlay is sufficient. Adrian Webb and Gerald Wistow estimated, in evidence given to the House of Commons Select Committee on Social Services, that the annual growth allowance needed to be between 3 and 4 per cent if the real level of services was not to be curtailed. This sum, they said, was necessary if local councils were to make provision not only for increases in the numbers of the old and other client groups, but also for changes in unit costs, and for the obligation to pick up the revenue consequences of joint finance projects.[48]

Mention of joint finance brings us to what has become a principal instrument of policies designed to deal with the overlap in responsibilities between the NHS and social service departments: it needs to be taken in conjunction with the statutory consultative machinery, consisting of Joint Consultative Committees (for elected or appointed members of local and health authorities) and Joint Care Planning Teams (which are multidisciplinary teams of officers). Joint finance consists of a special government allocation of funds which can be used to finance developments of interest to both parties. It is usually taken to mean the diversion of NHS funds to support local authority projects in the field of 'community care', but the allocation can also be drawn on to finance primary care and community health schemes run by health authorities, or projects put up by voluntary organizations. However, most of the money has been channelled towards social service departments. The scheme started in a smallish way in 1976/7, with an allocation of £20 million, but has since expanded considerably in three respects: in the size of the amount set aside, to around £100 million in 1984; in the ends to which the funds may be applied – joint finance is now regularly used to support local authority revenue expenditure as well as capital projects; and in the easing of the tapering arrangements. The last arise because it is a principle of joint finance that the sponsoring authority must in every case assume responsibility for the whole of the revenue bill after a set number of years. The period for which funds may be made available has risen from five to seven to ten years, and now may even be thirteen years when the project in question helps to empty one of the large old hospitals. However, this is only putting off the evil day: in the end, the local authority has to pay, or cut back on the expenditure.[49] Webb and Wistow argued before the House of Commons Select Committee that joint finance had been used 'to ease the transition' to lower growth.

One particular worry about joint finance is that, as the principal source of growth money around, it may distort the priorities of social service departments. The NHS does not have an equal interest in all client groups: for instance, it tends to be concerned with children only if they are mentally or physically handicapped. And local authorities assumed important new responsibilities in this area as a result of the Children and Young Persons Act of 1969. All residential penal establishments below the level of borstals or detention centres were redesignated as 'community homes' and put under the wing of social service departments: the Approved School Order was abolished, the approved schools becoming 'community homes with education'. At the same time local authority social workers took over from probation officers the responsibility for the supervision of young people 'in trouble', and were also assigned the task of working up new programmes to keep juvenile offenders out of custodial establishments. These programmes were lumped together under the rather opaque title of 'intermediate treatment'.

On the face of it, intermediate treatment has not fared badly over the past decade or so: it grew by no less than 32 per cent per annum between 1975/6 and 1979/80, a steeper rate of increase than was experienced by any other category of personal social service expenditure. But this expansion was from a very low base indeed: in 1977 local authorities were spending only about £1.5 million on intermediate treatment, compared with more than £25 million on community homes.[50] Social service departments have dragged their feet over the appointment of specialist intermediate treatment officers: some of them, indeed, appear to have done remarkably little to implement this part of the 1969 Act, even after nearly fifteen years. This poor showing must be both a symptom and a cause of the disillusion with the welfarist philosophy, the 'child care approach' to the treatment of delinquents, which we discussed earlier, and which strongly influenced the 1969 Act. David Thorpe and his colleagues have concluded that 'in terms of the usual outcome criteria, there is no method of dealing with juvenile offenders, no form of social work input (or input of any other kind) that has been shown to be more effective than any of the alternatives'.[51]

These sceptical words will not quite serve as an epitaph to this chapter, since there are other areas of social service department activity where the objectives are clearer, techniques are better understood, and methods are more closely attuned to intended results. Such conclusions have nevertheless sometimes been taken as an argument against experimentation, against the very possibility that carefully planned and monitored interventions will come up with answers to major social problems: but this does not follow. Still less do they make a case for more punitive methods of treatment: where outcomes are equal, there should surely be a presumption in favour of the more humane alternatives. However, that most compelling of arguments, that such methods are not only desirable in themselves, but also work, may have been mortally wounded by the experiences and the research of the past decade or so.

It was the fate of intermediate treatment – as of many of the other bold commitments entered into during the 1960s and early 1970s – that it had to be worked out in a more restrictive, less optimistic climate than that which gave it birth. It is difficult to imagine that social service departments would now be enjoined to go out and seek custom, as they were when they were required to survey the disabled population of their localities under the Chronically Sick and Disabled Persons Act of 1970. This act is also of interest – and a typical, if unusually advanced, child of its time – because it aimed to place new and binding obligations upon social service departments which could not be sidestepped on the plea that the money was not available. Local authorities must assess the needs of anyone who is permanently and substantially handicapped, and, under Section Two of the act, must, once the need is accepted, provide whichever out of a whole range of services is appropriate in the particular circumstances. However, as voluntary organizations representing the interests of the disabled have found, this part of the act is very difficult to enforce legally, since local authorities themselves are charged with determining the existence of the need, and how, if it is deemed to be present, it should be met.[52] Much has been done in the provision of aids and adaptations – often, latterly, with joint finance moneys – but local authorities differ in the scale of their expenditure in apparently arbitrary ways, and many social service departments clearly feel a need for some kind of valve to prevent too free a passage of public funds.

The hope of Townsend and his fellow Fabian writers that the personal social services would eventually become a 'fifth social service', similar in the size of their budget and their manpower to social security, the NHS, housing and education, was probably always misconceived: we are dealing here with too much of a mixed economy, dependent on self- and family care.[53] It is perhaps noteworthy, however, that, less than fifteen years after it was made, the plea seems to belong to another world.

11 Housing

Housing may legitimately be included in a study of social policy. A home, or at least a dwelling of some sort, is a necessary condition of health, security and welfare, the three objectives of social policy listed in the Introduction. Modern governments accept certain responsibilities concerning the quality of the commodity (a dwelling) and its availability to the individual consumer, in the discharge of which they intervene in, or interfere with, the operation of the market, in a manner characteristic of social services. To fulfil their objectives, public authorities may, as in other areas of social provision, employ three kinds of policy instruments, alone or in combination – they can encourage individuals or private concerns to behave in ways which lead towards them, they can curb or prevent action which is incompatible with them, or they can make and manage their own direct contribution to them. Differences between one housing policy and another depend very much on how these three types of action are used and combined.

However, there are important differences between housing and the other areas of social policy considered in this book. In particular, the private sector – a subsidized and assisted private sector, admittedly – dominates to an extent unparalleled elsewhere. The 1982 General Household Survey showed that 24 per cent of responding households owned their dwellings outright, 31 per cent were 'owner-occupiers with mortgages', and 12 per cent rented from a private landlord, rented from a housing association or obtained their accommodation with their job: there was thus a private sector total of 67 per cent in all.[1] These were Great Britain figures; if England and Wales are considered separately, the preponderance of privately owned housing becomes even more marked, for Scotland possesses a tenure pattern which neatly reverses the proportions of owner-occupiers and of council tenants prevailing south of the border. In addition, the 32 per cent minority which rents from a local authority or a New Town Corporation is consuming a 'marketed' service – provision is not free at the point of use or subject to nominal charges, as is largely the case in the National Health Service or the personal social services. Thus market considerations range more widely and penetrate more deeply than in other areas, and there are powerful private sector institutional actors, like construction firms and the building societies, to be taken into account.

Furthermore, housing presents some of the most elusive and intractable of all the problems with which social policy is confronted. In any area of the social services, 'need' is a word around which the inverted commas hover: so much depends on what is actually provided, and the aspirations and expectations to which that provision gives rise. In the mixed economy of housing, particular and major difficulties have been caused by the pronounced tendency for governments of both colours since 1950 to put their plans and ideas into separate boxes, so that they have had a policy for private rented housing, a policy for (encouraging) owner-occupation, and a policy for the public rented sector – largely regardless, that is, of the dynamics of the interrelationships between the different forms of tenure, and largely regardless too, as we shall see, of considerations of equity. Essentially, there are now two preferred tenures for long-term occupancy, owner-occupation and renting from a local authority, but the paths into either may be strewn with obstacles for many who wish to gain entry; they may not possess a high enough or secure enough regular income, for the first, or lack appropriate residential qualifications or other characteristics favoured by a housing department's points scheme, for the second. Thus the private landlord, winded but not yet quite *hors de combat*, continues to take up the slack, alongside the owners of sites for mobile homes, of especial importance in rural areas and in the South.

It is not, therefore, easy to measure even the current requirements for housing. The volume and urgency of concealed demand are difficult to estimate. In some respects, houseroom is a peculiarly elastic commodity. In times of shortage, people manage to make do with what they have. They stay in small homes after their families have outgrown them, and young couples begin their married life in a room in a parental house although they would much prefer to have a home of their own. On the other hand, houses once built are immovable and cannot follow shifting demand, so the geographical distribution of rooms does not coincide with that of people to live in them. And even in one locality the proportion of rooms per person (or persons per room) differs greatly from house to house. Overcrowding and under-occupation may exist side by side.

When one turns from an estimate of present needs to one of future needs the calculation becomes still more difficult to make. There are at least six questions here, closely bound up with one another, but in principle separable: How many houses should be built? What size should they be? Where should they be constructed? What kind should they be – separate houses, high-rise flats, low-rise flats, and so on? Should the emphasis be put on the rehabilitation and conversion of existing buildings, or on fresh construction? Should the new dwellings be erected for renting or for sale? All these are matters on which governments (and, indeed, local authorities) may be expected to have policies, of a greater or lesser degree of precision, but which their capacities to deliver will certainly be incomplete, and may be better described as limited. We will take these questions in turn, looking at the past record as well as probable future requirements as we go.

The computation of national totals of new dwellings required is not a simple matter of calculating the extent of any current housing shortage – the 'crude net deficiency', or the disparity between the number of structurally separate units of accommodation and the numbers of separately identifiable households – and adding on to that total an allowance for future population growth. The probable number of withdrawals from stock, which means policies towards demolitions, has to be estimated; and so has the demand for second homes. Most important of all, the magnitude of the demand for houses depends on the age composition and social structure of the population, and policy-makers must try to forecast these, even though it is hardly possible to do so with any degree of accuracy for as far ahead as the buildings they are planning are likely to survive. During the last couple of decades demographers have developed sophisticated techniques for the calculation of rates of new household formation.[2] However, many of the assumptions underlying these projections rest on the extrapolation of present trends, and most particularly the trend for the number of households to increase at a considerably faster rate than the total population. The tendency for young single people to set up house on their own, earlier marriage, a higher divorce rate (splitting one household into two), and the now widely accepted norm that old people should maintain a separate establishment for as long as possible in a longer average life-span, all increase the demand for more units of accommodation.

These trends also imply that more small dwellings are, and will be, required. Over sixty years, in the public and private sectors alike, the great bulk of new housing has been constructed with the nuclear family of husband, wife and two-point-something children in mind. In the late 1970s this was still broadly true of building for owner-occupation; between 1975 and 1979 75 per cent of the output of private builders in England and Wales consisted of three- or four-bedroomed houses or flats – and overwhelmingly of three-bedroomed houses.[3] However, during the same five years, nearly 60 per cent of the production for local authorities and New Town Corporations was made up of one- or two-bedroomed houses or flats, and preponderantly of one-bedroomed flats, usually built specifically for old people.[4] This is an important shift, in line with demographic trends, and one which one would expect to continue, and to be more and more reflected in what private builders put on the market. Nevertheless there is a caveat to be made. Projections in this area require some assumptions to be made concerning future economic developments. Greater material prosperity could lead to a demand for better space standards. This demand would not necessarily be restricted to the private sector. Local authorities have been pretty successful in resisting 'under-occupation' – those who seek this phenomenon would be advised to look especially hard at owner-occupied housing – but the envelope provided is usually designed to fit tightly around new occupants of council houses: prospective tenants who are deemed to need a certain number of bedrooms cannot expect to be allocated any extra. Thus old people may complain bitterly that they have nowhere in their purpose-built flats where they can put up relatives if they wish to stay.

Then there is the question of where the new homes should be built. Probably the most difficult factor to assess and allow for in making housing forecasts is the geographical shift of the population, or internal migration. A large number of vacant houses in Crook, County Durham, is of little use if the jobs are in Swindon. It is possible to exercise some influence over this kind of situation through regional planning, but in general the attempts of successive governments to revive declining areas have been disappointing: market forces tend to kick back. In any case, the immediate aim of plans for industrial and urban development has been to find ways of absorbing those who already lived in particular parts of the country, either by redeveloping areas threatened by decay or by trying to accommodate the 'overspill' from crowded cities. And here again demographic trends are forcing changes in the terms of the debate. Between 1971 and 1981 the areas which grew most notably in population were rural areas, in East Anglia, South Western England, the previously less crowded parts of the South East.[5] By contrast, virtually all the metropolitan districts, with a few exceptions like Rotherham and Doncaster, fell in population – the inner city areas often catastrophically, the suburbs markedly. And, for the first time, the population of nearly all the larger free-standing towns and cities, the old county boroughs now turned county districts, declined too. However, it is the future of the residential districts close to city centres which has given, and will give, the most cause for concern. They are now much less congested than they were, but all too often the sites of demolished buildings are occupied only by waste thickets of mugwort and buddleia bushes – a form of 'greening' which is welcomed only by insect fanciers. The decline in population has been accompanied by a decline in employment, and many of those who remain, especially among the families with young children, would like to go too, but are trapped by low incomes and poor job prospects. Should they be helped by public authorities to leave? It was this kind of issue which was highlighted by the Inner Area Studies, particularly that carried out in Lambeth.[6] These studies are further discussed in the next chapter.

Like the question of where to build, the question of what to build is fraught with difficulty. At first sight, the types of housing now on the market vary so enormously that they hardly seem to be members of the same species – from the bungalow to the tower block, the terrace to the housing estate, the luxury flat to the suburban villa and the commuter's residence. Actually, comparisons with other Western European countries suggest that the British housing stock is, in spite of its relatively advanced age, a fairly uniform and egalitarian one, scoring particularly highly in terms of internal space per head, in the enjoyment of the standard amenities, and in the possession of private land.[7] However, here again inner city areas pose special problems, since they contain concentrations of relatively unpopular forms of housing. It was here that the preoccupation of the 1950s and 1960s with making the maximum use possible of scarce and expensive land was felt most insistently. In Chapter 7 we discussed the rise and fall of high-rise housing: we must now consider the legacy. Most urban local authorities are now agonizing over what they should do with 'difficult to let' estates, and the demolition of some of the most unsatisfactory of these, often flatted developments erected fewer than twenty years ago, is being seriously contemplated.[8]

Perhaps the biggest change over the past decade and a half or so has been the retreat of slum clearance and the advance of government sponsored house improvement. The 1950s saw the demolition of most of the remaining areas which were universally regarded, not least by their inhabitants, as 'slums'. Clearance programmes more and more moved on to old but respectable districts of working-class housing, which had been passing into owner-occupation with the decline of the private landlord. This situation led to agitation over the terms of compensation, giving some legislative recognition in the Land Compensation Act, 1973, and to a growing feeling that clearance was a bulldozer solution in more ways than one, destroying as it did stable, or at least saveable, communities, and scattering their inhabitants to the four winds of distant council estates. Older people, especially, were often reluctant to move,[9] and the plight of elderly rebels against the local council, clinging despairingly to familiar bricks and mortar while demolition proceeded all around them, was featured in local newspapers up and down the country.

Thus the stage was set for a great growth of interest in the rehabilitation of older housing. The story here goes back to the Housing Act of 1949, which introduced discretionary improvement grants, discretionary, that is, on the decisions of local authorities. Take-up was slow at first, but was given a boost in 1959, when, provided that the house in question was deemed to have a minimum life of fifteen years, standard grants first became available as of right for such major amenities as a fixed bath, an indoor water-closet, and a hot water system. During the 1960s and 1970s there were several policy developments, most notably the innovation of area-based schemes of improvement. These started in a small way in 1964, reached their zenith in the General Improvement Areas of the Housing Act of 1969, and were finally consolidated with the Housing Action Areas of its successor of 1974. The 1969 Act also introduced payments for approved works of repair and replacement, such as for roofs, and for the first time provided moneys for neighbourhood amenities like tree planting and play-spaces in General Improvement Areas. Throughout there were increases in the maximum amounts of grant payable, and reductions in the proportions which owners had to find from their own pockets – governments made funds available for 60 per cent grants in GIAs, 75 per cent grants in HAAs, and, most recently of all, the budget of 1982 provided for a general availability of 90 per cent grants without proof of hardship, but only for a limited period of time.

Progress has by no means been linear, ever onwards and upwards. The great years for government-sponsored house improvement were the early 1970s, when the more generous amounts available and the relaxation of conditions previously imposed had their maximum effects. However, the total number of grants made in England and Wales fell abruptly between 1974 and 1975, from 232,000 to 127,000, and remained around the lower level for the remainder of the decade.[10] The early years of the 1970s were also ones of historically high levels of slum clearance, but here again there was a marked fall back, by about one-third, between 1973 and 1974, and again the later figure set the pattern for subsequent years. Thus there was no real transfer of energies from clearance to improvement, and one could argue that, contrary to popular belief, both went down together. The victory of improvement has been ideological more than it has been actual: the change in emphasis has commanded almost universal support, although the phenomenon known as 'gentrification' (the utilization of grants by members of the middle classes to do up desirable but decayed areas of housing) has aroused the hostility of some Labour councillors and housing professionals in places such as the London Borough of Islington.

A verdict on the drive towards improvement must therefore be tentative. There has been a very substantial reduction in houses without the standard amenities – it is estimated that between 1951 and 1971 the number of dwellings in England and Wales lacking a fixed bath and a hot and cold water supply at three points fell by 5 million, with a further substantial fall in the following years.[11] In these totals, demolitions have played their part, but their contribution has been smaller than that made by improvements to the existing stock. Between 1949 and 1976 more than 2.2 million grants were made for individual acts of house improvement, and although no-one has attempted to calculate the effectiveness of the grant-related induce-ment, this is clearly many more than would have taken place without the aid of grants.[12] However, many improvements have been effected without recourse to grant – between three-quarters of a million and a million baths, and 2.5 million systems for the supply of hot water were so installed up to 1971.[13] Central heating, an exotic rarity before 1960, was enjoyed by nearly one in two private households by 1976,[14] and this again is mainly attributable to private enterprise unassisted by the state. So the role of grants can be exaggerated, although it should be noted that most local authority and New Town Corporation houses completed since 1971 have contained central heating. Ironically, much of this is powered by expensive systems using electricity, and tenants have often experienced great difficulty in meeting the bills.

A central problem with encouraging house improvement as a major arm of policy is that is is, in principle, concerned with the well-being of houses rather than of their residents. The contradictions here were pointed up by the action of the 1974–9 Labour government, in response to the agitation over 'gentrification' to which we have already referred, in imposing a limit of rateable value above which houses could not qualify for grant. Inducements, like all other indirect methods of advancing policy objectives, require to be taken up, and the readiness to take them up has not been randomly distributed among the eligible population. In particular, private landlords have been largely immune to all blandishments, and Housing Action Areas, which were designed to cater especially for housing where private tenancy was the majority tenure, have altered this situation little. Powers to effect improvements by compulsion have proved slow, cumbersome and productive mainly of nervous breakdowns among housing officials, while the alternative of municipalization, in addition to these same defects, is extremely expensive, arouses ideological antipathy, and incurs the opposition of governments anxious above all else about the Public Sector Borrowing Requirement. So it is not surprising if, as seems likely, the grant system has mainly benefited younger people, in work, and earning average to higher than average incomes.

A question mark has to be set, too, alongside the capacity of grant-assisted improvement to fulfil the basic aim of safeguarding the existing housing-stock and bringing it up to standards acceptable to the next generation. Area-based schemes of improvement can be criticized on the grounds that the energies of local authorities and their officials have been disproportionately expended on particular smallish pockets of housing at the expense of a greater number of more scattered dwellings in essentially similar condition. Even if it was sensible to pursue an area-based strategy, it is clear that is has not been attempted on a big enough scale: the Department of the Environment itself calculated that there should have been more than half a million houses in Housing Action Areas as a result of the 1974 Act, but in the middle of 1980 there were only 150,000 houses in declared areas.[15] However, perhaps the most disturbing portent is the growing evidence of an impending crisis in house repair. The House Condition Surveys of 1971, 1976 and 1981 revealed a continuous increase throughout the decade in the number of houses in serious disrepair (defined in 1981 as requiring works in excess of £7000).[16] Many of those who live in the poorest stock are retired, unemployed or earning low wages, and would have great difficulty in financing the renovation, even taking account of grant. Moreover, the problem has started to spread to the nation's vast, and hitherto sturdy, inheritance of housing built between the wars. It may well be that sometime in the not too distant future large-scale slum clearance will have its time again.

The economist, Stephen Merrett – who claims allegiance to the ideas of both Marx and Keynes – has written about 'the partitioning of housing renewal'.[17] On the one hand, he suggests, there is rehabilitation, a policy essentially directed towards owner-occupiers and private landlords, with municipalization on the whole discouraged by governments; on the other hand, there is clearance, with private builders rarely being invited to participate in the ensuing new development except as agents of the local authority. This view would be more convincing if it were not for the fact that about one-third of all improvement grants approved in Great Britain in recent years have been for local authorities rather than for private owners; local councils have frequently had recourse to GIA procedures in order to deal with areas of purpose-built municipal houses which were rather lacking in modern amenities. However, if the example is dubious, the phenomenon to which Merrett draws attention is undeniably of great importance, and as a result the answers to the last of the six questions we posed earlier take us deep into party politics.

British policy, unlike that of most European countries, has been based on a sharp differentiation between the public and the private sectors, or between council houses and privately owned houses. In the context of new building this is tantamount to a distinction between houses to let and houses to sell. For economic conditions since the war, combined with statutory rent restriction and the unfavourable tax treatment of private landlords – there is no provision for depreciation allowances for houses and their capital equipment, analogous to that applicable to industrial plant – have progressively produced a situation in which it is no longer profitable to invest money in building dwellings for letting, except for a small clientele of well-to-do people who want a temporary home or a *pied-à-terre*. Attempts by successive Conservative governments to encourage private building or conversion for rent have proved to be the frailest of counterweights to this trend, and it is likely that the latest of these, the invention of 'shorthold' tenure in the Housing Act, 1980, will, like its precursors, disappoint its advocates. So it roughly true to say that while councils build only for letting, private builders build only for sale or self-occupation.

The political parties have differed in principle about the proportion in which these two methods of production and types of product should contribute to the total national stock of dwellings. The Conservatives have favoured private enterprise and home ownership; Labour has had a preference for the production by public authorities of houses for letting. These divergent views have been reflected in the methods adopted to encourage building. The standard form of assistance to local authorities is a subsidy to help meet the charges on the capital borrowed to finance the building, but subsidies can be of different kinds, designed to produce different effects. In the aftermath of war it was necessary to run a crash programme to cope with accumulated arrears. Aneurin Bevan, for the Labour government, decided that the operation must be a planned one and that 'the speculative builder, by his very nature, is not a plannable instrument . . . . We rest the full weight of the housing programme upon the local authorities'.[18] Private building was made subject to licence and a general subsidy was offered to local authorities on all domestic building.

The Conservatives, after their return to power in 1951, took the brake of the licence off private building, and in 1956 abolished the general subsidy for council houses and replaced it by subsidies for special purposes, such as slum clearance, redevelopment, New Towns and homes for old people. But these 'special' purposes covered a pretty wide area of cases, and the production of local authority housing remained at a high level (always over 100,000 houses a year) during the thirteen years the Conservatives stayed in office – it was not, indeed, until 1959 that the total of private houses completed exceeded that of dwellings for local councils. In 1961 the Conservatives reintroduced the general subsidy, at a lower level, and for the first time there was positive discrimination in favour of authorities in greatest financial need. Under Labour, the number of local authority starts edged up, to reach a peak of 192,000 in 1967, but thereafter it tailed off quite markedly, and was always smaller in volume than the private building of houses for sale.

Perhaps the most striking thing about these years, up to and into the early 1970s, is the enormous emphasis which almost everybody placed on the crude national totals of housing production. Political parties vied with one another in the making of promises for future performance and in the setting of targets; the success of Harold Macmillan in persuading the Conservative annual conference in 1950 to accept a target of 300,000 new dwellings each year, and then in making good this promise, probably established his claim to the premiership more than anything else. During the 1970s, however, the spirit evaporated from this apparently perennial contest. This can be illustrated by the party manifestos employed in the 1979 election: the Conservatives devoted much space in their offering to the electorate to encouraging home ownership, especially through the sale of council housing, but included no pledges about the new houses to be built, while Labour contented itself with a rather imprecise statement that it would continue with a 'substantial programme of housebuilding and house improvement'.[19] The change in mood was attributable, at least in good part, to a spreading fear that Britain has been running into an oversupply of housing. In 1951 there were about 750,000 more households than houses in England and Wales, with a specially grave shortage in the metropolis; in 1961 the census showed 'houses and households just about in balance overall though unevenly distributed';[20] in 1976 there were about 500,000 more houses than households, with, apparently, a small surplus even in Greater London.[21] Years of adding to stock above the levels of both demolitions and new household formation has led to a widespread fear that the country was 'overinvesting' in the production of dwellings. The belief that this was so has affected senior politicians of all parties, but perhaps a particularly significant sign that an era has ended is the fact that whereas Shelter, the radically-inclined housing pressure group, has drawn frequent and reasoned attention to the problems which are piling up as a result of cuts in housing budgets, its Director has none the less written that 'wealth in housing is increasing at the expense of wealth in the productive economy'.[22]

This shift in perception of the central problem of housing policy led to a redefining of the role of subsidies, away from the encouragement of new building and towards the support of the incomes of tenants. The first attempt at refashioning the system on these lines was contained in the Conservative Housing Finance Act of 1972. This once more abolished general subsidies and replaced them with a variety of grants for special purposes, including some of the former ones, but in principle directed to meeting permitted deficits incurred in executing programmes in conformity with statutory requirements. The most important of these were for raising rents to a 'realistic' level and granting rebates to families unable to pay at this level. The intention was that the basic costs of normal housing programmes should be met out of local revenue, primarily that received from tenants in the form of rents.

When Labour returned to power in 1974 one of its first measures was to repeal the Housing Finance Act. However, this action was more symbolic than real, since some of its main provisions remained in situ, including the national system of rent rebates and allowances which had been introduced. One feature of the act particularly hated on the Left had been the requirement that there should be phased and regular increases in council house rents, but these provisions had been overtaken by the decidedly unphased and irregular growth in inflation, which totally altered the rights and wrongs of the situation. Labour, in fact, never really made up its mind during its term of office about the beat to which it should march in housing matters. In 1975, Antony Crosland, as Secretary of State for the Environment, set up the Housing Finance Review, which turned itself into the Housing Policy Review in the course of its deliberations, and finally satisfied almost nobody, including the academics and housing professionals who nevertheless welcomed the comprehensive analysis of housing progress, problems and practices contained within the Review's three Technical Volumes.[23]

Under Labour, there were two important developments, although they were to prove of most significance after the Conservatives regained office in 1979. The first was the introduction of the Housing Investment Programme (HIP) system in 1977. Under this, each local authority has had to submit, every year, a bid for a share in a total of housing investment funds determined by the government. Allocations were made under four headings, covering new building; acquisition of existing properties, including slum clearance; improvement grants and loans for mortgages; and grants to housing associations: each was accorded its own cash limit. This scheme was represented as allowing local authorities greater freedom to choose their own priorities, but it was more a means of tightening central government control over particular areas of housing expenditure. The second innovation was the preparation of a new housing subsidy system. This was outlined in the Green Paper *Housing Policy* (1976), incorporated in the Labour government's Housing Bill (1979), and then enacted by the victorious Conservatives in the Housing Act, 1980. Consensus was not, apparently, insubstantial.

In order to calculate the new levels of subsidy, the Secretary of State makes an assessment of what he thinks each local authority ought to be contributing from local sources, and bases his payments accordingly. Powers were taken in a parallel act to limit recourse to the rates. For the first time, local councils were permitted to carry a surplus in the Housing Revenue Account – or make a profit out of council tenants, as opponents of the measure put it. Alan Murie has said that what has been provided for is 'a deficit financing not remarkably different from that introduced in the Housing Finance Act 1972'.[24] The aim of both schemes, of course, was to shift as much of the burden as was thought feasible on to the shoulders of that rather select band of council tenants who did not qualify for rebates. At the same time the government aimed to find in the housing budget a large part of the reduction in total public expenditure which it so much desired; in the 1980 Public Expenditure White Paper it provided for a planned cut of no less than 48 per cent between 1980/1 and 1983/4.[25] The starkness of these proposals was somewhat modified in the two following years, but the message remains clear. So far as new investment is concerned, depression in the public sector has been accompanied by depression in the private market, so that the total number of housing starts fell in 1981 to the lowest peacetime level for more than fifty years.

Meanwhile the overall structure of housing finance continues to resemble nothing so much as a weird contraption of wires and pulleys which scoops up money from one pocket and deposits it, apparently arbitrarily, in another. Much of the disappointment with the Housing Policy Review arose because it failed to deliver what Crosland had intended, a sustained and coherent assault on the inefficiencies and inequities of the existing system. Subsidies come in various shapes and sizes. As we have already indicated, some are directed at encouraging the production of certain kinds or qualities of housing, and others are openly measures for income support. Many, however, are an indeterminate mixture of both. Some important items of expenditure are essentially independent of tenure, like the payments which are made to recipients of supplementary benefit to meet their housing costs – though it should be noted that the DHSS will only cover the interest repayments due on a mortgage, and not the capital repayments. Most subsidies, however, are tied to the ways in which households hold their accommodation, and we must now look at these sector by sector.

We have already sketched the history of government subsidies for council housing, and there are only a few points which remain to be made. The state of a particular local authority's Housing Revenue Account depends on precisely when it went in for house construction, and the level of costs prevailing at the time. Briefly, if the municipal housing stock contains a goodly proportion of older houses, built at low rates of interest, and repayments on the loans for which have long been overtaken by average levels of rent, then the authority's financial situation will be much more favourable than if it has build extensively at high cost in recent years, employing loans which will have had to be re-financed at higher rates of interest during the inflations of the 1970s. Since local authorities pool rents, and pool the payments they receive from central government, it has always been almost impossible to work out the extent to which an individual tenant benefits from those Exchequer subsidies which are tied to the physical provision of dwellings. This is, however, a matter of diminishing importance, in so far as such subsidies have under the present Conservative government declined as a proportion of the total assistance extended to council tenants, while the avowedly income-related subsidy, the rebate system – latterly housing benefit – has risen markedly.

The enhanced prominence of rebates raises two points. The first is that this really is not a housing question at all, but a matter of income maintenance; it was a logical development, therefore, for the Social Security Advisory Committee (SSAC) to take over responsibility for advising on housing benefit in 1982. We therefore reserve further consideration of the scheme until the next chapter, including the dilemma of the poverty trap. The second point can perhaps best be left as a question: can one accept a system under which a large proportion of tenants on an estate, perhaps a majority, is considered unable to pay a full rent, and must therefore be granted a rebate after submitting to a means test?

One of the virtues of the much maligned Housing Finance Act of 1972 was that it covered both private tenants and council tenants and tried to treat them similarly. So for the first time tenants of private landlords, initially only those renting unfurnished accommodation, but soon those in furnished lettings too, became eligible to receive housing allowances calculated according to nationally laid down scales which permitted only minor local variations. Before the act came into effect such tenants were largely excluded from the system of publicly-financed subsidies which had grown up, unless they were on supplementary benefit, or happened to live in Birmingham, where an experimental scheme of allowances was instituted in the late 1960s. As the average household income of unfurnished tenants was lower than that found in the other tenure groups, this was scarcely a defensible situation, but it lasted a long time because governments had found another means of helping these tenants, one which was gratifyingly cheap in the demands it made upon public funds.

Old-style rent control simply froze the rent at the current level and gave the sitting tenant virtually complete security of tenure. This meant that, as market rents rose, tenants were to an increasing extent subsidized by their landlords, who consequently had neither a financial incentive nor, very often, the means to maintain their property, still less to improve it.

The first major attempt to secure a drastic revision of the system of general rent restriction was the 1957 Rent Act, which decontrolled a certain number of houses at a stroke by lowering the maximum rateable value at which dwellings ceased to be subject to control, and over the following years decontrolled many more 'by movement', that is, when one set of tenants left and new tenancies were negotiated. The consequences of the act were, generally, less dramatic than either its friends had hoped or its enemies had feared. Its main effect was probably to provide opportunities for landlords to take their money out of rented housing and place it in something more sensible, like gilt-edged. The provisions of the act were complex, and were widely misunderstood, whether intentionally or inadvertently – two years after it was passed it was found that some 20 per cent of the houses which remained controlled were being let at rents higher than those permitted by the law – but in most of the country there was little evidence of large-scale abuse. Ironically, the act was discredited more than anything else by the violent activities which ensured immortality for the name of Peter Rachman, but these had long predated its passing into law, and were not dependent on its provisions, even though the dual market in rented housing (with or without vacant possession) which the Act encouraged undoubtedly made life easier for him and his fellow operators.

Labour came back to office in 1964 pledged to take action. In 1965 the new government introduced rent regulation, a system providing for negotiation and arbitration, the idea for which had probably been derived from arrangements for settling disputed rents in the furnished sector which went back to shortly after the war. Rent regulation applied to all unfurnished properties below a certain maximum rateable value and subject to the decontrol provisions of the 1957 Act; the Government took powers to include controlled tenancies, by order, but did not implement them, which was very hard on the landlords of long time tenants who had to put up with the rents they received being frozen at 1957 levels for year after year. Applications for the fixing of a regulated rent could be made by tenant, landlord or a public authority to a new kind of official, a professional Rent Officer, who gave his judgement; only on appeal from one of the parties against this judgement did it go to an Assessment Committee, a body similar to the Rent Tribunals which adjudicated on furnished lettings. The act included guidance on the standard to be used in making the assessment: the Officer or Committee was to take account of 'the age, character and locality of the dwellinghouse and its state of repair', but to eliminate the effect of a competitive market by acting on the supposition that supply and demand were roughly in balance. The result was known as the 'fair rent': fair to both landlord and tenant. By this procedure rents could be either reduced or increased. At first reductions and increases occurred in about equal proportions, but by 1970 77 per cent of the applications led to an increase and only 17 per cent to a decrease.[26] Thereafter, the new rent could be registered, and became the official rent for at least three years; this minimum period was reduced to two years in 1980. During this time the tenant had full security of tenure: indeed, under the act it became difficult to evict tenants of unfurnished lettings, who could normally be got out only as a result of a court order, which would only be granted in a limited set of circumstances, such as the landlord proving he required the property for his own residence or that of a member of his family, or if there was a pattern of persistent rent arrears.

Many critics said that the 'fair rent' system would not work, and could not last, but by now it has a very permanent look about it. It tied together security of tenure and restrictions on the right of the landlord to fix the rent by fiat – as any system must if it is to afford the tenant a real measure of protection – but without embalming rents at a level which would soon come to seem ridiculous. It also restricted the involvement of the government to an absolute minimum – hence taking the issue 'out of politics' – and, since the new arrangements rested on voluntary referral by one or other of the parties involved, did so without overburdening the machinery which had been established. Certainly, the 'fair rent' is neither fish, nor fowl nor good red herring, neither a market rent nor anything else, but even that may be a strength if, as seems to be the case, the formulas chosen have been generally accepted. The 1970–4 Conservative government became so enamoured of fair rents that in 1972 they used a similar stratagem for determining the rents of the far larger number of council tenancies, but this was an aspect of the Housing Finance Act which failed to endure when Labour returned to power.

During the 1970s and early 1980s there have been a number of further changes affecting especially tenants of furnished lettings – a small group, accounting for no more than 2 per cent of all households, but one particularly vulnerable to exploitation because of their tenuous grip on the housing market. The process by which landlords could evade rent regulation by sticking a few bits of furniture into a dwelling was always highly questionable, and in 1974 the 'furniture test' was replaced by a 'resident landlord test': henceforth where the landlord lived on the premises, whether or not he let furnished, the tenancy would be covered by the less strict 'reasonable rent' provisions supervised by Rent Tribunals. Under the present government, Rent Tribunals and Rent Assessment Committees have been combined into one system, but they will be administering two separate codes, as before. It is important to note, however, that only 14 per cent of all private tenants are sharing a house with their landlord.[27]

We must now turn from these minority tenures to the established market leader. Governments can help owner-occupiers in two principal ways: by tax concessions with respect to interest on loans, and by enabling them to borrow on terms more favourable than those of the open market. In Britain, both methods have been made available, but the first is much the more important: British tax law exempts from income tax money spent as interest on a loan raised by mortgaging house property, although if a loan is for more than £30,000 interest payable on sums above that amount does not qualify for tax relief. It was arguable, when borrowers had to pay tax on the notional income received from the property in which they invested the borrowed capital, that they ought not to pay tax also on the income they had forgone in order to raise the capital. But when the tax (Schedule A) on the property was abolished in the early 1960s this argument lapsed; the concession, however, was retained. Reimposition of the old Schedule A, or a similar tax, has often been canvassed in the last twenty years. Such a step would, of course, affect all property owners, including the more than 40 per cent of owner-occupiers who own their own dwelling outright, and whose housing costs are proportionately lower than those of any other tenure group, accounting as they do for less than 7 per cent of their income on average. The sums involved here could be very large: Alexander Grey has estimated the net revenue from such a tax as £8600 million, enough to abolish domestic rates and have money left over to protect poor owner-occupiers.[28] However, there is a certain implausibility about proposals of this kind; nostalgia for Schedule A has always been considerably greater among economists and housing experts than among politicians and the majority of the electorate which lives in owner-occupied housing.

Shorn of its original rationale though it may be, the tax concession on mortgage interest repayments has plenty of currently proffered justifications. They would include the following: that it encourages owner-occupation, which many people believe is a socially desirable form of tenure; that is stimulates the building of much needed houses and so relieves the pressure on rented dwellings; and that it is fair that there should be some such system of assistance to the owner-occupier paralleling the subsidies given from both rates and taxes to rent-paying council tenants. Naturally, all these arguments have their critics, who have, however, their hands rather tied behind their backs, because the purchase of a 'home of one's own' is a widely accepted ideal – indeed, some would say, the only ideal in the whole system. Nevertheless, some commentators have expressed anxieties about the consequences for the marginal buyer of what they see as a headlong rush into owner-occupation on American or Australian lines – although there is as yet, despite the recession, only a little evidence of a rise in foreclosures of mortgages to justify such fears. Left-wingers dislike policies which rely on filtering (by which dwellings vacated by one income level are occupied by those on the rung below, and so on down to the bottom of the ladder, thus leading to a gradual improvement in general housing standards); Merrett has called filtering 'that recurrent rationalisation of inegalitarian housing policies in modern times'.[29] Finally, the argument about the desirability of establishing equity in shares of Exchequer subsidies may be accepted in principle, but may be partly countered by the observation that the balance of advantage has shifted in the last few years very much in favour of the owner-occupier. Although the average household income of mortgagors is not far short of twice that of council tenants (£169 a week in 1979 compared with £94),[30] one computation suggests that in 1982–3 the former would have been receiving £366 through tax relief or option mortgage subsidy, while the latter would have been getting, on average, £206 during that year in Exchequer subsidies or rate-fund contributions.[31] However, these calculations omitted the cost of income-related rent rebates, which benefit tenants only, and which, as we have seen, have been growing both relatively and absolutely in recent years.

The really indefensible feature of the system of financial assistance to owner-occupiers is that, since the larger a man's income the higher his rate of tax, the richer he is the more he benefits from the concession, and conversely the poorer he is the less he gains from it. The problem can therefore be tackled from either end, and an example of making easier the terms on which the less well-to-do can obtain mortgages was the 'option mortgage', which existed between 1967 and 1983. This offered benefits to people of modest or low incomes whose liability for tax was such that they could not get the full value of the concession, and were instead able to obtain a greater reduction of the interest payable on the mortgage by choosing to receive a government subsidy in lieu of the normal tax concession. Thus, at a point not very far along the upward slope of the income scale, would-be mortgagors had a difficult decision to make: whether to go for an option mortgage or choose the traditional tax concession. One could put this another way, and say that it was these aspirant house-owners who benefited least from either set of arrangements; and this cannot have been right. The option mortgage scheme, although no longer with us, is thus useful in illuminating the rather curious assumptions underlying the financial assistance extended to those buying a home. In 1983, both it and the system for standard rate taxpayers of claiming relief through their tax returns, were replaced by MIRAS (Mortgage Interest Relief at Source) under which most borrowers pay mortgage interest to their lender with the basic rate of tax already deducted. However, mortgage interest repayments continue to be offset against the higher rates of income tax in the same way as before. It must be a sign of the very sensitive politics of owner-occupation that the 1974–9 Labour government did not take the opportunity of abolishing this concession to an extremely well-heeled minority. One would not, perhaps, expect the present Conservative government, with a different ideology and clientele, to take such action; but that they were uneasy about the scale of the assistance accorded to high earning mortgagors was suggested by the retention, for four successive years, of the £25,000 upper limit on loans qualifying for tax relief bequeathed by the previous administration. In 1984, however, a new limit of £30,000 came into effect, so the gradual erosion of the advantage of tax concessions to high income earners has been halted.

The overriding commitment of the Conservative government to the expansion of owner-occupation has been most clearly demonstrated by its much publicized policies favouring council house sales, especially as encapsulated in the 'right to buy' provisions of the Housing Act, 1980. The gulf between the political parties is wide here, and some bitter engagements have been fought. The opposition has been somewhat muted, however, for two reasons. First, the government has, through legislation, availed itself of some extremely heavy weaponry to deter refractory housing authorities – Norwich City Council has been stripped of its powers under the act, for instance, for dragging its feet. Second, the Labour Party has had to make almost desperate attempts to come to terms with the evidence that the sales policy is popular, both among tenants and among the public more generally. So the policy has had a reasonably clear run, and the substantial variations among local authorities in the incidence of sales seem to be more attributable to differential demand than to party political factors.[32]

Tenure patterns have already been quite markedly modified. Between the general elections of 1979 and 1983 more than half a million dwellings, or about 10 per cent of the public sector stock at the earlier date, were sold in Great Britain. However, many commentators expect the pace of sales to slacken: the recession is taking its toll, in spite of the generous inducement of discounts of up to 60 per cent. There is also a dilemma of the government's own, that its desire to see council house sales pushed through and its desire to restrict public expenditure and reduce local authority manpower tend to contradict one another. In particular, sales are heavily dependent on the funds made available to local authorities for lending on mortgage: the government has failed in its efforts to tempt private-sector sources of funding into this part of the market on any significant scale, a fact which negates the possible public expenditure advantages of the policy. Incidentally, this also rather gives the lie to those conspiratorially minded people who profess to see as the engine power behind enforced sales the insatiable demand of corporate lenders and other private-sector interests, to be fed, like Moloch, with more and more business to replace that engendered by the drying up flow of previously privately-rented houses passing into owner-occupation.

More mainstream critics of the government's policy believe that sales of council housing in anything but small quantities will seriously detract from the ability of local authorities to meet the needs of their populations. They fear, in particular, and with evidence to support them, that the houses sold will be disproportionately of the most popular kinds suitable for young families – houses with gardens rather than flats. Such arguments illustrate the truth that the issue which is pointed up by the debate on council house sales is the future of public sector housing, not that of owner-occupation which may be taken as assured. At first sight, at least, the general approach to housing matters adopted by the Conservative Party and government possesses the quality of clarity: if one leaves aside, for the moment, the question of 'alternative tenures', the future pattern suggested consists of municipal housing catering for those who are 'in need' and owner-occupation providing for nearly everybody else. However, it is decidedly odd to posit a role for council housing based upon need, and to combine that with a stunning lack of curiosity about what those needs may be, how extensively they are encountered among the population, and hence about how large the public sector is required to be to meet them.

The position of the majority of the government's critics is, if anything, even more ambiguous. They are alarmed by the prospect of a municipal sector restricted to a 'residual' or 'welfare' role. Often the story of American federal housing is cited as a grisly warning, although it might seem unwise to extrapolate from a sector which accounts for no more than 2 per cent of accommodation in one country to a sector which makes up around 30 per cent of the housing in a different political culture. However, the basic problem with this line of argument is that it does not adequately confront two facts: first, that the critics themselves are usually deeply committed to an ideal of local authority housing which orders its priorities according to need (and thus fulfils a welfare function more effectively than at present); and, second, that over the past twenty years there have been substantial advances towards such a goal, amounting to a restructuring of the role allocated to council housing. The origins of municipal endeavour in this field may lie in a desire to house the respectable working class in stable, and quite probably skilled, occupations, but it has become more and more the sector which caters for the majority of the poor. As an example, we may note that, by the later 1970s, 56 per cent of all lone parents with dependent children were renting from a local authority or New Town Corporation.[33] The provision of council houses has always had – and particularly since the Greenwood Act and the coming of large-scale slum clearance in the 1930s – the character of a social service for a certain category of persons, namely those unable to obtain a home in any other way. What has happened is that this has been increasingly interpreted to mean that local authorities should become the principal providers for groups who would in the past have relied upon the private landlord for shelter.

The welfare orientation of local housing departments is clearly seen in allocation policies. This is an area which remains largely untouched by the central government's regulating zeal, and one must remember that there are 450 local housing authorities, with 450 sets of problems, 450 styles and qualities of management, and 450 separate allocations policies. However, with the larger authorities created by local government reorganization, there has been a good deal of streamlining and some standardization. There will almost certainly be a points system, and invariably special consideration is given to families in substandard housing, to large families, and to the needs of special groups, like the elderly and the handicapped. This emphasis on welfare considerations poses some problems of equity. A London Director of Housing wrote in 1973: 'Our allocation of tenancies in Camden goes four to one in favour of families with particular handicaps, as against those who remain for years on the housing list without the recognized stigmata which win them an immediate consideration. Is this right? we don't yet know.'[34]

Even more difficult questions are raised by the much more secretive practices sometimes termed 'secondary rationing'. These concern which particular flats or houses, out of a stock typically highly varied in kind and desirability, go to which particular applicants. As this usually means that such factors as rent-paying records and current housekeeping standards are matched up with the kind of offer to be made, the opportunities for the exercise of discretion based upon prejudice are substantial. As is usual in bureaucracies, the crucial decisions may be taken by persons occupying a relatively lowly position in the formal departmental hierarchy.

Doubts about local authority housing management extend to its relationship with existing tenants. Housing departments may be either fussy or unresponsive, or, quite frequently, both – fussy in the provision of sheafs of governessy rules like 'Not everyone is interested in gardening, but you are expected to keep your plot neat and tidy'; unresponsive in the difficulties which tenants encounter in their efforts to get repairs to their houses done. Some local authorities have tried to meet the later criticism by instituting much more decentralized, estate-based schemes, and the government has also taken a hand in the form of a provision in the 1980 Housing Act which requires local authorities to consult with 'secure tenants' about any matter of housing management which substantially affects them. (The act also compels authorities to publish outlines of their schemes for allocating dwellings and for dealing with requests for transfers made by established tenants). However, these provisions are a decidedly watered down version of the Tenants Charter adopted by Labour towards the close of its term of office, and, in general, the schedule of rights and obligations remains biased in favour of the local authority and against the tenant.

A common response to such criticism which is made by convinced supporters of local authority housing is well summed up by Valerie Karn when she writes: 'Unlike the inequalities of a market system the defects which mar public housing are not intrinsic – they have arisen out of its use as a means of buttressing rather than undermining an essentially hierarchical social and economic structure.'[35] However, the optimism implicit in these words seems scarcely justified: reliance upon sensitive management by a class of underminers of the hierarchical social and economic structure appears to be all too extrinsic. Contemporary housing departments share with the early twentieth-century Poor Law the feature of not having attracted sufficient officials of a calibre and status to command respect – it is estimated that only 3.5 per cent of their staff hold the professional Institute of Housing qualification.[36] In any case, it is not certain that better training and more professional standards of work would encourage the rather subversive qualities which Karn desires. More generally, it is unrealistic to expect bureaucracies not to produce, among other more desirable things, bureaucratic distortions, and to believe that they can be insulated from assumptions widespread in the society of which they form a part. In particular, there are two recurrent, and surely inherent, problems which they encounter. First, it is not easy to see how they can provide for discrimination in the good sense without also furnishing opportunities for discrimination in senses regarded as bad. Second, where we are dealing with publicly answerable suppliers of scarce commodities – in this case, desired forms of housing space – we have to recognize that the exercise of a welfare role will be tempered by the obligation to safeguard public money and to collect from debtors.

The administration of public housing in Britain is very localized. In this may be sought the reason why housing departments have been reluctant to assume responsibilities for certain overlapping groups, like younger single people and the geographically mobile. Local authorities have long seen it as their prime duty to provide for natives, and not for strangers. This may be fading, under pressure from governments who fear that the present structure of council housing rewards immobility and retards economic adjustments which they see as essential. Nevertheless, it continues to colour much local administration, and indeed is still quite frequently taken to ludicrous lengths – persons on waiting lists would be well advised to invest in a good map which clearly marks borough boundaries before changing one private landlord for another, lest they jeopardize their chances of rehousing. Fears by local authorities that they might be compelled to rehouse outsiders against their will have also affected their approach to homelessness. This was one of the main reasons why the local authority associations lobbied hard and successfully during the progress of the Housing (Homeless Persons) Bill through Parliament to secure an amendment which would absolve their members of the responsibility for providing permanent accommodation for those deemed to be 'intentionally homeless', that is, whose circumstances were thought to be their own fault.

In view of all this, it is not perhaps surprising that governments have become inclined to listen, over the past twenty years or so, to the band of enthusiasts, of very varying political views, who have been promoting 'alternative tenures', designed to perform functions previously carried out by private landlords and to avoid the starkness of the choice between renting from the local authority and conventional owner-occupation. In the growth of this movement, dislike of the exclusions wrought by a market system, and distrust of the other, plusher bureaucracies epitomized in the building societies have been motivating forces, but probably a bigger part has been played by dissatisfaction with the narrow way in which local authorities have often conceived their role, and especially by the belief that for local housing departments to assume a virtual monopoly of the provision of rented housing in their localities would be a highly undesirable development. In order to advance their case, such critics could note that Britain was an odd one out among Western democracies in according so major a role to local authorities in this field. In Europe, the normal pattern is to have one or more public or quasi-public finance corporations or banks through which funds are channelled, as loans or as subsidies, to housing associations, individuals or public authorities according to the intentions of the national housing policy. Thus in France the *Crédit Foncier*, the *Caisse des Depots* and other similar financial institutions channel funds to a variety of recipients, but especially to the housing corporations and societies grouped in the so-called HLM (*Habitations a Loyer Modéré*) organization. This replaced the pre-war *Habitations a Bon Marché* and the change of title from 'cheap' to 'at moderate rent' indicates the extension of its operations upwards into higher income brackets.[37] The corresponding Italian organization is the *INA-Casa* and in both countries a part of the money invested in housing is provided by a pay-roll tax on industry. Housing societies and co-operatives occupy a central position in these systems, since they stand between direct public provision of dwellings for letting to the poorer families and the independent buying and building of houses by the well-to-do, and serve in particular the needs of the middle range of families with moderate incomes. For a long time, however, British housing policy failed to make significant moves in the same direction.

Housing trusts and associations had existed in England since the nineteenth century as private voluntary organizations to build homes for certain classes of persons in certain areas. Some, like the Peabody fund, were charitable (though paying a limited dividend to investors), and others were co-operative. The Housing Act of 1936 gave them a legal status within the category of Friendly Societies, and they were allowed to borrow from the Public Works Loans Board on the same terms as local authorities. After the war scant attention was paid to their interests, and Beveridge, writing in 1948, said of them that 'housing societies today, from the government of the day, get warm words and cold comfort'.[38] The situation remained virtually unchanged until 1961, when a Housing Act authorized the advancement of direct loans to housing associations up to a total of £25 million to help schemes approved by the minister. This was by way of experiment, and was followed in 1964 by an act setting up a Housing Corporation to encourage the establishment of non-profit housing societies to 'provide and manage rented houses, or houses on a co-ownership basis'. The corporation was authorized to devote up to £100 million of public funds in advances to projects of this kind in partnership with the independent building societies, who agreed to put up twice the amount. For some time the success of the project seemed very dubious (although co-ownership schemes started to thrive, in a modest kind of way), but in 1974 the prospects for the housing association movement were transformed, partly by a much greater injection of funds from the central government, and partly by the elevation of the Housing Corporation into the dominant promotional and supervisory body in the field. From then on, any housing society which wished to have recourse to the public funds made available had to register with the corporation, and such registration would only be affected if the corporation's enquiries satisfied it that the association in question was financially sound and operationally capable. In 1977 – which was to be the high point – about 10 per cent of all housing starts in Britain were of dwellings constructed by or for housing associations.

There is a broad swathe of land lying between owner-occupation and traditional public sector housing, capable of producing a diversity of crops, some of them decidedly unusual in the British climate. On the boundary with owner-occupation can be found self-build schemes, and co-ownership schemes in which members acquire a stake, or share, in the property itself as well as a tenancy on favourable terms. At the other extremity are cost-rent projects, and also management co-operatives, the role of whose members is restricted to a collective responsibility for some or all management functions. In the middle come par value co-operatives, where the stake of the individual co-operator consists of a single share, repayable on leaving. There are also many registered charities providing for special groups like the elderly and the disabled. Thus there is a bewildering variety of different kinds of scheme, and a bewildering number of separate associations (about 3000). Housing associations have suffered in the general cutback in housing investment – the scale of funding in the mid 1980s is running at about half the level prevailing in the late 1970s. Their future contribution is not at all clear, perhaps because the crucial question of the role they should be performing remains unresolved – in particular, whether the provision they make should be supplementary or complementary to local authority provision. Cullingworth makes this point, and goes on to say: 'The evidence suggests that there is little demand for alternative forms of tenure *as such*, but rather a series of perceived problems relating either to the management of or the access to the traditional tenures'.[39] Thus it is implied that alternative forms of tenure are a bit of a digression, and attention should return to ironing out the creases in the traditional tenures.

Doubtless this a sensible view. The flexibility of owner-occupation, as well as its popularity, has been shown by its spread to groups who would not, in the past, have been able to contemplate the possibility – and it should be remembered that the recent growth in owner-occupation is by no means a phenomenon restricted to Britain, but has occurred not only throughout Western Europe, but in Eastern Europe as well. Indeed, some countries, like France and Belgium, now have proportions of their householders in this sector close to that of Britain. Local authority housing departments, too, have, in spite of their low professional base, generally proved more responsive and adaptable than their critics have often given them credit for. Even such features of the present system as the 'intentional homelessness' clause of the Housing (Homeless Persons) Act 1977, to which we have already referred – reviled as it has been by all good radicals – could be defended on the grounds that the act would probably have been unworkable without a measure of local authority discretion, and that there had to be a learning process. After all, local authorities do accept about two-thirds of those who present themselves as genuinely homeless, and hence requiring priority treatment.

However, there remain strong arguments for encouraging as diverse a band of suppliers as possible – private landlords (with checks) as well as housing associations (with checks). Perhaps the most important reason for this is one we have so far only hinted at, but now requires to be made flatly. That is that there is a very pronounced bias, within the main tenures, in favour of those who are already established, and against those who are striving to become established. Mortgage repayments fall heaviest in the years when family commitments are heaviest, and income is most stretched, and lighten when the children have fled the nest. In addition, and to some extent admittedly conversely, the system tends to encourage 'buying up', moving to larger and more expensive accommodation, and hence obtaining an even larger share of tax reliefs: fewer than half of new mortgages now go to first-time buyers. Those council tenants who are thought to be deserving of the biggest discounts on purchasing are those who have occupied their existing dwellings the longest. As for those who remain in council property, well, apart from the wait they will probably have had to endure to get into the sector in the first place, they may have to produce the right number of children, of the appropriate sexes, before being permitted to graduate from a fourth-floor flat to a house with a garden.

There may be good reasons for some of these features of our present arrangements taken individually; together, they give cause for disquiet. We have never had an integrated housing policy in this country, and since the failure of the Housing Policy Review there seems to be less and less demand for one. Indeed, we are surely dealing with an area of public policy in retreat. In this chapter, we have explored some of the causes of this – the belief that the problem of housing shortage is no longer with us, the failed Utopias of municipal housing as characterized by semi-derelict urban estates. The consequence has been that real cuts can be made in housing expenditures with apparent impunity. However, perhaps the best indication of the withdrawal of public concern has been the way in which the sale of council housing, an issue which would have been regarded as peripheral at any time in the last fifty years, has moved to

212 *Beyond the welfare state?*

the centre of government policy. George Boyne has written:

> Throughout this century housing policies have concentrated on issues of quality and quantity. The sales policy may be an electoral strategy, an economic policy or a moral crusade. It is not a housing policy as traditionally conceived or a policy of housing needs as traditionally defined.[40]

The question is thus: Will these 'traditions' reassert themselves?

12 Poverty

When social policy consisted of a Poor Law and little else it is obvious that the focus was wholly on the lowest depths of social life, on poverty. It combined a rescue operation for those whose destitution drove them into its arms with a punitive expedition against those who were able, but unwilling to work. There was no need for such a policy to define 'the poor', since they simply constituted the immeasurable pool from which was drawn the very clearly defined category of 'paupers'. Rowntree's 'poverty line' marked a step forward, because it defined poverty in terms of the level below which life became a sort of social non-existence, irrespective of whether the poor appealed for help (and so became paupers) or not. This was primary poverty – inescapable, unconditional, and, in one sense of the word, absolute. It was not a status, but a condition. A second step forward was taken when the poverty line passed from Rowntree to Beveridge and became the 'subsistence level'. Then instead of serving only to measure the level *below* which poverty existed, it acquired the positive function of fixing the level *up to* which family incomes must be raised, and thus prepared the way for a recognition of a *right* to welfare. For the subsistence level is, so to speak, the underbelly of the 'national minimum', to which, by definition, all 'nationals' are entitled.

Thereafter, poverty was generally regarded by those concerned with social policy as something which must sooner or later – and if possible sooner rather than later – be eliminated. This was part of the simple philosophy of the welfare state, and it is vulnerable to sophisticated criticism. Much time has been spent defending the unassailable view that poverty is a relative concept, because the condition to which it refers differs from place to place and from time to time. This is obviously true, but preoccupation with it distracts attention from the subtler question: what kind of meaning can we give to poverty when it is used of a particular community at a particular time? One answer given is that, even in this limited context, it is wholly relative in meaning, and can refer only to a position on a scale of inequality, and not to a condition of life. You may say that A is poorer than B, but not that A is poor and B is not. However, the term 'poverty' may be retained (in this view) to denote an arbitrary statistical category, such as the bottom 20 per cent on the inequality scale. This of course implies that poverty is always with us, and can never be abolished unless inequality is abolished too. Others, while still insisting that poverty is relative, not absolute, allow that the comparison by which we recognize it is not just a step in the process by which we compare each level with the one above it right down the scale, but comparison with the *average* standards of the community as a whole, so that 'the poor are those who fall sufficiently far below these average standards'.[1] But how far is sufficient? We can only infer that the comparison made here is not in fact with an average, but with a minimum, and that poverty is a condition of life which lies below the minimum which that particular civilization can accept as part of itself. A minimum is a value judgement, an average is a mathematical calculation. So, though it is still relative, there is a flavour of absoluteness about the concept, in the sense in which we can say something is 'absolutely intolerable'. It is with this meaning that we shall use the term 'poverty' in this chapter.

One obvious objection to this approach is that poverty conceived in these terms is not something whose frontier can be determined by drawing a 'poverty line'. Abel-Smith and Townsend, in their report *The Poor and the Poorest* replaced it with a band, ranging up to 140 per cent of the then National Assistance Board scales, but even this, though admirable for its purpose, does not dispose of the criticism. Furthermore, although national assistance and, later, supplementary benefit rates obviously provide an authoritative statement of the levels of living which successive governments have believed are appropriate for claimants, their reliability as objective indicators of poverty may be called into question. This is not only a matter of the inconsistent ways in which these offical schemes have treated different kinds of income and different groups of beneficiaries. There is also the fundamental objection that if a government has a sudden unwonted rush of generosity, correcting the scales by more than is necessary to cope with inflation, then the amount of poverty discovered by using entitlement to benefit as a measuring rod will automatically rise, which, as the philosophers would say, is counter-intuitive.

It was in order to deal with problems such as these that Peter

Townsend, in his more recent mammoth study, *Poverty in the United Kingdom*, has devised a measure called the 'deprivation standard of poverty' based on deviations from the 'style of living' of the population as a whole.[2] So that he could compute this measure, Townsend built up a list of no fewer than sixty indicators – possessing or lacking this or that amenity, participating or not participating in this or that activity. He then went on to suggest that his survey results indicated a sharp disjunction at about 150 per cent of supplementary benefit levels – a threshold, below which deprivation increased disproportionately. His claim to have established a more objective and reliable measure of poverty has not, however, been universally accepted.[3] The major difficulty is that a number of the indicators contributing to scores on the deprivation index may be guides to differences in tastes rather than to differences in the opportunity to participate: people may *choose* not to have a cooked breakfast most days of the week, or not to give their children a party on their birthdays. And of course the fact that not having this or doing that correlates quite strongly with other, less disputable, indicators of deprivation does not help to sort out this conundrum; it merely leads into a circular argument, and suspends a question mark over the validity of the overall scores of deprivation which are arrived at. However, a poverty line such as Townsend's is, nevertheless, based on the evaluation of a great deal of evidence about how ordinary people live, and about how they think and feel. Poverty defined as income is an exiguous concept, but it provides a nucleus to which specific kinds of want can be attached to build a much richer concept whose integrity is the product of two qualities present in all its components, deprivation and urgency. Of all these accretions the most important are housing, the physical environment, education and those physical and mental disabilities which exacerbate and are exacerbated by poverty in the narrower sense. These are the poverties of our civilization.

That this idea of poverty as a sub-minimal social condition has been strongly represented since the war among those concerned with social policy, both in theory and in practice, cannot be doubted. It is also true that it has been severely criticized as misleading and dangerous, on the grounds that in theory it encourages the propensity to study poverty apart from its social context, and in practice it may lead to the treatment of poverty as a painful sore on an otherwise healthy body which can be removed under a local anaesthetic. To the first comment one may reply that, if wisely used, this approach may be profitable because it directs attention to qualitative inequalities and inter-class attitudes associated with them, and because it raises questions about the nature of the social conscience (if any) of the society studied. Those who offer the second comment argue that the real problem towards which action should be directed is inequality – in its many different forms – rather than sub-minimal poverty. It is perfectly true that the former represents the context within which the latter must be attacked, but a policy inspired by resentment of inequality can, as has often been seen, be distorted or even frustrated by the strength of its appeal to selfish interests, whereas a policy inspired by resentment of sub-minimal poverty appeals to feelings of altruism, which are not always easily awakened. So the spate of single-minded campaigns directed by anti-poverty pressure groups on behalf of the old, sick, disabled, homeless and generally disadvantaged have contributed something essential to the advance of social policy. It is true that pressures of this kind can be an embarrassment as well as a stimulus to policy-makers who are tackling difficult problems of priorities, but the course of events does not suggest that they have led to the issue of sub-minimal poverty being considered apart from its wider context. The trend has rather been in the opposite direction, away from the piecemeal or patchwork treatment of symptoms towards a more systematic and comprehensive view of the problem area of which poverty is a part.

However, this broadening out from the tried and familiar concept of sub-minimal poverty carries a risk which policy-makers have felt acutely, that they might find themselves in a boundless wilderness spanning the totality of economic and social relationships. They have therefore found a need to fence the terrain off into manageable tracts, in order that limited energies and resources might be deployed to best (or to most apparent) advantage. Two ways of attempting this have come to be of particular importance. The first leads to a concentration on impoverished geographical areas which are then treated as total communities, whose whole life must be reanimated and raised to a higher level at which poverty, in the narrower sense, would cease to be an acute problem. The second focuses attention on groupings within the population, like the elderly (or perhaps the very old among the elderly), the younger physically handicapped, or, especially recently, the unemployed school-leaver. These are all sections of the population known to be liable to suffer from income poverty and other deprivations and demoralizations. Again, the aim is to narrow the gap of disadvantage. Both these approaches could be called 'positive discrimination' although the term has usually been reserved for the first of them. One general problem here is that however priority districts and priority groupings are defined they will be found to contain more non-poor than poor, and at the same time will fail to include many of the poor. For instance, only a small minority of the deprived (by any measure or criterion) lives in those inner areas of our major cities which have been the subject of so much nervous pulse-taking by politicians and administrators.[4]

Positive discrimination in favour of selected districts has taken several forms in this country. The earlier experiments followed, in a modest and unslavish fashion, initiatives embarked on as parts of President Johnson's War on Poverty, declared in 1964. First came the Educational Priority Areas (EPAs) selected as districts within which the problem was 'one of an entire community at social and educational risk'.[5] Unlike the American Head Start, the plans were based on the idea of equal partnership between action and research, and the 'compensatory education' of the USA – which tried, by intensive application, to make good what the young had missed, on the assumption that schooling was the key to opportunity – was rejected in favour of the 'community school' as an agency of community development. There was much emphasis, too, on pre-school education as an integral part of the system. Results here were inconclusive, although there was some agreement that this was of particular importance for immigrants hampered by cultural and linguistic obstacles.[6]

The Urban Programme, the next arrival, appeared in the wash of Enoch Powell's notorious 'rivers of blood' speech in April 1968, although the stress on the problems of districts with high concentrations of immigrants was soon toned down by a very wide definition of the areas which could qualify for the 75 per cent grants on offer for approved projects. In the words of the first circular (October 1968) 'areas of special social need' were to be identified through a high incidence of such manifestations as large families, overcrowding, unemployment, poor environment, concentration of immigrants, children in trouble or need of care – a very far-reaching list. This is the programme which has carried with it the most in the way of resources,[7] but its impact on deprived urban areas has been small compared with that of redevelopment and house-improvement – and an early decision was to exclude nearly all housing projects from those eligible to obtain grants. Edwards and Batley described it as a 'piecemeal subsidy programme', regarded by both the central and local authorities as useful in plugging a few of the gaps in statutory social welfare provision.[8] As time has gone on, it has been used more and more to channel through local authorities grants to voluntary organizations for worthwhile, but minor, ventures.

The Community Development Project launched by the Home Office in 1969 was described as 'a neighbourhood-based experiment aimed at finding new ways of meeting the needs of people living in areas of high social deprivation'. Twelve areas of different character were chosen for the experiment, which, like the EPA projects, included both action and research. The original assumption that urban deprivation was rooted in the characteristics of local populations – a sort of social pathology – was soon abandoned in favour of a more structural approach in which specific issues were chosen for treatment by plans of action which involved participation by the citizens. Much attention was paid to assessing the merits and defects of different strategies, such as that of local co-operation (or consensus), intra-structural conflict, community organization (to make popular wishes and individual claims effective), political pressure and planning at regional and national level. Experience soon indicated that 'community action' (or 'development') as an end in itself was not enough, and one could not expect a community to pull itself up by its own bootstraps. The question is, said the First Inter-Project Report 'whether a clear enough awareness of the underlying issues can be developed to stimulate a powerful movement for change from a local base'.[9] This seemed to be answered in the negative, when several of the project teams aroused the enmity of the locally powerful, who declined to participate in what they saw as tax-supported Marxism (or, at best, trouble-making). The Home Office itself became indifferent about the fate of those it had sponsored: after 1974, individual local authorities were allowed to decide whether their CDPs should continue or not, and in 1977 the CDP Information and Intelligence Unit was closed down.

In these innovations of the late 1960s and early 1970s the initiative had been taken by the Home Office, anxious that with the loss of its responsibility for children's services it would be left with negative and politically rather unpopular areas of policy, like prison administration and immigration control. Its primacy in the field of inner city affairs appeared to be endorsed with the setting up of its Urban Deprivation Unit in November 1972. However, the government department centrally concerned with local government and with urban policies was the Department of the Environment, and in the same year that body tired of its subsidiary role in the game, and commissioned six Inner Area Studies from independent consultants.[10] This led to a significant change in direction, for these were research studies pure and simple, with no experimental component, and provided the opportunity for fresh looks at what was happening in inner city areas, shorn of preconceptions about the pathology of their inhabitants. In particular, the researchers in Lambeth, Birmingham and Liverpool documented the erosion of the industrial base, and thereby sparked off a debate about the desirability of post-war dispersion policies.

New emphases, therefore, were contained in the Labour government's White Paper, *Policy for the Inner Cities*, published in 1977. First, much more in the way of resources was to be made available, through a re-jigging of the rate-support grant (the post-1979 Conservative government has tended, in its successive grant settlements, to shift the balance back again towards the shire counties). Second, there were promises of new initiatives to produce employment opportunities (and New Towns, not for the first time since 1945, went quite out of fashion). Third, there was much stress on the need for fresh mechanisms to advance interdepartmental co-operation, at both central and local government levels. This firm setting of the problems of urban deprivation within the context of general economic trends (particularly those relating to employment location) was welcomed by many academic commentators, but it added to the complexity of the task of co-ordinating policy. In 1981, the riots in many inner areas produced a head of steam in favour of further urgent – some would say showy – political initiatives. Even before these events, the Conservatives had added a number of new programmes to the existing mosaic, such as the twenty-five Enterprise Zones, in which some planning controls were removed in order to encourage development, and what have been called the 'In-Town New Towns' in the docklands of London and Liverpool. However, only in Northern Ireland has commitment to large-scale spending to relieve unemployment remained respectable, and, at least until late 1984, there was a dampish pocket of 'non-Thatcherite' ministers (James Prior, Nicholas Scott, Chris Patten) to bear witness to the different emphases deemed appropriate in the province.

The dilemma of how to strike a balance between problems of acute urgency and the broader long-term issues in which they are embedded arises in all branches of social policy. The easiest way to explain this is to consider the second approach noted earlier – policies directed towards groupings in the population – and to take a few examples. The aged poor have been, for a long time, an ostensible object of public compassion, and proposals to improve their lot have played a prominent part in party political programmes. They were given pensions and then, when everyone got pensions, supplementary pensions, and then, when the depth of the poverty of the poorest was uncovered, they were given allowances additional to their supplementary pensions, such as additions for heating, and also a special weekly rate, which was called 'long term' even though it was denied to the longest term of that singularly unfavoured group, those required to register for employment. In addition, a patchwork of aids grew up – home helps, meals on wheels, the services of chiropodists and so forth. These were subject to constant revision, were largely though not entirely limited to the relief of poverty, and were administered by several different agencies. But increasingly though has been given, not only to the aged poor, but to the problems of old age in general, and some attempt has been made to shift the emphasis to the still broader concept of the problems of ageing as a process and an experience. This trend was neatly summed up in a White Paper published in March 1981 and entitled *Growing Older* (Cmnd 8173). The subject chapters in this start with 'Income', and then following on with 'Entering retirement'. 'Retirement: a time of opportunity', and 'Where to live'. Later chapters are concerned with the various divisions of social care, such as 'Care in hospitals and nursing homes'. Thus there is growing up a policy for old age, interested in the role of each item in a continuum stretching from pre-retirement courses to the geriatric ward, and in the relevant areas poverty is absorbed into the general policy.

The case of the disabled is similar. Disablement is not poverty in the ordinary sense, but is is a form of deprivation which poverty exacerbates. It took a vigorous, single-minded campaign to win recognition of the extent and urgency of the needs of those included in this admittedly far from homogenous category. But categorization was a necessary prelude to action. Then came some piecemeal measures such as new welfare services, attendance allowances for severe cases, and the reservation of certain jobs for the employable among the disabled. Experience of these various programmes indicated that disablement needed to be viewed in a wider context. So pressure developed for a policy, or one might say a charter, for the disabled, in deference to which the Labour government of 1974 appointed a Minister for the Disabled.

In housing the balance between the particular and the general was different. The major problem which confronts a housing policy is how to ensure that building goes on and that the dwellings constructed are available to people of all incomes throughout the population; it is concerned with inequality rather than with poverty in the absolute sense. Dealing with exceptionally poor housing conditions or providing for the homeless must be harmonized with the demands of the policy as a whole. However, the effects of the housing programme – or the lack of one – on poverty are immediate. 'Housing policy', said the West London branch of the Family Service Units, 'largely controls where our work will lie.'[11] It is all too easy, because of the peculiar difficulties of this branch of government and administration, to allow quite unacceptable conditions of squalor and an alarming amount of homelessness to continue to exist. In the last chapter we described the pressures which led to the passing of the Housing (Homeless Persons) Act 1977, noting the anxiety of many local councils that they should be permitted to decline to assume full responsibility for those whose plight is regarded as their own fault. And there are indeed real problems of priority and of equity here, deepened because this is an area of social administration where the Poor Law principle that people should have a 'settlement' still has life. Local housing authorities fear that those who have been subsisting quietly on the waiting list for council accommodation may be elbowed out by newcomers whose problems may be more floridly presented but whose needs may be no greater, or perhaps may be less great. The basic problem of how to devise a policy which can simultaneously and effectively provide immediate relief for urgent poverty and deal in a fair and even-handed fashion with less insistent social and economic inequalities has not yet been solved.

But the area in which this dilemma presents the gravest difficulties is that of social security, in the sense of cash benefits. The Beveridge plan was an attack upon want, just as Bevan's health service was an attack upon disease, but both relied for their purpose on universal measures. Selective treatment of the poor was residual in Beveridge's plan and totally absent from Bevan's. But selectivity broke into both, on a large scale in social security through national assistance and supplementary benefits, and in a more limited way in the health service, through charges (for medicines, spectacles, dentures and dentistry) from which the poor were exempt. A new kind of duality was added with the introduction of graduated insurance: a duality of purpose. For social security was coming to be directed both at staving off want and at providing for all, when earnings ceased, a pattern of incomes based on the principle of equitable (or legitimate) inequality. The critical question was whether these two aims could be pursued through a single universal system, or whether there must be two distinct but related sets of apparatus to cope with them.

So far there has not been much attempt at fusion. The Conservative government of 1970–4 became enthused with a new piece of machinery, tax credits, designed to be both universal in its application and at the same time selective on behalf of the poor, but the government fell before anything definite had emerged; its post-1979 successor has so far (in 1984) appeared to be content to abandon it in the rusty scrap-yard of good ideas. For its part, Labour introduced the Castle scheme, as we have seen: this should have the effect, in the early years of the next century, of lifting a certain proportion of old people off supplementary benefit, but, whatever the intention, it seems unlikely that it will prove to be radical enough to make much of a dent in the dual system. Indeed, events of the 1970s and 1980s appear rather to confirm its permanence.

Three developments were especially important in the strengthening of means-tested benefits. First, in 1970, came a new selective aid for the working poor in the shape of the family income supplement (FIS). This started life as a rather hastily cobbled together expedient, but fifteen years on it seems to be a well established feature of the social security scene. FIS has been acclaimed – and condemned – as the first measure of direct supplementation of wages by public authorities since Speenhamland in the 1790s. However, the lines between the latter-day descendants of the Old and the New Poor Laws – FIS and supplementary benefit – have become steadily less clear cut. FIS can be claimed by anyone who works full-time, defined as thirty hours a week (twenty-four hours for a single parent), but anyone who works part-time may be eligible for supplementary benefit. And the emphasis is on 'anyone', since in November 1983 Britain implemented a European Economic Community directive of 1978, by which national social security systems had to give equal treatment to men and women. Thus either partner in a marriage of cohabiting relationship may now be entitled to either FIS or supplementary benefit. This explains how FIS, although nowadays mainly assisting single parents and their families, could be obtained, in 1984, by the working wives of striking miners.

Second, supplementary benefit has itself been reformed, in ways which put into effect the view of a team of officials who reported in 1978 that 'the most realistic aim is to fit the scheme to its mass role of coping with millions of claimants in known and readily definable categories for the forseeable future ...'[12]. As in 1966, when supplementary benefit replaced national assistance, one of the aims of the 1980 remodelling of the system was to tidy up the accretion of discretionary allowances and grants; thus, single payments for clothing and footwear, formerly almost routine for longer-term claimants, became very difficult to obtain. The main feature of the reform, however, was what is sometimes called the 'legalization' of the scheme. As far as possible, discretion has been replaced by rules and regulations codified in statutory instruments laid before Parliament. People should know where they stand better than they did before, but the variety of common human needs is such that any attempt to cover all likely contingencies in advance is bound to involve regulations of a fiendish complexity, requiring frequent emendation. The well-schooled claimant, therefore, needs to have access to up-to-date editions of two massive tomes – the S-code (the internal rule-book issued to supplementary benefit officers) and the so-called Yellow Book, more correctly termed *The Law relating to Supplementary Benefits and Family Income Supplements*. Both of these are public documents, but the net result of the changes may well have been to increase bewilderment, as well as throwing into sharp prominence the issue of the availability of sources of impartial and informed advice.

Third, a dual system to rival the dual system emerged in the early 1970s, based on rent rebates (for council tenants), rent allowances (for the tenants of private landlords) and rate rebates (particularly helpful to elderly owner-occupiers). This created what became known as the 'better-off' problem, since some people would obtain more on supplementary benefit, while others would find that the rebate system treated them more kindly. Under the 1974–9 Labour government officials of the DHSS were charged with the duty of explaining to claimants which of these would be in their best interests to obtain, but in 1980 this was abandoned as an economy measure. Conservative ministers became convinced of the case for a radical simplification, under which local authorities would assume administrative responsibility for all payments to tenants in respect of housing costs, including those hitherto made by DHSS as part of a supplementary pension or allowance. Such a scheme would have the gratifying side effect of reducing the need for civil service manpower.

Housing benefit was introduced in two stages, in November 1982 and April 1983. The first stage, which applied to council tenants only, passed off smoothly enough: many claimants had an entitlement to supplementary benefit which exceeded their housing costs, and, as in such cases the only money transaction was between the DHSS and the local authority, these tenants were in effect being transferred to what was termed in the jargon 'rent direct'. Even here, however, there were confusing complications where heating charges were included in the rent, or there was an adult non-dependant in the household. And the second stage of the introduction of the new scheme, which extended it to private tenants, was in many areas a fiasco: the government was fortunate that the media did not regard the plight of poor people as particularly newsworthy. Local authority administrative systems buckled under the strain, and there were many stories of tenants running deeply into rent arrears as a result of delays in the processing of their claims. There *were* teething problems, but the difficulties with the scheme were not just transitory, since it has not solved the 'better-off' problem. Indeed, under housing benefit, *two* systems of regulations and calculations were replaced by *three*: first, standard housing benefit, which is the old rebate and allowance system under a new name; second, certificated housing benefit, which goes to those in receipt of supplementary pensions and allowances, and, as its title suggests, involves a 'certificate', which is sent by the DHSS to the local authority; and, third, housing benefit supplement, which is an addition to standard housing benefit obtainable by those householders whose incomes are below supplementary benefit levels after they have paid their rent and rates. The last was designed to protect those who would otherwise be worse off as a result of the new arrangements, but its invention compounds confusion. The chief trouble is that many of those entitled to housing benefit supplement will approach their local council first, rather than the supplementary benefit (DHSS) office, but housing department officials are not skilled in SB assessments, and eligibility may be missed. The amounts of housing benefit supplement awarded may well be small, but it is a form of supplementary benefit, and hence entitles recipients to lump-sum payments for items like furniture, and acts as a passport to benefits such as free school meals and free prescriptions.

It should not be thought that groups like the long-term unemployed who have exhausted their entitlement to insurance benefits are relatively worse off than their counterparts in countries like France and West Germany. Continental public assistance schemes are often based on the local commune or some other small unit of government, and may be subject to restrictive rules of a kind long given up in the

United Kingdom – enjoining support from family members inside or outside the household, for instance. International comparisons suggest, too, that the scale rates of means-tested benefit are somewhat higher in Britain, when expressed as a proportion of average earnings, than they generally are elsewhere.[13] That the British dual system does not treat the very poor too harshly requires acknowledgement, which it often fails to receive. The price, however, is a mind-boggling complexity. It was noted in 1982 that DHSS staff 'rely on over 100 bulky instruction manuals – closely printed, frequently amended, and full of cross-references', in order to administer the more than thirty benefits for which the department was responsible.[14] Furthermore, the unusual weight accorded to the means-tested element in the system produces three familiar problems, which ensnare would-be reformers.

The first of these may be termed the 'dilemma of the gap', that is to say of the gap in value between a social insurance benefit and the larger amount received by those getting the full supplementary pension or allowance: the latter but not the former includes a sum for rent or mortgage interest payments, and for rates. The dilemma arises because poverty can be seen both as a condition and a status: a condition of material want and a status of dependence on discretionary aid. Most reformers would like to do something about both aspects, that is, to raise the income of the poor and to reduce the number dependent on supplementary benefits, but it is very difficult to do both at once within the framework of our present system of social security. If you raise pensions without also raising the SB (supplementary benefit) rate, you narrow the gap and reduce the number of people dependent on SB, but you do not increase their incomes unless the addition to the pension is more than enough to fill the gap. An increase sufficient to do this would be immensely costly, and it would still benefit least those who need it most. If insurance benefits and SB are increased *pari passu* there is some gain for everybody (including those who do *not* need it), but the gap remains and the number of people in the *status* of poverty is unaffected. This is the course of action generally adopted, because it seems to be the simplest. It made it possible for the Labour government of March 1974 to announce immediately the biggest increase ever made at one go, because it could add that there would be a similar advance in SB. Thus the gap remains, and the number dependent on supplementary means-tested pensions is unchanged until some more drastic reform of the social security system is undertaken.

The second dilemma is that of the 'poverty trap', and it springs from the same source, namely the fact that any benefit or concession given on condition of poverty must inevitably be reduced or withdrawn if and when income rises. The gap is one example of this, but there are others. The most obvious are family income supplement and housing benefit (including rate rebates), where the regulations lay down exactly how the benefit is to be reduced as the income rises. The significance of the procedure is greater in the case of the FIS than of pensions, because its beneficiaries are working and may expect their earnings to rise. The FIS is, in effect, a part of the wage, and, since it is calculated at 50 per cent of the gap between actual earnings and the income prescribed to meet the family's basic needs, any addition to the family earnings is automatically cut by 50 per cent through the corresponding reduction of the supplement. This is called the 'withdrawal rate' and has the effect of a 50 per cent tax on the additional earnings. The withdrawal rates differ as between one kind of benefit and another, and when a family is in receipt of many of these, including FIS, standard housing benefit, free school meals, free medicines etc., the total withdrawal rate is very high, and the situation may further be adversely affected by a rise in insurance contributions and income tax. It is actually possible for an increase in earnings to cause a decrease in net income. In 1983–4 a couple with two children would have been better off (by about £4) earning £80 a week rather than £100.[15] Such calculations presume that those affected are actually obtaining the benefits for which they are eligible, but this is an unrealistic assumption, since take-up usually falls a long way short of the maximum possible: this is especially true of families with children, on whom the poverty trap snaps tightest.[16] However, any government which tried to offer this as a plea in mitigation to the charge of failing to tackle the problem of the trap would be parading as a kind of virtue what has always been regarded as one of the prime defects of most means-tested systems – that they fail to relieve poverty efficiently because they rely on people having a good idea of their entitlements and on their being prepared to push themselves forward to make a claim.

Thus the problem here is the existence of a host of separate and uncoordinated benefits, in cash or in kind, for the partial relief of poverty. The details change from time to time, in accordance with no coherent pattern or strategy. Thus, the chaos of differential rent schemes, rebate schemes, and no schemes at all, which confronted council tenants in different parts of the country before 1972 was then replaced by a single, national scheme, which could only be varied by individual housing authorities in minor ways: while free school meals have moved in the opposite direction, from nationally set income scales and conditions of eligibility to local discretion – since 1980 many LEAs have restricted the benefit to the children of the recipients of SB or of FIS. Estimates of the number of means-tested benefits in use vary, and one official statement put it at forty-four. But it would be quite wrong to imagine that all these are for the relief of poverty in the absolute sense. They include grants for various kinds of training, for university education and for several sorts of Legal Aid to which people with quite substantial incomes are entitled. There are others where there is unlikely to be a strict application of a withdrawal rate, such as home helps and 'meals on wheels', and others again, like old people's homes, where inmates pay what they can afford (retaining a personal allowance) and receive the same treatment whatever they pay. However, the extended use of discretionary, means-tested benefits has produced a situation which is in some respects both chaotic and inequitable.

The third dilemma is that of the discrepancy between economic and welfare values. Here too there is an overlap with the previous category, since one example of this dilemma, and of a solution to it, is family income supplement, which brings the market value of a man's labour – or, more usually, a woman's labour – up to a level acceptable by welfare standards. In the case of those out of work, economic values clearly prevailed until 1970, because of the supplementary benefit 'wage stop', which was designed to ensure that an unemployed man should not draw in benefits a weekly sum larger than he would be likely to earn if he found work. The introduction of family income supplement modified the rule, as calculations of SB thenceforth assumed that claimants would be in receipt of their notional entitlement to that benefit. Finally, and after much criticism, the practice was abolished in 1975, but the flavour of less eligibility lingers in the British social security system. Governments appear to endorse the widespread belief that 'too generous' benefits will have dreadful effects upon work incentives. This was a principal reason for the abolition of earnings-related short-term unemployment benefits, and also must serve to explain the persistent refusal to extend to those required to register for employment the privilege accorded to every other group of long-term claimants, that of receiving the long-term supplementary benefit rate. This step was publicly urged on several occasions by the now disbanded Supplementary Benefits Commission, and was a priority for improvement selected by the team of officials charged with reviewing the supplementary benefits scheme in 1978. (Since the team worked on the assumption that no net additional resources would be made available for a reformed scheme, the scope they envisaged for improvements was in any event extremely limited.) Since 1980, the newly appointed Social Security Advisory Committee (SSAC) has taken up the cause, in its annual reports for both 1981/2 and 1982/3, but with no more success than its predecessors.

Most calculations of the relationship between levels of benefit and levels of earnings – such as those made by the DHSS Cohort Study of unemployed men[17] – confirm that income often falls very sharply with the advent of unemployment. The Cohort Study found that a third of the men who were unemployed for at least three months in 1978 had a total income out of work which was less than half of their previous income in work: since then, the abolition of earnings-related supplement to unemployment benefit will have considerably increased the numbers with such low replacement rates. On the other hand, about 9 per cent of those included in the Cohort Study were actually receiving the same as, or more than, they had obtained when in employment. However, around a quarter of these were occupational pensioners, who, before a change in rules in 1980, were able to draw their pension in addition to unemployment benefit. The remainder usually had large numbers of children and a low earning potential. But the problem of work incentives may be understated if we concentrate on this quite small minority of claimants, for there are many more who would be only a little better off in work than on benefit, once work expenses and the incidence of taxation and social security contributions is taken into account.

These three dilemmas all involve the use of benefits which are selective in terms of a means-test. Selectivity, or discrimination, can also operate positively in terms of categories for which the existence of a need is *presumed*. We may take as examples the disabled and one-parent families. The crucial point in the demand for a true disablement income is the insistence that it should be based on the assumption that a certain degree of disablement creates a certain degree of need, and that this should be measured not only by loss of earning power, but should also apply to those who have never entered the labour market, or have not recently been in it, like the disabled housewife. As for single-parent families, it seems beyond question that they, as a category, experience much absolute poverty, and that our present patchwork system of social security is singularly ineffective in meeting their urgent needs – the failure being least evident in the case of widows, most glaring in the case of unmarried mothers. A detailed study of the situation in five selected areas was published in 1973. It was found that in all the areas the mean incomes of fatherless families were less than half those of two-parent families, that the rate of mental trouble was three times as high in unmarried as in married mothers, and that the mean percentage drawing SB in the five areas was 2.6 per cent among two-parent families, 15.4 per cent in motherless families, and 53-5 per cent in fatherless families.[18] In response to such findings, a few variations were inserted into the repertoire of benefits, most notably the child benefit increase described in Chapter 8. However, the proportion of lone parents in receipt of SB was still 44 per cent at the time of the Supplementary Benefit Review in the late 1970s.[19]

Recent measures have been directed towards helping those single parents who want, and are able, to earn: a new and lower level of weekly earnings eligible for supplementation by FIS has been specified for single parents only, and the SB earnings disregards have been increased through the addition of a tapering sliding-scale, which also benefits single-parent families only. However, none of these changes has altered what is perhaps the principal bugbear of many divorced and separated women, that they are dependent on maintenance supplied by their former marriage partners, which all too often means that their family's income is uncertain as well as low. The progression from voluntary arrangements which break down, through the courts and a court order which is also only intermittently complied with, and then back to the courts, perhaps for an attachment or earnings order, is a familiar one, very wearying for the women concerned, and productive of the maximum ill-feeling on the way. Quite often the problem is that a single income from employment is required to be stretched to provide for two households and two sets of young children. The case for classing one-parent families as a special category deserving to be treated with positive discrimination is an overwhelming one, and there is a long way to go before it is fully accepted.

However, there is one awkward problem which arises over the definition of the category. For its essential feature is the absence, not of a marriage contract, but of a family which has the support of a man and a woman who share the burden between them. Therefore, a man and woman living together as man and wife do not qualify for supplementary benefit, if the man is working or is otherwise ineligible:

a widow may also lose her national insurance benefits if a man moves in with her. The principle here may be reasonable, and certainly the poverty campaigners have found it difficult to suggest a coherent alternative. In theory the rule accords to cohabitation the status – and responsibilities – of marriage, but a man has no legal obligation to maintain the children of his common-law partner, and he does not obtain the same favourable tax allowances as he would if his marriage-lines were in order. The state thus appears to be trying to have things both ways in certain respects. Furthermore, the application of the rule is exceptionally problematical: for example, a couple may be deemed to be living together as man and wife when it is agreed on all sides that no sexual relationship exists. The result is that a woman may be completely unsure about where she stands, and may be deterred from entering into a permanent relationship with a man for fear of jeopardizing the financial security of her children.

Children are more generally a category of persons which our social and economic systems expose to a special poverty risk. It arises because the family is a closely-knit, self-contained consumer unit whose income from the market is determined without reference to its collective needs. That is why the problem is viewed as one of family poverty rather than simply of child poverty. The corrective chosen has been, not to institute a family wage, but to supply financial support to the family independently of the market, as a sort of social, or welfare, service. In this country, as was explained in Chapter 8, this support takes two main forms, child benefit and the family income supplement. Now child benefit, as we said in that chapter, is not in its nature an anti-poverty measure, but a modification of the general system of income distribution in favour of families with children. Since the abolition of 'clawback' – by which increases in cash payments for child support were partly recouped from the better off by means of a higher tax bill than they would otherwise have incurred – child benefit has been totally non-selective, and hence is quite unlike family income supplement and the rest of the panoply of means-tested schemes. We have already seen that there are grave doubts about whether child benefit either is or will be generous enough to even up the financial circumstances of those with and without children at the same level of original income. There must, therefore, be even graver doubts about whether it can possibly prove an effective instrument in the elimination of child poverty. We may be getting the worst of both worlds, with a selective system which is cumbersome, invidious, and likely to suffer from a low rate of take-up, coupled with a non-selective cash distribution, which the Treasury has appeared to be anxious to rein back, because it spreads its benefits widely and expensively rather than concentrating them on the poor: each one pound per week increase in child benefit costs £550 million in a full tax year.

In spite of all its limitations, child benefit is of great importance in that it represents a first attempt to unify the systems of income taxation and income maintenance. This is also the essential element in some more comprehensive plans, applying to more areas than family support, and of which the prototype was negative income tax as first suggested by the American economist, Milton Friedman, in 1963. The idea is quite simple, though the variants which have been suggested are many and the calculation of their effect on personal incomes and on public finance is a highly complicated affair. Everybody would make a full return of income, and this figure would be used as an assessment both of the tax payable by those with incomes above the amount fixed as a tax threshold and for the cash supplements payable to those with incomes below it. Thus, if NIT is used for the relief of family poverty, tax allowances for children would have to be reinstated. It would then be possible to add up the amount of income which each family, according to the number, status and age of its members, is considered entitled to enjoy before it is called on, or can afford, to pay any income tax. The tax-free allowances, that is to say, represent an income deemed sufficient to meet the family's needs, and NIT offers an alternative to those allowances for those – the ever-diminishing number of those – who do not fully benefit from them because their income is too low to be taxable. But the tax threshold does not have to be the same as the poverty line (or guaranteed minimum); it can be substantially higher, on the grounds that a family should not be made liable to tax the moment it struggles out of poverty. So the crucial question to decide is to what level in relation to the threshold should incomes which are below it be raised by NIT. On this opinions have differed, with some saying about 30 per cent of the way up, others 100 per cent.[20]

There is a rather different approach to this problem which includes what is called the 'social dividend', and also the tax credit plan proposed by the Conservative government in 1972.[21] The social dividend method, instead of paying 'negative tax' as an addition to incomes below the tax threshold, makes a grant to all, free of tax, in the same way as child benefit, but universally. Taxation then falls heavily on all incomes other than this dividend. The grant would replace all the personal allowances now enjoyed by income-tax payers, and could be so adjusted as to replace as many of the cash benefits received through social assistance and flat-rate social insurance as the planners wished. The effect, as James Meade explains, would be that 'those who start with Earnings above the average will lose more in tax than they gain in Social Dividend and those with Earnings below the average will gain more in Social Dividend than they lose in tax', and no family's income would fall below whatever is set as the national minimum.[22] The Conservative tax credits represented a more modest version of the same idea. The scheme was intended to cover employed persons earning more than a given minimum and pensioners, but not the self-employed. All those covered would receive tax credits in respect of each member of the family: the figures suggested – which we cite purely to give an idea of the relativities chosen – were £4 for a single person, £6 for a married man and £2 for every child, irrespective of age. If tax due on the family income exceeded the credits given, the balance would be paid to the Inland Revenue, if credits exceeded the tax due, the balance would be paid to the taxpayer. The personal tax-free allowances would have disappeared, as would also family allowances and FIS. It was expected that the need for supplementary benefits would have been much reduced, although no claim was made that poverty would be abolished through the scheme. The principle was simple, but disagreements about the probable effects of the system were extensive and profound.

Negative income tax schemes, and their variations, went out of fashion in the early 1980s, but there are signs of a revival of interest in them, and it is not unlikely that at some stage something like the tax credit scheme – perhaps a bolder variant – will be adopted. An example of such a 'bolder variant' is the scheme recommended in the Institute of Fiscal Studies' report by Dilnot, Kay and Morris, which we referred to in Chapter 8. The IFS authors start by advocating the abolition of the contributory system. They then suggest that the principal social security benefits, both means-tested and non means-tested, and most tax allowances – relief on mortgage interest repayments being an exception, for reasons which are not fully explained – should be replaced by 'benefit credits' which would vary according to family circumstances. However, the proposals depart considerably from those of earlier schemes in that the suggested 'benefit credits' would be withdrawn from medium-income (and, of course, higher-income) families *entirely*: thus, 63 per cent of the households currently in receipt of child benefit would lose all their entitlement to child support. Dilnot, Kay and Morris note that the largest gains under their scheme would be made by single people and two-earner couples without children, but try to turn this into a kind of advantage with the observation that 'this is an unavoidable result of any policy which reduces social benefits in order to reduce taxation'.[23] Their proposals, too, would *increase* the marginal tax rates suffered by a substantial minority, especially the heads of large families. The authors are frank: 'Some sort of poverty trap is the price we unavoidably pay for guaranteeing households a minimum level of state support.'[24]

Dilnot, Kay and Morris, with their single-minded concentration on the goal of relieving sub-minimal poverty, at least remind us that there are hard choices to be made. There are drawbacks which affect all NIT-type schemes. They may, for example, be too objective, too standardized. There is always the old problem of the great variation in housing costs, which, in spite of the IFS authors' attempt to incorporate housing benefit into their scheme, would almost certainly mean that this major element in the family budget would have to be handled separately. More generally, any decision on the income required to satisfy the needs of a family which is applied uniformly throughout a whole category is a presumption about an average. It cannot be totally fair and, unless a very broad margin of safety is allowed, much of the unfairness will take the form of deprivation. A particular worry concerns the extent to which such a scheme would react sensitively to emergencies, and would meet the needs of those whose circumstances undergo frequent change. In spite of cumulative PAYE, the income-tax system works in good measure at least a year in arrears, and this will not do at all for the paying out of benefits. However, it should be possible to devise a scheme which will deliver at least *some* of the advantages so often cited in favour of 'big bang' or 'at a stroke' schemes of social security reform. These advantages may be listed as the following: that they integrate procedures for collecting and distributing income in such a way as to simplify administration and dispose of anomalies; that, since benefits do not have to be claimed, there is no problem of 'take-up' but everybody gets automatically what they are entitled to; that the only disclosure of means required is an ordinary income-tax return, which should not be humiliating; that the assessment of needs is objective and standardized, not discretionary; that it should be possible through such a scheme to provide a guaranteed minimum income which would virtually eliminate family poverty.

A scheme of the kind we have been discussing might provide the cash element in that 'infrastructure of universalist services' demanded by Titmuss, above and on the basis of which discrimination could take place. But not necessarily discrimination of the kind exercised in the award of supplementary benefits, which involves a penetrating inquiry into means, and a discretion which, even now that there are detailed published regulations, depends a lot on the personal judgement of the individual on the case. Titmuss saw the answer in 'categorical' services, provided as social rights 'on the criteria of the *needs* of specific categories, groups and territorial areas and not dependent on *individual tests of means*'.[25] Another possible development is suggested by an observation made by Barbara Rodgers about a trend she found in some countries to make use of 'an assistance scheme which emphasizes needs rather than means, and which attempts to meet the individual's needs with service as well as cash allowances'.[26] If the infrastructure looked after all major problems of income redistribution, it is not improbable that most of the unsatisfied cases would call for welfare services as well as cash assistance, which could be jointly dispensed without humiliating effect.

Here, however, a word of caution is necessary, one which takes us back to the beginning of this chapter, and indeed to the beginning of the book. Arrangements on these lines already exist, in a modest form. Under Section One of the Children and Young Persons Act 1963, social workers may make cash grants to clients in order to obviate the necessity of taking their children into care. As we noted in Chapter 10, Bill Jordan has harshly criticized these payments, partly because he believes that social services departments are more and more taking over functions that are properly the responsibility of the DHSS's local offices, but also because he fears that the controls inherent in the bestowal or denial of small helpings of public money are contaminating the relationship between social worker and client. Such arguments serve to pose a question – is it perhaps the case that the principles of 1834 did their work so well, were so deeply absorbed by the British people, that they still discolour all the services which descended from the Poor Law, and indeed the British welfare state more generally?

That there is something peculiar about British attitudes to poverty is indicated by the strength of the feeling against 'scroungers', which has erupted on several occasions, most recently during the late 1970s. It was shown, too, in the results of a survey carried out for the

Commission of the European Communities, and published in 1977.[27] Respondents from all nine member countries were shown cards on which four possible causes of poverty were listed and were asked which came closest to their own opinions. The French and the Italians were especially prone to blame the plight of the poor on the injustices prevalent in their societies, the Danes to see poverty as an inevitable concomitant of progress in the modern world, while the Irish, more frequently than others, opted for lack of luck. However, 43 per cent of the British respondents chose 'because of laziness and lack of will-power': this was well above the Irish proportion, nearly twice that found among the Germans, not far short of three times that of the French, and four times that of the Danes. And Peter Townsend's findings, though shorn of the comparative dimension, broadly concur. 'Among all sections of the (British) population', he notes, 'there was a tendency to adopt individualistic rather than institutional explanations of poverty.'[28] The attitudes of the poor did not differ much from those of the larger number who had never been poor. Some 38 per cent of them did not believe that 'real poverty' continued to exist: many of those who did recognize the persistence of the phenomenon attributed it to 'a mixture of ill-luck, indolence and mismanagement' and did not see it, as Professor Townsend thinks they should, as 'a collective condition determined principally by institutionalized forces, particularly government and industry'. The challenge for reformers is that survey results tend to suggest that 'relative poverty' is a construct which engages the attentions of academics but of few people otherwise, while poverty understood as destitution or subsistence strikes a ready chord of popular recognition, but is thought either to be no longer with us, or to affect mainly the undeserving.

In the 1980s the terms of debate have in any case tended to move against the povery campaigners. Positions long thought to be secured against attack now look in urgent need of refortification. This applies particularly to the indisputable achievement of the poverty lobby of the 1960s in winning acceptance for the view that supplementary benefit levels should be regarded as a state-sponsored minimum. This has been largely taken for granted for twenty years, and leading reformers would much prefer to go on taking it for granted, while pressing the case that a more accurately computed poverty line would entail more generous amounts of benefit. In a recent Fabian pamphlet Peter Townsend calculates that the SB allowance for a child under 11 years of age provides approximately 50p per day for food and drink. 'In 1984', he says, 'this would have covered the cost of a large loaf of bread, or one pork chop, or two twelve ounce tins of beans, or a fair-sized cabbage.'[29] He then goes on to observe that 'neither the Government nor DHSS officials ever attempt to defend the rates they pay by reasoned exposition of a low-budget plan'.

This is a well-taken point, although it invites the response that the obvious rational alternative to the present rather hit-and-miss methods of determining levels of benefit would be a basket of goods approach, under which each item in a notional poor household's budget is first costed separately, and then added together to arrive at an appropriate sum – and it is by no means certain that higher totals would thereby result. However, basket of goods approaches seem to be on no-one's current agenda, and the reason why it may be a dangerous stratagem at the present juncture for the poverty lobby to emphasize the arbitrary nature of levels of benefit is somewhat different. The government might welcome demonstrations that the amounts currently established have no particular intellectual validity, because they have increasingly come to see poverty as a residual in quite another argument, one concerned with the 'stickiness' of real wages. If, so this argument runs, wages could be forced down to market clearing levels, then Britain could emulate the United States, and absorb many of the unemployed in what the Chancellor, Nigel Lawson, has called the 'low-tech and no-tech' jobs of the private services sector. It is with this in mind that there has been an assault (at the time of writing a purely verbal one) on that pale shadow of minimum wage legislation in Britain, the Wages Council system. It may also explain the importance the government attaches to its plans to put out to tender ancillary services in the NHS (see Chapter 9), and more generally its desire to draw the teeth of militant, or just plain effective, trade unionism. However, if the low-paid are to make sacrifices for the greater good of others, the poverty line for those out of work needs to be reset, too, at new and lower levels.

This drift of thought is open to attack from the left as a whole, from neo-Keynesians of every stamp, from Tory paternalists, and from assorted sceptics, who note the contribution which deficit financing has made to the relative boom which the American economy has enjoyed in recent years. To moral objections may be added economic ones – it is doubtful if markets can be 'cleared' at any feasible levels of wages, and the spur to efficiency would be weakened if employers were let off pressures on the wages front. So opposition to the Treasury analysis runs both wide and deep, and the government has been cautious: the best evidence of a concerted effort to restructure both wages and benefits concerns the 16 to 18 age group. Here two programmes have had a major impact, the Manpower Services Commission's Youth Training Scheme (YTS) and the Young Worker's Scheme, catering in 1984 for 320,000 and 130,000 young people respectively. Both of these subsidize employers taking on 16 and 17 year olds who receive relatively low levels of allowance or remuneration – £25 a week in the case of the YTS, under £40 for those employed according to the terms of the Young Worker's Scheme. These sums need to be compared with the average earnings of around £60 enjoyed in early 1984 by the rather small number in the age group who had obtained unsubsidized jobs in the open market.[30] It is not surprising that the supply of apprenticeships has shrunk rapidly.

However, less has been done on the benefits side, although there has been some cutting back, both in supplementary benefit and in housing benefit for households containing earning children. The figures quoted above also require to be considered alongside the £16.50 (again in 1984) allowed for the unemployed under 18 year old school-leaver in supplementary benefit, and the nothing in cash payments given to those staying on at school or college to take traditional full-time courses. True, in the latter circumstances, *parents* continue to receive child benefit, and if their incomes are low enough may also be able to obtain small weekly sums from their local authority. But educational maintenance allowances, as these are called, are real poor relations of the social security system, being highly variable in amount and method of assessment; the Child Poverty Action Group found that they did not exist at all in the areas of five specially mean local education authorities in 1982.[31] There seems no obvious reason why young people should be deterred from remaining in full-time education, nor why those who stay on should not be judged as capable of looking after their money as those on government training schemes.

What this example illustrates is that there has to be some *extension* of benefits if the government's objective of a fairer and more coherent system is to be realized. At the time of writing, the whole matter is before the Review of Benefits for Children and Young People, one of the four major reviews of the social security system established by Mr Norman Fowler (see Chapter 8). The emphasis so far has been on 'withdrawing the ladders' rather than on 'scotching the snakes' which face young people, to employ *The Economist*'s phraseology.[32] This is a dilemma which is by no means confined to youth benefits. It does not seem to be very near resolution.

13 Problems and prospects of the 1980s

When the last edition of this book appeared, in 1975, it was possible to write of a basic agreement about the purposes and instruments of the welfare state. As was said then, and as we have noted in Chapters 7 and 8 of this edition, even where the political debate was most intense, as over pensions reform, the sound and the fury concealed the fact that much of the argument concerned details rather than fundamentals. True, the confident bipartisanship of the 1950s, the Butskell years, had given way to a much more anxious kind of consensus, one which prescribed the most comprehensive reorganization of the administrative apparatus of the social services for nearly thirty years. Nevertheless, the outlines of the post-war settlement, though more and more insistently questioned from a variety of standpoints, remained very much in place.

It would seem sensible to start with a consideration of the principal components of this settlement, and of the 'social democratic' consensus which guaranteed it, as they were at the time of its high point, in the 1950s and the early 1960s. It rested on three main pillars. First, there was the belief in the desirability and feasibility of continuous economic growth: governments, advised by Keynesian economists, could control the macro-economic aggregates, and could thereby help to provide for a steady increase in levels of living. Second, there was a largely unquestioned faith in the effectiveness and responsiveness of parliamentary democracy, roughly as developed by 1950. Alongside this went a system of central and local administration, which prided itself on its impartiality and incorruptibility, and whose self-assessment was very widely accepted. Both the parliamentary institutions and the administrative systems could be confidently packaged for export to a quarter of the globe. And, third, there was an acceptance of the necessity for high, and growing levels of public expenditure, particularly but by no means solely, on social welfare: such expenditures would help to dissolve social tensions, and were seen as supportive of, rather than contradictory to, the economic aims espoused by governments. Certainly, as we saw in Chapter 7, there were some heated disagreements about whether (and how) welfare spending could be held down to the relatively sluggish rates of growth of the British Gross Domestic Product. By and large, however, 'incremental statism', Raymond Plant's term for the sum of these three elements, reigned supreme.[1]

Eight years on from 1975, things seem very different. Indeed 1975 was itself a grim curtain raiser – a year in which industrial production fell in the United Kingdom, unemployment moved up to 4 per cent, and the inflation rate came very near to hitting the 25 per cent level.[2] The art or science of economics was thrown into disarray: the old verities, that high levels of inflation and unemployment could not co-exist, and that there was a ready comprehensible, and attainable, trade-off between the two, no longer seemed to hold water. If such a Phillips curve exists, then it is one which now prescribes what are historically very high totals of unemployment: between 1975 and 1984, while the year-on rates of price inflation fell from 24 per cent to under 5 per cent, unemployment rose from around 4 per cent to nearly 13 per cent (from 1.25 million to well over 3 million). Governments seemed to be rather like signalmen, who were no longer sure that trains would arrive on their line according to any timetable, and if they did appear had no confidence that slamming the levers would have any effect on the vehicles' speed or trajectory. There was increasing talk of 'overload', meaning that governments had taken responsibilities which they were not well fitted to perform, and that demands were being made upon them which they could not meet.[3] It became less easy to dismiss the dominant politicians, academics and men of business of the 1930s as men who failed to pursue perfectly obvious courses of action: indeed, in some areas, like measures to combat youth unemployment, there seems to have been almost a retreading of the steps of the actors of that period, the same plays with much the same dialogue. It is the prosperity of the two decades after the war which now appears mysterious. Confronted with the apparent failures of many confidently advocated nostrums – incomes policies, devaluation, 'breaks for growth', administrative restructuring, industrial modernization led from Whitehall – successive administrations embarked on courses of damage limitation, courses which we will try to trace shortly.

Failure and bewilderment have produced a marked revival in ideological modes of thinking. There has been, for example, a growth of a species of left-wing radicalism more penetrated by Marxist assumptions than ever before in Britain. However it would seem sensible to concentrate, for the moment, on developments to the right of the political centre, on the grounds that one should pay particular attention to the propositions of those who are in a position to dispose. The 1983 general election result put paid to two decades of shuttlecock politics, during which those who called an election, after having governed for a full term, invariably proceeded to lose it. Although the Conservative domination may be less securely grounded than at first appears – owing as it does so much to the electoral system and to the stark divisions among the party's opponents – nevertheless conventional psephological wisdom would suggest that their majority is unlikely to be shifted in fewer than two elections. Thus it is of obvious importance that a large section of the Conservative Party, including most of the current leadership, has been captured by a latter-day economic liberalism which has intellectual affinities with the public choice school in the United States. There has been a proliferation of right-wing research and propaganda units, the Adam Smith Institute, the Centre for Policy Studies, the Social Affairs Unit, set up to promulgate the newly fashionable doctrines. The most august of them, the Institute of Economic Affairs was, when sparring partner of Richard Titmuss in the controversies of the late 1950s and early 1960s, widely thought of as slightly ridiculous, or at least to be seated below the salt: it has now attained academic respectability and political influence.

The New Right has employed arguments like the following: that the state is increasingly led to do things which, although perhaps good in themselves, could be more efficiently done in other ways; that its undertakings are often extravagant and wasteful for reasons which are inherent in the nature of public action; that public employees, including the most senior of them, are as self-interested as any other groups of economic actors and see this self-interest as being best advanced through the inflation of their programme budgets; that the goods and services known as 'welfare' are no different in principle from any other bundle of goods and services; that the market is a more sensitive register of preferences than are elections, and that politicians habitually and cynically stoke up demand for publicly provided services in order to win the latter; that bureaucracy flourishes where it is least appropriate; and that government policy shows signs of lacking a consistent system of values, without which it cannot clearly define its responsibilities, and that this is a natural result of the great range and complexity of its interests. Running through many of these postulates is the belief that social policies are no more than a sub-set of economic policies, and certainly in times of economic and financial stress the lines of demarcation between the two, so carefully delineated by Richard Titmuss a generation ago, no longer seem as clear-cut or as persuasive. Thus what Bleddyn Davies has termed the 'enclave' theory of social administration has undeniably lost power.[4] This is the view which presents the welfare state as a walled garden, where, sheltered from the buffeting winds of the economic market, fruits can be grown of a kind and a quality unattainable if the plants had to take their chances among the weeds outside. The principal ideologists of the social democracy of the 1950s and 1960s paid rather little attention to the problem of production: both Crosland and Titmuss, the former more explicitly than the latter, saw it as having been essentially solved, and believed that the pressing questions concerned the distribution of the surplus which had been generated.[5] It is worth noting, in passing, that some of the organisms which have led to the decomposition of social policy as a clearly defined separate entity were present even in the social democratic formulation, because of the emphasis upon distribution. This was illustrated by the brief popularity of the phrase 'the social wage' in the mid 1970s, as the government sought to persuade trade unions and other citizens to moderate their wage demands and to pay their taxes willingly. If the provision of services and benefits in kind was to be treated as a form of income like any other, then at the very least questions were being implicitly raised about how people would prefer to receive this extra income.

How can we, then, distinguish the aims of social policy from those of other areas of public policy? There are many possible ways of going about this task, but the most helpful classification for our present purposes is that which distinguishes three types, which we may call the elimination of poverty, the maximization of welfare and the pursuit of equality. The first is the most limited of the three and concentrates on the lowest socio-economic stratum of society: in the case of services, other than those concerned with income maintenance, the adjective 'residual' is often employed to describe them. The second is much broader, being concerned with the welfare of all, not only of the poor, with the objective of achieving an optimum rather than a minimum. The third is the translation into action of a political philosophy whose implications, if pressed to the hilt, are very far-reaching indeed. The three aims are not mutually exclusive: in the period immediately after the Second World War, policy pursued the first of these aims in its social security measures, and the second in health and welfare, while believing that in doing so it was making some progress towards the third. In the 1960s and early 1970s, the middle objective became dominant in nearly all areas of provision, and this may still be the case today, although that is a matter for later discussion.

In all these approaches need is a key concept. This is a word which some economists and philosphers have wished to see banished from the lexicon, on the grounds that a 'need' is merely a demand which has been elevated to a special status for persuasive or tendentious purposes.[6] In one sense, such critics are wrong, since needs may not be expressed as 'demands', and indeed may not be felt by those who are held to possess them:[7] thus, if an old lady lives in squalid conditions without modern amenities like running hot water, it makes perfect sense to say that she is in need of a change in her environment, even though all the problems of paternalistic government are raised if someone is sent in to clean the place up, or she is rehoused against her will, or is forcibly removed to an old people's home. On the other hand, the 'anti-needologists' are quite correct in their perception that the determination of need involves a process of licensing some wants and refusing to license others. Accredited licensers in the field of social policy include Parliament, local authorities and professionals working in particular services. All will be influenced, to a greater or lesser extent, by political pressures, by social approval or disapproval, and by values deeply held in our society. The ensuing hierarchies in which they arrange needs are unlikely to be entirely morally coherent, although they will be considerably more so than the patterns thrown up by that other licenser of some wants and refuser of others, the economic market.

It should be noted that these processes occur quite as much in the setting of minima (the meeting of need) as in the setting of maxima (the meeting of needs). However, there are some free market economists who would allow that the guaranteeing of subsistence levels is an appropriate, indeed a necessary, function of the state, while believing that governments have no right to go beyond that point; it is not easy to see why, on their own premises, they permit such kind-heartedness in cases where the destitution in question arises out of a failure to insure or to save.[8] Need, as Alan Williams has noted, is a very hard concept to exorcise;[9] it has a habit of breaking through the back door after having been thrown out at the front.

When we say that the aim of a policy is to maximize welfare, or anything else, we mean that it is trying to do the best it can for all concerned with limited and inadequate resources. Its most fundamental task, in such circumstances, is to establish a system of priorities, on the basis of which it can balance competing claims among programmes. Battles over priorities are, however, far from being a matter internal to social policy. Social welfare expenditures have to be weighed against other demands on the public purse, and more fundamentally still, public expenditure as a whole has to be considered in relation to all the claims upon resources generated in the economy. The latter has become very much a mater of controversy in the past decade or so, and this was heightened by the electoral victory of a Conservative Party with decided views on the matter. The first words of the first White Paper on its future spending plans published by the incoming Conservative government (November 1979) proclaimed that 'public expenditure is at the heart of Britain's economic difficulties'.[10]

However, the cutbacks set in motion in 1979/80 were only episodes in a story which dated back several years. It would therefore be unwise to presume that they were the consequences of the implementation of something called 'Thatcherism'. It was the previous Labour government which introduced cash limits in 1976, and Tony Crosland, a man who, as his widow says, 'believed high public expenditure was morally right',[11] who popularized the phrase 'the party's over'.

There were two main reasons for the Labour government's retreat from positions it had previously occupied. The first was the experiences of its first year in office. In addition to the horrific inflation rate which we have already noted, there was the fact that in 1975 public expenditure amounted to 57.9 per cent of the Gross National Product. Roy Jenkins joined with Milton Friedman to proclaim that this was very near the upper limit compatible with the maintenance of a mixed economy and democratic institutions. In fact, the figure was highly suspect. Not only did it rest on certain accounting conventions about what was included in public expenditure – so that this expenditure could be cut 'at a stroke' when these conventions were revised, as they were shortly afterwards – but it also involved a substantial element of double counting, since it included transfer payments, which do not use up real resources in competition with the private sector, but simply recirculate incomes which have already been generated in the economy. As Alt and Chrystal say in their recent text-book of political economy, 'percentages are meaningless if they are not constrained to add up to 100 per cent when the motion is implicitly one of sharing a cake'.[12] However, the government was not deflected by such arguments from its concentration on the totals taken into its coffers, even if they were to be paid out that very same day. Admittedly, this was as much for political as for strictly economic reasons. Government spending has to be financed through taxation or borrowing. It was believed that the taxpayer was already near the upper limits of what he could be parted from without turning unpleasant, while more and more borrowing, at very high rates of interest, would not only feed inflation, but would also involve the creation of a heavy and continuing burden of debt, which would become relatively all the greater if the government succeeded in its aim of eventually bringing inflation down.

The second reason for the government's change of course was more directly concerned with the performance of British industry. The leaders of all the main political parties were much impressed by the 'crowding out' hypothesis, especially in its influential popular formulation by Bacon and Eltis.[13] These authors made a distinction between 'marketed' and 'non-marketed' goods and services and asserted that the latter lived off the former. From this it was easy to move to the conclusion that public spending was parasitical or at least a luxury to be considered once the staples had been paid for – a strange reversal of an orthodoxy of the 1960s which claimed that social investment, especially in education, was the X-ingredient which held the key to economic prosperity. There was much loose talk to the effect that the growth in public spending had to be curbed, if 'room' was to be created for the task of preserving and adding to 'real' jobs in 'productive' industry. Such language made for confusion between how something was paid for (i.e. money over the counter, or through rates and taxes) and its economic value, and for an even more serious confusion between the latter and the moral worth of the activity in question.

The Labour government, chaperoned by the International Monetary Fund, was quite successful in containing and restraining public expenditure. If one uses the same kind of indicator as we criticized earlier, but simply as a rough measure, public spending was brought down from 46.3 per cent of GDP, at market prices, in 1974/5 to 42.5 per cent in 1978/9. The advent of a Conservative government which, unlike its predecessor, marched forward to battle with gusto, might have been expected to have a substantial additional impact: the new administration believed that tax cuts were good in themselves, releasing pent-up energies which would be directed towards wealth-creation, espoused a monetarist philosophy in which the Public Sector Borrowing Requirement was a key economic indicator, and dreamed of 'rolling back the frontiers of the State'. So it was no surprise that the incoming cabinet rejected the plans which Labour had bequeathed – the previous government's final Public Expenditure White Paper (Cmnd 7439, January 1979) had provided for a resumption of the upward march of public spending – and continued Labour's practice of squeezing where it could.

It is therefore ironic that the out-turn so far has borne more resemblance to the Labour government's aborted plans than to the Conservative's own more restrictive ones. Public expenditure in 1983–4 was back to more than 44 per cent of GDP. This reflected the poor performance of the economy and the continuing costs of the recession, but is striking none the less. Not only has social security spending grown sharply in response to the increase in the numbers of the unemployed and pensioners, as one would have expected, but the NHS and the personal services have grown, too, in volume terms. As we saw in earlier chapters, there is some doubt about whether these increases will have been sufficient to take full account of changes in client population, but there seems to be little substance as yet in the charge that the vital organs of these services have been affected, at least in most of the country and in most areas of provision. And where there have been volume cuts, they have usually been decremental – that is, a little has been taken off each year, a process which is easily reversible if the will to expand should reassert itself.[14] Thus, education spending has clearly declined, but not in line with the fall in school rolls.

True, there have been some quantum cuts, meaning the excision or severe attenuation of whole programmes or areas of service. Earnings-related short-term national insurance benefits have gone completely, and school meals have become in many parts of the country a shadow of their former self, because local education authorities are now obliged to provide them for those children eligible for free meals only. In both these instances, however, there are some special circumstances: in the former case, one has to take account of the government's anxiety about the 'replacement ratios' of those out of work (see Chapter 12), while meals were regarded as a core area of the education service by neither the majority of teachers nor the Department of Education and Science. Perhaps the most obvious candidate to be considered a service which is being deliberately residualized is council housing, both through the sales policy and because it is expected that public expenditure on housing will have fallen by a staggering 70 per cent between 1978/9 and 1984/5.[15] The seeds of this assault on public housing were sown, it might be suggested, in the 1960s with the hubris of certain architects and the growth of doubts about the quality and responsiveness of housing management. However, even this is not as simple as it appears. Not only is there room for differing interpretations of the significance of the fall in the council sector owing to sales – about 8 per cent of local authority and New Town owned dwellings in the UK were sold off between 1979 and 1983, and this has to be set against the admittedly scanty total of addition to stock – but also the housing budget has always been peculiar in that a very high proportion of it is expended in the form of capital payments. And in all areas of public spending, it is expenditure on the capital account which has suffered the most to date. Indeed, capital cuts are the perfect example of 'soft' cuts, along with those made in budgets for the maintenance of buildings. Future projects have, by definition, no material existence, and it is always easier to axe them than to cut into established programmes, staffed as they are by protesting employees and serving protesting consumers. The costs of reductions in the capital programme are mainly borne by the private sector construction industry – which is not a result which a Conservative government might have been expected to welcome. Furthermore, in 1980–1 capital expenditure fell so far that it was actually less than the Public Sector Borrowing Requirement; in other words, the government was borrowing to finance its pay bill and its social security obligations. This also was not a course which one would have expected that a financially prudent Conservative administration would have followed.

On the whole the evidence seems compatible with what Alt and Chrystal term a 'permanent income model' of public expenditure.[16] Such models suggest that government budgets are pretty insensitive to ideological inputs – the political preferences or prejudices of particular administrations – but respond to demographic changes (whether an increase in old people or to a decline in schoolchildren) and to alterations in the external context in which national economies have to operate. In recent years, the most important of the latter were, first, the breakdown of the Bretton Woods agreement in the late 1960s and the move to floating exchange rates (only thereafter could the principal Western European economies allow themselves the luxury of home-generated inflation, instead of having to keep in line with American experience); and, second, the energy crisis of 1973, when the OPEC countries imposed what was in effect a heavy tax levy upon all other national economies. Alt and Chrystal suggest that for a time after 1973 'government expenditure continued to grow until it was clear that the income losses would be sustained'.[17] Then, in 1976–8 the brakes were slammed on, and levels of public expenditure were readjusted to the new levels of GDP. The plateau then arrived at has since been broadly maintained, they suggest.

Such an interpretation of the trends and outcomes of the past decade rests on the empirical generalization that the inertia commitments of governments are such that it requires the impact of something very heavy indeed to stop the machine from steadily coasting along (or for that matter to lift it up to new and higher levels of expenditure: wars have fulfilled this function during the twentieth century). It says little about the strategies followed by the present government (which are puzzling) and nothing about its current intentions (which are unclear). At the time of writing, doubts about the latter have been heightened by conflicting interpretations of the administration's policies and attitudes towards the National Health Service. On the face of it, the government is committed to maintaining the NHS as the optimum-aiming and sometimes optimum-achieving service which it has been since 1948; some very explicit and much publicized pledges to this effect were made by Mrs Thatcher and her close associates during the 1983 election campaign. However, the election was soon followed by a Circular (HC(83)16) demanding, in the middle of a financial year, that health regions meet precise manpower targets by the end of it – all the prescribed totals represented cutbacks either in planned (and partly achieved) growth since April 1983, or to levels below those prevailing at that time. The government maintained that this intervention was necessary because health authorities had lost their grip of their own manpower, but no evidence was adduced to support this claim, unless the growth in the total number of NHS employees of about 50,000 from 1979 to 1983 should itself be taken to constitute such evidence. Moreover, there was no explanation of why cash limits (including enforced 'efficiency savings') had to be supplemented in this apparently arbitrary way.

Consider further these facts. First, one thing which has *not* been deflated under the present administration is the propensity to prepare and pass through Parliament hefty pieces of legislation, stuffed full of clauses imposing new duties upon local authorities and others, laying down detailed procedures which have to be gone through, and so on.

Most of these acts are largely uncontroversial in party political terms – indeed, they often fit squarely into the old-time liberal consensus. Recent examples in the social policy field would include the Education Act 1981, which passed into law some of the chief proposals of the Warnock Report on special education; the Criminal Justice Act 1982, which made substantial changes to the provisions relating to the sentencing of young offenders, including the abolition of most sentences of imprisonment for those under 21; and the Mental Health Act, 1983, which in broad terms has reinforced the rights of the mentally disordered and obliges social services departments to ensure that the social workers who exercise responsibilities under the legislation have been specially trained for the task. The important point to note here is that all these measures will be expensive to implement, but the government has made no extra funds available for the purpose.

Second, again in relation to local authorities, the government has devised an amazing variety of mechanisms for controlling their expenditure. First, there is the GREA (Grant Related Expenditure Assessment) system, under which the government calculates, by formula, how much it thinks each local authority ought to spend in order to provide a common level of service. Rather less rational has been a series of 'targets', essentially historically based, as they depend on how much expenditure has risen since an arbitrarily selected base-year, 1978–9, just before the Conservatives took office. Then there is the manpower watch, designed to monitor the progress of local authorities in achieving staff numbers which the government believes to be appropriate. Furthermore, controls over capital differ from those over current expenditure, and, though both have been steadily tightened, the situation remains that local authorities may be unwilling to spend on permitted capital projects because of fears of the 'revenue consequences' of such expenditure, and if they do go ahead may have to mothball the much needed new facilities because they are unable to staff them. This apparent idiocy may also affect health authorities, and, as we have seen, the government has embarked on the melancholy progression of setting up a battery of separate kinds of control, which may very well conflict one with another, in relation to them, too.

We may also note that Whitehall no longer seems interested in what it buys with its money, in respect of personnel, equipment, and so on, since the old system of making calculations for grant purposes in volume terms has been superseded: cash alone now counts, with no arrangements for mid-year or retrospective adjustments to take account of unanticipated rises in real costs. And even this is not quite all the story as the government's legislation to abolish the Greater London Council and the six English metropolitan counties bears witness. Many of the powers of these authorities will be transferred to centrally appointed or indirectly elected *ad hoc* boards. The administration has also armed itself, in the Secretary of State for the Environment's words, 'with a general power, to be used if necessary, for the limitation of rate increases for all authorities'. This 'rate-capping', as it is called, means that English and Welsh local authorities are for the first time losing their right to determine their own rate poundages. This path has already been trodden in Scotland: in 1981/2, the Scottish Office took action against seven 'high-spending' local authorities under the Local Government (Miscellaneous Provisions) (Scotland) Act 1981. Subsequent academic investigation has failed to reveal any consistent criteria underlying the choice of villains, or victims: an alternative 'hit-list' could easily have been drawn up.[18]

Possibly this twisting record suggests no more than that elaborate strategies are necessary to curb the spenders. However, in addition to the desire to reduce the overall share of public expenditure in the national economy, one should note three other commitments of the present government which were either contained in the 1979 election manifesto, or have been developed since, presumably in response to experience. These were, first, the strengthening of certain traditional functions of the state, such as law and order; second, the contraction of the sphere of public administration in some other respects – these were vague at first, but have since been filled out with the help of the doctrine of 'privatization'; and, third, the encouragement of decentralized decision-making, through the freeing of local government from 'unnecessary' controls, or economic enterprise from 'unnecessary' regulation. Together these could add up to a plausible intellectual position, one which has been dignified with the title 'central autonomy'.[19] This asserts that a strong government is one which would deny the claim of powerful interest groups to partnership in the determination of policy, and which would use its powers to curb the ability of these groups, and also of subordinate assemblies like local authorities, to act in ways which would be detrimental to the liberties of citizens. Also, such a government does not dissipate its energies, but sticks to what experience has shown it does best. The implementation of a programme based on this philosophy would require the maintenance of a most careful balance between centralizing and decentralizing tendencies, and perhaps it is not surprising that the Conservative attempt to do so has toppled over in the direction of centralization. There has always been something of a paradox in the postulate that one can use the institutions of the state to contract the state.

An alternative interpretation of recent events would flatter the government somewhat less, as it would suggest that what we have been seeing is a prolonged exercise in the spreading of blame: the British economy – except for the rate of inflation – has failed to respond sufficiently to the medicines which have been administered, so both responsibilities and problems have been exported from the central government to local authorities, private companies, voluntary organizations or individuals. According to this way of looking at things, the line between the public and the private loses some of its significance. 'Privatization' becomes not only a way of providing opportunities for profit, but also a matter of the transfer of costs and risks.

However, there are some difficulties with this view. First, even where the cost-cutting ambitions of the government are overt, the execution of the policy may produce a different outcome: we saw in Chapter 8 how the savings envisaged in employers' assumption of responsibility for short-term sickness benefits failed to materialize. Second, it fits rather badly with the complaint that the government has been bent on concentrating power in its own hands rather than trying to disperse it. In fact, there seem to be few relevant examples in the social services, and those there are often involve complex transfers. An instructive example is the decision in 1980 to permit supplementary benefit moneys to be more freely used than before to pay the board and lodging charges in residential rest homes and fees in private nursing homes. This represented a shift from cash-limited local authority expenditure on old people's homes and domiciliary services like home help, to non cash-limited, 'demand-led' central government expenditure. The result was that rest homes mushroomed, and the bill borne by the public purse escalated even faster, especially after the establishment of maximum local limits in 1983; these soon became regarded by proprietors as minimum levels and they raised their charges accordingly.[20] These charges bore no relation to the quality of the accommodation and service provided, and illustrate the logical and empirical point that, contrary to the view which government spokesmen have sometimes expressed, 'privatization' *increases* the need for regulation by public authorities.[21]

All this discussion of financial stringency and the effects of Conservative political domination may seem incredibly remote from the third of the aims of social policy which we distinguished earlier, the pursuit of equality. On the face of it, the gulf between this and the first aim we outlined, the establishment of minimum levels of provision, seems to be so wide as to be practically unbridgeable – and certainly those who urge that the state should restrict itself to the relief of poverty are invariably vociferous assailants of 'egalitarianism'. However, there is a rather obvious conceptual confusion here. Everything depends on where the lines are drawn. As we saw in Chapter 7, the success of the poverty campaigners of the 1960s – such as it was – was due to the acceptance of their argument that the poverty line has been set too low, thus paving the way for a modest and temporary reduction in the gap between the incomes of those dependent on state benefits and average earnings. There is actually no reason why equality could not be achieved by holding everyone down to minimum levels – puritanical communist regimes like that of Albania aim for just this. If one turns from income maintenance to other services, one comes to another set of arguments of the 1960s, those concerned with 'territorial justice'. The essence of this is the belief that the quantity and quality of service provided should not differ according to a presumed arbitrary factor, those of where people happen to live. In the past, the assumption has always been that any levelling would be upwards, not downwards. However, generous social arrangements are not the same as equal ones. Those who aim for the establishment of optimal public welfare services, but who also value diversity and local autonomy, may perhaps sometimes be too eager to pin on themselves the label of 'egalitarian'. One should always ask exactly what it is that it is hoped to equalize, and at what level.

The relation between the maximalization of welfare and the pursuit of equality is thus a subtle one. At times they appear to come into direct conflict with one another. One familiar example of this is to be found outside our subject area, in education. It is the mutual recrimination between those who favour selection and streaming and those who want comprehensive schools and mixed ability classes. The former accuse the latter of sacrificing educational potential to their egalitarian faith, and of pursuing the goal of equality by levelling down. Rather similar is the contention that to forbid specialists serving in the NHS to engage in part-time in private practice would be to give effect to egalitarian principles without sufficiently exploring the consequences for the efficiency of the service. In Chapter 9, we argued that the Utilitarian test of aggregate utility was appropriate in considering such controversies; that is to say, one should judge developments according to whether they lead to an increase in the total supply of the scarce resources of medical care, or whether they simply redistribute, almost certainly in the direction of inequality, those resources which have already been created.

It might appear that we have in the NHS itself the perfect example of a policy in which welfare and equality are successfully and harmoniously adopted as the twin aims of the enterprise. Here the optimum is relatively easily defined – it depends on the state of medical knowledge, of clinical and nursing techniques, and of good practice generally, as professionally approved at any particular point in time. And it is perfectly true that the health of all is the target, and the principle that like cases should be treated alike is the rule of action. But this is only one kind of equality. It was the free services in health, education and welfare that Abel-Smith had in mind when he declared that 'the main effect of the post-war development of the social services, the creation of the "Welfare State", has been to provide free social services to the middle classes'.[22] It is perfectly true that the universal free health service did not enlarge the disposable income of those who had a free service already (by national health insurance) while it did enlarge that of the middle classes, by reducing their medical expenses, and thus increased inequality in one sense. Critics on the left can also point to the continuing disparities in health status – discussed in Chapter 9 – and to the greater ability of the middle classes to get what they want out of the NHS.[23] However, the latter phenomenon affects all universalistic services, and it would be fairer to say that the coming of the NHS led to a major improvement in the quality of the service, especially for the working classes, and to the creation of an area of general experience in which the treatment received was unaffected by class distinctions, both in principle and to a considerable extent in practice. There remains something special about the NHS, according to popular sentiment and in reality. The goal is the optimum satisfaction of needs: all operations undertaken in pursuit of this goal must be governed by the principle of fairness; the reduction of inequality is an expected consequence of this and is always present, just round the corner, ready to break in as a positive motive.

The positive as regards money benefits, including social insurance, is rather different. Titmuss has suggested that in analysing the areas of social policy in this area use could be made of the distinction between 'adequacy' and 'equity' as the criteria on which decisions may be based.[24] Adequacy refers to what is required to satisfy measured needs: the word tends to obliterate the distinction between the minimum and the optimum which we have been careful to establish, but will serve as a handy term for all assessments of requirements which pay attention only to situations existing at particular points in time, and which regard the circumstances which give rise to the dependency as irrelevant. Equity, however, implies conformity with a principle of justice and all such principles are essentially backward-looking, basing current treatment on the previously acquired characteristics or the previous actions of those whose cases are under consideration. Thus the award given to a man who has lost a leg has varied according to whether he lost it fighting for his country, in an industrial accident, as a result of a criminal assault upon him or by falling downstairs at home. These distinctions have been held to be equitable, though the need to be satisfied is the same. Indeed, the need is the same if a man's limb has to be removed because of injuries received while seeking to evade arrest after he has been caught committing an armed robbery. Differential treatment applies to dependents, too. Margaret Wynn pointed out in the early 1960s that the benefit awarded for a fatherless child depended on the status of the mother (widowed, divorced, or deserted) and of the child (legitimate or illegitimate) and if the father was dead, whether he had died of an illness, was killed in an industrial accident or fell in battle.[25] The differences arose because these individuals had been assigned to different categories, presumably on grounds of alleged equity. It has often been suggested that these disparities have been allowed to remain through inadvertence and the difficulty and expense involved in trying to iron out the categories; they are, this view continues, unfairnesses to be rectified by giving proper weight to the principle of adequacy. If this is so, they are remarkably long-lasting oversights – nearly all of the apparent anomalies which Mrs Wynn charted two decades ago still remain in place today. This suggests that there is something deeper at stake here, like considerations of relative desert. Indeed, the recent tendency has been to multiply categories of this kind rather than to replace then with a scheme which would treat all similar needs alike.

Social insurance raises some subtle questions. Why, we may well ask, including those that devised the Crossman and the Castle Plans, think it proper to incorporate into their arrangements for social insurance systems which reflect, if only up to a limiting ceiling, the inequalities of income created in the economic market? (This has indeed become the characteristic version of the optimum in this area of social policy). One answer relies on equity. It points to three features of these schemes. There is a contractual element in them, since those who receive larger benefits pay larger contributions; there is an element of merit in them, since they take account only of income earned by the labours of the insured; and they often include some measure of income redistribution from richer to poorer, which may be seen either as the only practicable way of making the awards to lower earners adequate, or as a way of somewhat reducing the general inequality of incomes in the society on grounds of equity – or both. But another approach is possible, which argues that needs vary in relation to income, and that unequal benefits are provided for the satisfaction of unequal needs. This can be expressed by saying that if a man's pension falls below a certain proportion of his pre-retirement income, he suffers hardship, because real needs, developed during his more prosperous years, cannot be met. This same entanglement of adequacy with equity also haunts and perpetually bedevils attempts to work out an incomes policy for salaries and wages. It reveals itself when (and this happens) a professional man says, in the same breath, 'I find it impossible to live on £20,000 a year' and 'this is a miserable sum in view of my long training and the vital importance of my services.'

It may be added in parenthesis, that if the concept of need is allowed to become as subjective as this, reflecting the personal reactions of individuals to their circumstances rather than a generalized evaluation of typical and relevant experience, we soon find ourselves involved with the much abused concept of 'relative deprivation'. It was invented for the study of the reaction of American soldiers to the deprivations of war service; it has been twisted into a term to express the view (as one American writer puts it) that 'needs stem not so much from what we have as from what our neighbours have'.[26] It may be that social policy should pay attention to expressions of this kind of subjective need as an aid to the discovery of effects of inequality which are obstacles in the way of the welfare that it is trying to maximize. But to do more than this would be to risk losing sight of its chosen goal. The question of the inequality of incomes in society at large raises issues far beyond the scope of social policy as generally understood.

This discussion is not of purely academic interest: it has a direct bearing on the problem of how to establish and implement a *right* to welfare. Rights in the full sense of the word can be attached only to categories of persons (citizens, wives, employees) or of circumstances (unemployment, invalidity, defamation). The members of a category, especially a broad one, are never a wholly homogenous group. When, as normally in a court of law, the claimant's right is first established, and the damages are then assessed by act of judicial discretion, the heterogeneity does not matter. But when, as in social security, a right is conceived as determining both the entitlement to be paid and the amount due, then, in a broad category, only very rough justice can be done. In the article we quoted earlier, Titmuss declared that in some countries attempts to satisfy more exactly the entangled criteria of adequacy and equity by splitting up and refining the categories risked becoming self-defeating. In the first place the tests to which a person had to submit in order to establish his membership of a particular category might turn out to be indistinguishable from, or at least as troublesome as, a means test. He instanced 'income-conditioned entitlement tests within "as-of-right" programmes'.[27] This was rather laconically expressed, but some of the new benefits for the disabled introduced in the past decade or so and discussed in Chapter 8, fit the description admirably. Second, the more complex and precise the system of rules and regulations defining the rights, the more sure they are, at some points, to curtail rather than enlarge the services available. The function of all boundaries is to shut out as well as to let in. Here again events since Titmuss's death prove his prescience. The new supplementary benefit scheme introduced in 1980, with its sheaves of detailed regulations incorporated in statutory instruments laid before Parliament, has probably reduced the scope of creative discretion rather more than that of punitive discretion.

It is not being suggested here that attempts to establish rights to welfare are misguided or doomed to failure; far from it. The point being made is a double one: that rights are not as absolute as some people think. They are fenced in by qualifying conditions – tests of sickness, unemployment, retirement, age, income and so on. And discretionary awards are not left to the mercy of human caprice, but are governed by principles which may be as powerful as the rules which govern the administration of rights. In the case of both types of service the spirit in which they are administered may well be more important than the form in which they are described. One may still well ask whether it makes sense to talk of a 'right to welfare' when discretion enters into the making of any part of an award. It is argued here that it can, if three conditions are satisfied, and that if they are not no social rights can be really safe. These three conditions are: first, that the basic principles and aims of the social policy of a country are understood and accepted by the great majority of its citizens, and progressively absorbed into their culture; second, that the agents who carry out the policy are trained and equipped to accept and to discharge the responsibility which falls on all members of the personal service professions of translating these principles and aims into action in individual cases: third, that all claimants for benefit or service know, or can easily find out, what their rights are in each particular case and are able, by themselves or with the help that is made available, to present and press their claims on those who have the powers to meet them. We need to consider these conditions in turn.

Throughout the 1950s and 1960 supporters of the welfare state convinced themselves that the first condition was either already realized, or was in the process of being realized – there might be a few residues, survival of attitudes of the Poor Law era, but these affected mainly the elderly and would disappear or at least greatly diminish with the passing of time. Events of the late 1970s – such as the outbreak of 'scroungerphobia' or the results of the EEC survey of attitudes to poverty discussed in the last chapter – indicated the continuing strength of some fiercely individualistic assumptions among at least a substantial minority of the British population, and led many advocates of high levels of welfare spending to the reluctant conclusion that they were less in step with their fellow citizens than they had supposed. This alarm tended to be reinforced by the answers given to a standard set of opinion poll questions: in May 1979, at the time of Mrs Thatcher's first victory, equal numbers of Gallup's respondents said that they would prefer tax cuts, even if they meant some reduction in welfare services, as favoured the extension of welfare services, even if this meant some increase in taxes – about 37 per cent of the voters surveyed chose each of these alternatives. However, opinions in this area are not very stable. A more recent Gallup poll posing these questions (March 1983) found over twice as many opting for more welfare spending as for tax cuts.[28] It seems that, just as the demand for social expenditure, which helped to boost Labour in the early 1960s, was largely satisfied after 1964, so the appetite for reductions in taxation which aided the Conservatives in 1979 was sated soon afterwards. This is all the more remarkable, since the tax cuts never actually materialized, except for a minority of the more affluent.

The second condition is a matter of the extent to which those who work in the social services have the well-being and interests of their patients, clients and customers as their paramount concern. In other words, it depends on how far they have ingested the principles of disinterested service – the Victorian nature of this concept is indicated by the fact that even the mightiest in the land, like leader-writers in the quality newspapers, no longer seem to appreciate the correct meaning of the word 'disinterested'. Success in the fulfilment of this condition depends quite largely on maintaining the status and the power of the 'free' professions *vis-à-vis* the bureaucracy. Good professional practice requires a mixture of detachment and personal involvement which is unusual among relationships, and hence there is always a strong emphasis upon training. However, professionalism in the welfare services, like so many other concepts, faces in two directions at once. The other face may be experienced by the victims of bungled routine operations, where the intervention of medical protection agencies may impose a wall of silence. Some of the mental hospital scandals, too, which we discussed in Chapter 9, have concerned the introduction of eccentric clinical regimes – the inquiries into events at the Napsbury and South Ockendon hospitals will serve as examples – and the NHS seems to be singularly poor at meeting this particular challenge.[29] Occasionally, therefore, the interests of clients or patients may be better protected by strengthening the bureaucracy *vis-à-vis* the 'free' professions. It is usually the other way around, but not always, so it is not possible to offer any confident, generalized, policy prescription.

The situation in services which employ very few professionals of any kind, like social security, is rather different. There the obligation to provide courteous, fair and humane treatment can only be discharged by means of controls exercised through managerial hierarchies. It is a common observation that the higher one goes in these hierarchies, the more likely one is to encounter an open-minded and non-punitive approach. However, there are clear limits set to the generosity of those who work in such services, managers and managed alike, by the requirement to protect public money, while state-employed professionals, too, have obligations to their employing authorities as well as to their clients. Recent events have tended to strengthen the position of the financial controllers relative to such professionals – indeed, one development has been the way in which formerly untouchable groups like hospital consultants have reluctantly had to turn themselves into second-order financial controllers. Their resentment at their enforced complicity in the provision of services which they may well regard as sub-optimal is creating a most powerful set of pressures against further restrictions of public expenditure. However, once again, it should not be presumed that cash-limiting is never in the interests of clients – geriatric and psychiatric patients probably will only be able to exercise their right to a good level of service if the appetite of consultants in the more prestigious specialities for expensive equipment and pharmaceutical preparations is restrained. Furthermore, it is instructive to look at those areas of public administration which have so far avoided cash limitation: it would be a salutary experience for judges and magistrates if they had to compute the public expenditure costs of the sentences they handed out, and the freedom of general practitioners to prescribe may have benefited the drug companies rather more than the doctors' patients.

In spite of all these difficulties, it is the third condition which is the most troublesome. In an interesting and challenging book, *Social Theory and Social Policy* (1971), Robert Pinker has argued that 'in all industrial societies . . . citizenship is a range of skills rather than a status transmitted from generation to generation'.[30] The rights of citizenship are a reality only for those who have a belief in their authenticity and the skills needed to exercise them, and this belief and these skills are developed through experience and socialization in the context of a class society. Consequently, to make a claim for a social service as of right can seem to some a mark of status and to others a brand of inferiority. This is one way of describing what is in fact the chief barrier to the fulfilment of the third condition listed above. It is created not only by the stigma or sense of shame attached to any request for aid, but also by dislike of being involved with officials, fear of not being able to restrain angry reactions if one's appeal is rejected, ignorance of what one's rights really are and by the procedure to be followed in presenting them, apathy induced by a long experience of frustration and deprivation – in a phrase, lack of capacity to feel or act as a full and equal member of the community. There is a marked contrast between the power of organized labour and the relative ineffectiveness, when in need or trouble, of many a working-class man or woman. One of the outstanding features of the past two decades or so has been the spate of activities undertaken by both the authorities and by voluntary associations and pressure groups of many kinds in an attempt to break through this barrier, by spreading information, offering help and stimulating active participation in community affairs.

The form of participation in the field of social policy by persons outside public administration which has the longest tradition is that of the voluntary organizations. They have been, and still are, of many kinds. Beveridge pointed out that the two springs of voluntary action in the field of welfare were mutual aid and philanthropy, both of which originated in personal contacts within small groups or communities.[31] The two differ in three important ways. Mutual aid is a system of help between equals whereas philanthropy has been essentially assistance given by the privileged to the under-privileged. Mutual aid is self-contained and concerned only with its internal affairs, whereas philanthropy attacks national social problems, and often sees its main task that of forcing governments to take action. This was obviously the case with some of the great pioneers, like John Howard, who gave his name to the League for Penal Reform, or Florence Nightingale on behalf of several causes. A good modern example is the Family Planning Association, which has combined active philanthropic works with a campaign (now crowned by success) for the inclusion of family planning in the National Health Service. Third, when mutual aid expands it develops into large-scale organization of a business of quasi-commercial character – great national provident associations like BUPA and Blue Cross. When philanthropy expands to national proportions it creates services which run parallel with the public social services, and are well fitted to supplement or to co-operate with them. It was the Charity Organization Society which first injected into the rather chaotic world of philanthropy of the mid nineteenth century those principles of orderly procedure and efficient management which made this development possible.

In due course the voluntary bodies, with their up-to-date administration and their large national federations, came to look and to act more and more like a public service. The way was opened for a partnership in which the two sides met well-nigh on equal terms. The principles and practices by which they worked had been shaped more by private than by public influences, and the prestige of the voluntary organizations stood high, while the public services were limited in scope and lacking in experience. However, the rapid expansion of public service during and after the Second World War made the statutory services undoubtedly the senior partner, so much so that many people thought that voluntary action had had its day and would decline into comparative insignificance. But this did not happen: the

partnership continued, taking various different forms. Voluntary
action plays an important part in initiating projects, some of which
may subsequently be taken over by public authorities. In the case of
evacuees during the war, according to Titmuss, voluntary bodies
'helped to hold the line during the period while the official machine
was beginning to take efficient action' and handed over to the official
machine when it was ready.[32] Sometimes voluntary organizations
implement by their services obligations which have been accepted by
government, and do so on lines approved of by the government and
under its supervision. Examples of this were the Home Office
Approved Schools (now renamed Community Homes with Education,
and under local authority tutelage). Very often voluntary bodies offer
services similar to those provided officially, but carry them into areas
or types of cases which it is beyond the capacity of the public services
to reach. Thus, on the one hand, they very often assume responsibility
for services of an intimate or social nature, like marriage guidance
counselling, or voluntary visiting and luncheon clubs for old people,
while, on the other hand, it is often thought appropriate that they
should provide facilities for stigmatized groups which the statutory
authorities wish to keep at arm's length, perhaps for political reasons
– examples could be hostels for discharged prisoners, treatment
centres for alcoholics or drug addicts, almost anything concerned with
the single homeless. Usually, in such instances most of the money will
come from public sources.

All these voluntary undertakings are examples of and given by one
class to another, or better, by the secure to the insecure. This is an old
pattern, but there have been important recent developments in two
respects. First, there has been an enormous increase in the amount of
social research being conducted, and a great deal of it is focused
directly on current social problems, with the purpose, not only of
collecting and interpreting the facts, but also of suggesting action.
Second, pressure groups have multiplied and in some cases they form
a very direct link between the social scientists and the political
activists, who are often the same people. Outstanding examples of
this are the Child Poverty Action Group, the Disablement Income
Group, and Shelter. Typically these organizations combine lobbying
with direct work among those whose cases they are pressing. Shelter,
for example, helped to finance the Family Squatting Advisory
Service, to which most lawful squatting groups in London were
affiliated. It was even prepared to give tactical and legal advice to
those squatting unlawfully[32] – making an interesting amalgam of the

strategies of confrontation and co-operation.

Mutual aid groups as well as philanthropic ventures have flourished in the 1970s. In addition to such old established types as tenants' associations and pensioner's action associations – co-operative organs for the protection of the interests of their members – there has been a proliferation of self-help groups. Many of these have been in the health field – Alcoholics Anonymous, weight-watchers, associations for sufferers, or the relatives of sufferers, from almost every variety of debilitating disease. A rather different example is the spread of pre-school playgroups; although some of these are run as businesses and others were established by existing voluntary organizations or the churches, many more started with groups of mothers getting together and opening up in any available premises. This development has created a whole new area of social service, and a whole new area of local authority regulation too. The latter has generally received the wholehearted support of local branches of the Pre-school Playgroup Association; this is an interesting pattern which seems to be normal in such circumstances. Playgroups tend to be thickest on the ground in the leafier stretches of suburbia, and one of the strongest criticisms of such voluntary effort, or at any rate of its results, is that it is least in evidence where the needs are greatest. True, there are examples of bodies formed and manned by the insecure and disadvantaged themselves, such as claimants' unions. This movement began in 1968 and was in full swing by 1970. Its main purpose is to help members, all of whom are unemployed and drawing social security, to prepare, present and defend their claims and able to work for changes in the law.[34] It should be noted that many claimants' union activists, especially in London, have been unemployed graduates with far left opinions, so their representativeness has inevitably been in doubt. During the past few years, claimants' unions have tended to fade, and to some extent the same fate has befallen the more radical pressure groups; faced with a less than sympathetic government, they have been forced to put their energies into defending gains which they had thought quite secure. Nevertheless, prospects for the future continue to depend on how these various forms of participation develop and how successful they are in maintaining their independence of public authority while preserving a constructive and responsible relationship with it.

One area in which this is of especial importance is race relations. The needs of immigrants are not in essence different from those of the native population, among whom also there are poverty, unemployment, derelict housing, educational backwardness, invalidity and deprivation. But all these troubles are magnified in a group which enters the society laterally from outside instead of growing up vertically from within, a group which is culturally alien, linguistically handicapped and often, in addition, visibly distinguished by colour. In principle social policy makes no distinction between immigrant and native: their rights and claims are the same. In practice, they present different problems which in the case of immigrants call for special skills and understanding on the part of the people who interact with them, whether they be housing officers, teachers, the police, child care officers, social workers, or nurses. But to regard immigrants, and more especially coloured immigrants, as a special category to be accorded positive discrimination would almost certainly increase their detachment from, and impede their integration with, the rest of the community, which is the opposite of what is desired.

For a time governments chose to stay on the sidelines, but they adopted a more central role in 1968, when the Community Relations Commission was established by statute as the successor to the non-staturory National Council for Commonwealth Immigrants. Its task was the positive one of furthering community developments in areas with a large immigrant element, while the Race Relations Board tried, by conciliation and if necessary by prosecution, to curb the expression of racial prejudice in acts of discrimination. Subsequently these two bodies were merged into the Commission for Racial Equality (CRE); the change in title indicated that a change was also taking place in the way the problem was viewed. Now there is much more concern about the circumstances and prospects of the second generation, those educated and often born in Great Britain. It was their frustration – especially over unemployment and 'being picked on' by the police – which was one factor (but only one factor) in the wave of violent disturbances which swept many British cities in the summer of 1981. When particular attention is paid to the needs and interests of black Britons, this is not a privilege, but a means of ensuring that the opportunities and assistance provided them are in substance equal to those enjoyed by others. This principle is recognized today, particularly in projects for priority areas of mixed population. But progress is slow, precisely because it involves changes in the complex of community relations to which there is still considerable resistance, both conscious and unconscious.

The problem with participating communities, whether comprising single estates or whole neighbourhoods, is that they are often defensive and inward-looking; they are organized for the purpose of keeping others out. And the more representative their tenants' or residents' associations – and, for that matter, their local parish or district council – the worse the situation may become for outsiders or minorities. Such necessary projects as hostels for the adult mentally handicapped or day centres for the mentally ill may have a hard job to find welcoming hosts. And almost no-one wants permanent gypsy-sites – the cry is always (and it is a perfectly rational one): 'Not on our patch!' Those charged with the planning of unpopular projects often seek sites where the 'antis' are likely to be negligible or containable, which may mean the more dislocated areas of multi-occupation within cities, or around the poorer and less organized council estates on the urban fringes.

One of the biggest emergent dangers is that social policy may find itself administering more and more to underclasses. This term may be used to comprehend not only those relatively small groups which have always been discriminated against by settled society, such as gypsies or the single homeless, but also much larger minorities, like the long-term unemployed, working-class people in the less skilled and less stable jobs, residents of the more blighted inner city districts or of towns created by heavy industry from which the industry has departed, council tenants who have no hope of buying, many black people. These categories overlap, and 'underclass' is a rather imprecise description, but it can be employed to signify that, increasingly, some of the most important lines of division in British society run through the working class, rather than between it and the middle class. This is not in itself new: one of the commonplaces of Victorian England was that there was a gulf between the roughs and the respectables, between the casually employed and the labour aristocracy. The post Second World War welfare state (and indeed post-1911 welfare provision) helped to smooth out such distinctions, together with the rise of the Labour Party, which is itself now finding its remaining pockets of majority support among the marginal groups we have enumerated. The question to which we must now turn is whether or not social policy is losing its integrative function.

Studies of means-tested benefits suggest that stigma in a narrow sense – fear of being demeaned through having to make a detailed statement of circumstances – is not a very significant factor in low take-up, compared with ignorance of entitlements and the small amounts often obtained once the application is processed.[35] In the broader sense suggested by this discussion of underclasses, however, stigma clearly remains a most important matter. The favoured method of beating it back has been to cover the engine of redistribution with heavy camouflage. Who pays what and who gains what is obscure, and to some extent this obscurity has been intended. One hand collects in vast sums of money through taxes and insurance contributions; the other hand pays it out immediately, in the form of both benefits and services in kind. Right-wingers complain about the extent of the overspill to the non-poor; left-wingers object to the way in which so many of the benefits of social expenditure accrue to the middle classes. They are saying not dissimilar things in different languages.

However, we must reiterate that a welfare state dedicated to delivering the optimum has objectives which differ from one concerned solely with the relief of poverty; it is charged with meeting need, providing for dependencies and fostering potentialities wherever they may occur in the social structure. Certainly this should be without fear or favour, and critics are right to be worried about the ability of the articulate or the well-off to manipulate the system. Nevertheless, the correct basis for the distribution of most health services is the existence of treatable medical conditions; for family allowances, the presence of children in the household; and for places in higher education, the location of relevant abilities or talents, although here motivation and effort also rightly play some part. In all these instances – and many others could be cited – the application of appropriate criteria may result in variations by income and social class, but in ways and directions which differ from service to service, so that the existence of a fair or an unfair distribution cannot simply be adduced from the presence or absence of transfers to the poor.

It is not, in fact, on the benefit side but on the contribution side that the system has relapsed into total incoherence. In only one part of the edifice which has been created, national insurance, is there meant to be a clear relationship between what is paid in and what is received, but even this has always been somewhat spurious, and has become more so as governments have played around with entitlements, and have more and more assimilated the contribution system to PAYE. Furthermore, the latter has been attempted only half-heartedly, so that the lack of fit between the two systems has produced a crazy pattern of marginal rates of income taxation. And, of course, this is compounded by the withdrawal of means-tested benefits as income rises.

The British system of income taxation levies tax at the standard rate over a very broad band of incomes. A taxpayer has to have a taxable income of £14,600 (1983/4) before becoming liable to the lowest of the higher rates of tax – and of course this calculation is made *after* allowances and the deduction of permitted expenses. On the other hand, the standard rate begins to bite only a very small distance up the income scale. For a two child family the tax threshold is currently set at only a little above 40 per cent of average earnings. This is a very different pattern from that which prevailed in the early years of the welfare state after the Second World War, when the tax threshold cut in at a point only a little below average earnings. Tax now falls upon supplementary benefit levels of income, and four-fifths of all the families receiving family income supplement pay part, or all, of it back in tax. This does not seem a very sensible way to proceed. It suggests that radical egalitarians should perhaps themselves be rooting for tax cuts, even if of rather different kind than those favoured by Conservatives convinced of the disincentive effects of high levels of taxation upon managerial incomes.

Although there is a possibility of some interim arrangements, probably in the form of an earmarked tax covering both social security benefits and the bulk of National Health Service expenditure, we are told that progress towards the full integration of the tax and social security systems must await the computerization of the Inland Revenue and of the principal social security benefits. According to the DHSS's *Social Security Operation Strategy*, the latter process is not due to be completed and on stream until 1994/5.[36] There appears, therefore, to be plenty of time during which a sparer and more rational system could be devised, one which relies less on complicated sleights of hand – that is, between the clawing-in hand and the paying-out hand. If however, the problem of the poverty trap is to be overcome, it will have to be a system which accepts the necessity for some overspill – or, in other words, that a controlled proportion of cash benefits will be going to the not-so-poor as well as to the poor.

It is also around the mid 1990s, and into the next century, that there will be a real economic (as opposed to a political or ideological) problem about the financing of public expenditure. This will be caused by the decline and eventual disappearance of North Sea oil revenues and by expected increases in the number of old people, the latter coinciding with the build-up of the expensive commitment to provide earnings-related pensions. (It is worth recalling that the first big wartime birth cohort does not actually reach the age of 60 until the year 2002). However, recent estimates would suggest that if one assumes an average annual growth-rate of about 1.5 per cent per annum (a median assumption), then, at least until the beginning of the 1990s, currently projected levels of public expenditure can be met at present tax rates and with a fall, rather than a rise, in borrowing as a percentage of GDP.[37]

It is also by sometime early in the next decade that we can expect planning to have made another of its periodic resurgences in popularity (though whether under the aegis of technocratic Conservatives or that of one or other of their varieties of political opponents it is obviously impossible to foretell). The unsettled argument concerning the correct units for planning in social policy – whether it should be based on client groups, type or professional orientation of service, or geographical areas – will then doubtless be resumed at heightened levels of intensity. Meanwhile, we might do worse than to ponder the words of a French spokesman at an international conference on social security planning held in 1972 under the auspices of the International Social Security Association. He drew attention to a situation from which, he thought, social policy has some difficulty in extricating itself. He said: 'The evolution of social expenditure is still planned as a burden, certainly inevitable but all the same troublesome, in a national accounting system entirely conceived in terms of market values, and not as a desirable result, positive and conducing to the increase of available wealth.'[38]

References

Chapter 1   The legacy of the Victorian era

1   Leonard Woolf, *Sowing* (Hogarth Press 1960), pp. 151 and 160.
2   e.g., J. A. R. Marriott, *Modern England 1885–1932* (Methuen 1934), p. 155.
3   G. M. Trevelyan, *History of England* (Longmans 1926), p. 50.
4   R. C. K. Ensor, *England 1870–1914* (Clarendon Press 1936), p. 109.
5   Royal Commission on Labour, 1894, vol. xxxv, p. 36.
6   Cited by Sir Ivor Jennings in H. J. Laski (ed.), *A Century of Municipal Progress* (Allen and Unwin 1935), p. 57.
7   Children's Employment Commissioners, 1864, quoted in B. L. Hutchins and A. Harrison, *A History of Factory Legislation* (London School of Economics 1911), p. 224.
8   Harold E. Raynes, *Social Security in Britain* (Pitman 1957), p. 175.
9   A. Bevan, *In Place of Fear* (Heinemann 1952), pp. 73–4.
10   David Roberts, *Victorian Origins of the British Welfare State* (Yale University Press, New Haven 1960), p. 315.

Chapter 2   Problems and policies at the turn of the century

1   Edward R. Pease, *The History of the Fabian Society*, 2nd edn., (Fabian Society 1925), p. 13.
2   Godfrey Elton, *England Arise!* (Jonathan Cape 1931), pp. 123-30.
3   John R. Commons, *History of Labour in the United States*, vol. 3 Macmillan Co., New York 1935), pp. 128 and 219.
4   R. C. K. Ensor, *England 1870–1914* (Clarendon Press 1936), p. 111.
5   Richard Hofstadter, *The Age of Reform* (Jonathan Cape 1955), p. 166.
6   Charles Booth, *Life and Labour of the People*, vol. 1 (Williams and Norgate 1889); R. Seebohm Rowntree, *Poverty, a Study of Town Life* (Macmillan 1901).
7   L. G. Chiozza *Money, Riches and Poverty* (Methuen 1905), p. 5.
8   D. Lloyd George, *Slings and Arrows* (ed. Philip Guedalla) (Cassell 1929), p. 6.
9   Parliamentary Papers (1904), vol. xxxii, p. 92.
10   Royal Commission on the Housing of the Working Classes, First Report, 1885, p. 4 (Cd 4402).

11   J. M. Mackintosh, *Trends of Opinion about the Public Health, 1901–1951* (Oxford University Press 1953), pp. 42–3.

12   A. V. Dicey, *Lectures on the Relation between Law and Public Opinion in England during the Nineteenth Century*, 2nd edn. (Macmillan 1914), p. 64.

13   R. L. Hill, *Toryism and the People* (Constable 1929), pp. 5–6.

14   Dicey, *Lectures on the Relation between Law and Public Opinion*, p. 256.

15   S. MacCoby, *The English Radical Tradition, 1763–1914* (Nicholas Kaye 1952), pp. 201–2.

16   *Fabian Essays* (Jubilee Edition 1948), pp. 194–7.

17   *The Nineteenth Century* (1899), pp. 10 and 23–7.

18   'Lord Rosebery's Escape from Houndsditch' in *The Nineteenth Century*, 1901, p. 366.

19   W. S. Churchill, *Liberalism and the Social Problem* (*Speeches 1906–1909*) (Hodder and Stoughton 1909), pp. 71–8.

20   *Fabian Essays*, p. xxii.

21   ibid., p. 137.

22   Helen Bosanquet, *The Strength of the People* (Macmillan 1903), p. 208.

23   William Stanley Jevons, *The State in Relation to Labour* (*The English Citizen*) (Macmillan 1882), pp. 9 and 12.

24   E. Halévy, *History of the English People in the Nineteenth Century* (trans. E. I. Watkin and D. A. Barker), 2nd edn., vol. 5 (Ernest Benn 1951), p. 231.

Chapter 3   The problem of poverty

1   Emily Greene Balch, *Public Assistance of the Poor in France* (American Economic Association, Baltimore 1893).

2   George P. Nelson (ed.), *Freedom and Welfare–Social Patterns in the Northern Countries of Europe* (Arbejds– og Socialministeriet, Copenhagen 1953), p. 457.

3   Jean S. Heywood, *Children in Care* (Routledge and Kegan Paul 1959), pp. 71–2.

4   *Provision for Old Age by Government Action in Certain European Countries*, P. P. (1899), vol. xcii; *Memorandum on New Zealand and Germany* (1908), vol. lxxxviii.

5   K. de Schweinitz, *England's Road to Social Security* (Oxford University Press 1943), p. 180.

6   S. and B. Webb, *English Poor Law Policy* (Longmans 1910), pp. 214–15.

7   W. H. Beveridge, *Unemployment – A Problem of Industry* (Longmans 1912), pp. 154–6.

8   Grace Abbott, *From Relief to Social Security* (University of Chicago Press, Chicago 1941), p. 17.

9   W. J. Braithwaite, *Lloyd George's Ambulance Wagon* (Methuen 1957), p. 136.
10 S. and B. Webb, *English Poor Law History*, part ii (Longmans 1929), pp. 529–31
11 Majority Report of the Royal Commission on the Poor Laws and Relief of Distress (1909), vol. xxxvii, p. 294, para. 220.
12 ibid., p. 421, para. 604.
13 ibid., p. 529, para 10.
14 Minority Report, pp. 284–5.
15 Beatrice Webb, *My Apprenticeship* (Longmans 1926), p. 195.
16 Minority Report, p. 405.
17 ibid., pp. 670–3.
18 Majority Report, p. 597, para. 4.
19 S. and B. Webb, *English Poor Law Policy* (Longmans 1910), p. 302.
20 W. S. Churchill, *Liberalism and the Social Problem* (*Speeches 1906–1909*) (Hodder and Stoughton 1909), p. 87.

Chapter 4   The coming of social insurance

1   L. K. Frankel and M. M. Dawson, *Workingmen's Insurance in Europe* (New York Charities Publication Committee (Russell Sage Foundation), 1910), p. 395.
2   H. du Parcq, *David Lloyd George*, vol. 4 (Caxton 1912–13), pp. 643 and 778.
3   Majority Report, p. 528, para. 2.
4   Beveridge Report (*Social Insurance and Allied Services*), p. 12, para. 24.
5   A. Birnie, *Economic History of Europe* (Methuen 1957), pp. 223–4; *Provision for Old Age by Government Action in Certain European Countries*, P. P. (1899), vol. xcii.
6   Dermot Morrah, *A History of Industrial Life Assurance* (Allen and Unwin 1955), pp. 29–35.
7   Gertrude Williams, *The State and the Standard of Living* (P.S. King and Son 1936), pp. 67–8.
8   *Provision for Old Age* [. . .], pp. 14–19.
9   Minority Report, p. 274.
10 W. H. Dawson, *Social Insurance in Germany* (T. Fisher Unwin 1912), pp. 14 and 19.
11 *Memorandum on Old Age Pensions*, P. P. 1908, vol. lxxxviii, p. 393.
12 J. M. Mackintosh, *Trends of Opinion about the Public Health* (Oxford University Press 1953), p. 33.
13 W. J. Braithwaite, *Lloyd George's Ambulance Wagon* (Methuen 1957), p. 71.
14 The *Lancet* (1895), p. 476.

15   I. G. Gibbon, *Medical Benefit: A study of the Experience of Germany and Denmark* (P. S. King and Son 1912), pp. 27 and 236–9.
16   Dawson, *Social Insurance* . . ., p. 85.
17   Majority Report, p. 630; W. S. Churchill, *Liberalism and the Social Problem* (*Speeches 1906–1909*) (Hodder and Stoughton 1909), p. 254.
18   S. and B. Webb, *English Poor Law History*, part ii (Longmans 1929), p. 663.
19   W. H. Beveridge, *Unemployment – A Problem of Industry* (Longmans 1912), p. 322.
20   Frank Tillyard, *Unemployment Insurance in Great Britain* (Thames Bank 1949), pp. 3–4.
21   Churchill, *Liberalism* . . ., pp. 309 and 315–16.
22   W. S. Churchill, *The Second World War*, vol. 4 (Cassell 1951), appendix F, p. 862.
23   E. M. Burns, *The American Social Security System* (Houghton Mifflin Co., Boston 1951), p. 36.
24   Braithwaite, *Lloyd George's Ambulance Wagon*, p. 121.

Chapter 5   The inter-war years

1   C.W. Pipkin, *Social Politics and Modern Democracies*, vol. 2 (Macmillan Co., New York 1931), p. 196.
2   Keith Feiling, *Life of Neville Chamberlain* (Macmillan 1946), pp. 459–62.
3   Pipkin *Social Politics*, pp. 202–5.
4   Paul Douglas, *Social Security in the United States* (McGraw-Hill, New York 1936), p. 11.
5   Arnold Wilson and G. S. Mackay, *Old Age Pensions* (Oxford University Press 1941), p. 203.
6   ibid., pp. 88–9.
7   Beveridge Report, appendix F, p. 287.
8   R. C. Davison, *British Unemployment Policy since 1930* (Longmans Green 1938), pp. 111 and 128.
9   W. H. Beveridge, *Unemployment – A Problem of Industry* (Longmans 1930), pp. 288–9.
10   Douglas, *Social Security* . . . pp. 12 and 130; *The Social Welfare Forum* (Columbia University Press, Columbia 1962), p. 9.
11   D. V. Glass, *Population Policies and Movements* (Clarendon Press 1940), ch. 3.
12   Norman Wilson, *Municipal Health Services* (1938), pp. 87–99.
13   André Rouast et Paul Durand, *Sécurité sociale* (Dalloz, Paris 1960), pp. 473–505; Henrich Braun, *Industrialisation and Social Policy in Germany*, (Carl Heymanns Verlag, Köln, Berlin 1956), p. 90.

14 George P. Nelson (ed.), *Freedom and Welfare – Social Patterns in the Northern Countries of Europe* (Arbejds- og Socialministeriet, Copenhagen 1953), pp. 446–60.

15 Hilary M. Leyendecker, *Problems and Policy in Public Assistance*, (Harper and Bros, New York 1955), pp. 52–5 and 82–5.

16 Edith Abbott, *Public Assistance*, vol. 1 (University of Chicago Press, Chicago 1940), p. 125.

17 Marian Bowley, *Housing and the State 1919–1944* (Allen and Unwin 1945), p. 3.

18 G. Slater, *Poverty and the State* (Constable 1930), pp. 243–8.

19 Bowley, *Housing and the State, passim*; John Greve, *The Housing Problem* (Fabian Society 1961), p. 11.

20 Pipkin, *Social Politics . . .*, vol. 2, pp. 156–7.

21 Alva Myrdal, *Nation and Family* (Harper and Bros, New York 1945), p. 242.

22 ILO, *Housing Policy in Europe* (1930), *passim*.

23 Davison, *British Unemployment Policy . . .*, ch. 5.

24 A. C. F. Bourdillon (ed.), *Voluntary Social Services* (Methuen 1945), p. 164.

25 ibid., p. 57.

26 ibid., p. 26.

Chapter 6   The war and the welfare state

1 R. M. Titmuss, *Problems of Social Policy*, in *History of the Second World War* (UK Civil Series 1950), p. 507.

2 ibid., p. 504.

3 A. G. B. Fisher, *Economic Progress and Social Security* (Macmillan 1945), p. 23.

4 Beveridge Report, para. 459.

5 ibid., para. 8.

6 ibid., para. 14.

7 ibid., para. 31.

8 *Social Insurance*, part 1, (1944), para. 1 (Cmd 6550).

9 H. D. Henderson, *The Inter-war Years and other papers*, ed. Henry Clay (Clarendon Press 1955), pp. 192–207.

10 Bulletin of the International Social Security Association (1959), vol. xii, no. 8–9.

11 *Hansard* (Lords) (1953), vol. 182, cols. 675–6.

12 Arnold Wilson and G. S. Mackay, *Old Age Pensions* (Oxford University Press 1941), p. 193.

13 W. H. Beveridge, *Insurance for All and Everything* (*Daily News* 1924), pp. 6–7.

14 J. L. Cohen, *Social Insurance Unified* (P. S. King and Son 1924), p. 23.

15   Beveridge Report, para. 288.
16   ibid., appendix F, para 6.
17   ibid., para. 294.
18   ibid., para. 369.
19   *Social Insurance*, part 1, paras., 12–13.
20   *Hansard* (Lords) (1953), vol. 182, col. 677.
21   Beveridge Report, para. 302.
22   *Hansard* (Lords) (1945–6), vol. 143, col. 78.
23   Henry Brackenbury, *Patient and Doctor* (Hodder and Stoughton 1935), pp. 149–50.
24   Joan S. Clarke, in W. A. Robson (ed.), *Social Security* (Fabian Society 1945), pp. 92 and 121–3.
25   Consultative Council on Medical and Allied Services, First Interim Report (1920), vol. xvii, para. 3.
26   Royal Commission on National Health Insurance (1926), vol. xiv, p. 138.
27   ibid., p. 152.
28   Harry Eckstein, *The English Health Service* (Harvard University Press, Massachusetts 1959), p. 142.
29   A. Massey (ed.), *Modern Trends in Public Health* (Butterworth 1949), p. 130.
30   Aneurin Bevan, *In Place of Fear* (Heinemann 1952), p. 73.
31   Vincent Brome, *Aneurin Bevan* (Longmans Green 1953), p. 198.

Chapter 7   Re-assessment of the welfare state 1950–70

1   EEC, *Exposé sur la situation sociale dans la Communaute*, p. 71.
2   Report of the Committee on the Economic and Financial Problems of the Provision for Old Age (1954), Cmnd. 9333.
3   Iain Macleod and J. Enoch Powell, *The Social Services – Needs and Means* (Conservative Political Centre 1952), p. 5.
4   R. M. Titmuss, 'Crisis in the Social Services', *Listener* (14 February 1952).
5   *The Times* (26 February 1952), p. 5.
6   *Crossbow* (Autumn 1960), p. 25.
7   Alan Peacock, *The Welfare Society* (Liberal Publication Department on behalf of the Unservile State Group 1961), p. 11.
8   Geoffrey Howe, 'Reform of the social services' in *Principles and Practice* (Bow Group 1961), p. 61.
9   *The Cost of the National Health Service* (1955–6), Cmnd 9663, p. 9.
10   White Paper on Provision for Old Age (1958), Cmnd 538.
11   ILO, *The Cost of Social Security 1949–1957*, p. 205.
12   *The Times* (24 May 1961), p. 17.
13   David Butler and Donald Stokes, *Political Change in Britain* (Macmillan 1969), p. 343.

14 Hansard (Commons) (7 February 1966), vol. 724, cols. 37 and 56.
15 *Housing Statistics Great Britain*, no. 12 (HMSO February 1969), p. 23.
16 Keith Banting, *Poverty, Politics and Policy* (Macmillan 1979), p. 70.
17 ibid.
18 Frank Field 'A pressure-group for the poor', in David Bull (ed.), *Family Poverty-Programme for the Seventies* (Duckworth 1971), ch. 12.
19 Banting, *Poverty, Politics and Policy*, p. 103.
20 *Social Trends*, no. 4 (1973), tables 49 and 50.
21 Brian Lapping, *The Labour Government 1964–70* (Penguin 1970), p. 32.

Chapter 8   Social security

1 E. M. Murphy 'Methods of financing social security: an introductory analysis' in *Methods of Financing Social Security*, International Social Security Association, Studies and Research no. 15 (Geneva, 1979).
2 International Labour Review, vol. vii, p. 566; J. E. Russell (ed.), *National Policies for Education, Health and Social Services* (Russell and Russell, New York 1961), pp. 275–76.
3 Paul Fisher 'Developments and Trends in Social Security, 1967–69', *International Social Security Review*, vol. xxiv, no. 1 (1971), p. 24.
4 Social Security Pensions Bill, Second Reading debate (18 March 1975), *Hansard*, col. 1486 ff.
5 Richard Crossman, *The Politics of Pensions* (Liverpool University Press 1972), p. 21.
6 *Occupational Pension Schemes*, Third Survey by the Government Actuary (1968), pp. 7–13.
7 Barbara N. Rodgers, John Greve and John S. Morgan, *Comparative Social Administration* (Allen and Unwin 1968), pp. 34–5 and 289–90; EEC Social Policy Series no. 17 (1966), *Supplementary Social Security Schemes*.
8 Occupational Pensions Board, *Improvement protection for the occupational pension rights and expectations of early leavers*, Cmnd 8271 (HMSO) 1981).
9 *Pensions: Britain's Great Step Forward*, Leaflet no. 25 (DHSS 1975), p. 14.
10 National Association of Pension Funds, *Survey of Occupational Pension Schemes* (1983).
11 Scott Report, *Inquiry into the Value of Pensions*, Cmnd 81476, (HMSO) 1981).
12 A. W. Dilnot, J. A. Kay and C. N. Morris, *The Reform of Social Security* (Institute of Fiscal Studies 1984), p. 13.

13   R. M. Altmann and A. B. Atkinson, 'State pensions, taxation and retirement income 1981–2031', in M. Fogarty (ed.), *Retirement Policy: The next fifty years* (Heinemann Educational Books for the Policy Studies Institute 1982), p. 92.

14   According to the Office of Population Censuses and Surveys, Government Actuary Department's official central projection, *Population Trends*, no. 23 (Spring 1981), HMSO.

15   Sir John Walley, *Social Security – Another British Failure* (Knight 1972), pp. 146–7 and 170–1.

16   The new contribution structure was introduced in the Social Security Act 1975.

17   Occupational Pensions Board, *Solvency, disclosures of information and member participation in occupational pension schemes*, Cmnd 5904 (HMSO 1975), and *Greater Security for the Rights and Expectations of Members of Occupational Pensions Schemes*, Cmnd 8649 (HMSO 1982).

18   Centre for Policy Studies, written evidence to the Inquiry into Provision for Retirement (1984).

19   *Report on a Survey of Occupational Sick Pay Schemes* (HMSO 1977).

20   *Income During Initial Sickness: a New Strategy*, Cmnd 7864, (HMSO April 1980).

21   Michael O'Higgins, 'Privatization and social security', *Political Quarterly* (April–June 1984).

22   House of Commons Social Services Committee, Second Report, *The Government's Proposals for Income during Initial Sickness*, memorandum by M. O'Higgins (HMSO 1981).

23   House of Commons Social Services Committee, *Report on the Age of Retirement* (HMSO 1982).

24   B. Showler and A. Sinfield, 'Unemployment and the unemployed in 1980' in *The Workless State* (Martin Robertson 1981), p. 22.

25   F. Field, 'Killing a commitment: the Cabinet v. the children', *New Society* (17 June 1976).

26   Jean Coussins and Anna Coote, *The Family in the Firing Line*, Poverty pamphlet 51 (Child Poverty Action Group 1981), p. 21.

27   Dilnot, Kay and Morris, *The Reform of Social Security*, p. 43.

28   *Guardian* (3 April 1984).

Chapter 9   Health care

1   *Medical Care under Social Security in Developing Countries*, International Social Security Association, Studies and Research no. 18, (Geneva 1982).

2   'Selection of patients for dialysis and transplantation', *British Medical Journal*, 2 (1978) pp. 1449–50.

3 Doubtless spurred on by the revelation that Britain was at the bottom of the league table of the OECD countries (including apparently Greece) the Secretary of State has recently (1984) announced a crash programme for renal dialysis and transplantation facilities.

4 Thomas McKeown, *Medicine in Modern Society* (Allen and Unwin 1965), p. 13.

5 A. L. Cochrane, *Effectiveness and Efficiency: Random Reflections on Health Services* (Nuffield Provincial Hospitals Trust 1972), pp. 50–4.

6 M. M. Hauser (ed.), *The Economics of Medical Care* (Allen and Unwin 1972), p. 19.

7 Rudolf Klein, 'An anatomy of the NHS', *New Society* (28 June 1973).

8 Christopher Ham, *Policy-Making in the National Health Service* (Macmillan 1981).

9 *A Review of the Medical Services of Great Britain*, Report of the Medical Services Review Committee of the BMA (1962).

10 *Management Arrangements for the Reorganized NHS* (The Grey Book), (HMSO 1972), p. 12.

11 *National Health Service Reorganization: England* (HMSO 1972), para. 134.

12 *National Health Service Reorganization: Consultative Document* (1971), para. 20.

13 *Management Arrangements for the Reorganized NHS*.

14 Ruth Levitt, *The Reorganized National Health Service* (Croom Helm, London 1976), p. 26.

15 *Management Arrangements for the Reorganized NHS*, paras. 1.22–1.27.

16 Nick Bosanquet (ed.), *Industrial Relations in the National Health Service – the search for a system* (King Edwards Hospital Fund for London 1979), p. 1.

17 Report of the Royal Commission on the National Health Service (1979), Table 12.1, p. 163, Cmnd 7615.

18 ibid., para. 4.12.

19 Levitt, *The Reorganized National Health Service*, p. 162.

20 Report of the NHS Management Enquiry, 6 October 1983, both quotations p. 12.

21 Maurice Kogan *et al.*, *The Working of the National Health Service*, Royal Commission on the National Health Service, Research Paper No. 1 (HMSO, London 1978), p. 44.

22 *NHS Reorganization: England*, para. 66.

23 Rudolf Klein and Janet Lewis, *The Politics of Consumer Representation; A Study of Community Health Councils* (Centre for Studies in Social Policy 1976), p. 13.

24 ibid., p. 135.

25   Royal Commission on Medical Education (1968), Cmnd 3569, paras. 133–7.
26   *Doctors in an Integrated Health Service* (HMSO, Edinburgh 1971), para. 107.
27   Report of the Committee of Enquiry into Mental Handicap Nursing and Care (HMSO 1979), Cmnd 7468, paras. 159–61.
28   Report of the Royal Commission on the National Health Service, para. 6.38.
29   See J. P. Martin, *Hospitals in Trouble* (Basil Blackwell 1984).
30   *Better Services for the Mentally Handicapped* (HMSO 1971), Cmnd 4683; *Better Services for the Mentally Ill* (HMSO 1975), Cmnd 6233; *Growing Older* (HMSO 1981), Cmnd 8173.
31   *Department of Health and Social Security Health and Personal Social Services Statistics for England 1980–81* (1982), tables 2.4 and 2.7.
32   Joint Report of the Royal College of Physicians and the Royal College of General Practitioners, *The General Practitioner in the Hospital* (1972), p. 3.
33   *The Field of Work of the Family Doctor* (HMSO 1963).
34   J. Enoch Powell, *A New Look at Medicine and Politics* (Pitman 1966), p. 33.
35   *Hansard* (Commons), 1982–3, Written Answers 10 March 1983, vol. 38, col. 482.
36   A. Cartwright and R. Anderson, *Patients and their Doctors 1977*, Institute for Social Studies in Medical Care, Royal College of General Practitioners, Occasional Paper no. 8 (1979).
37   *The Future Structure of the National Health Service* (HMSO 1970), p. 1.
38   *Inequalities in Health: Report of a Research Working Group* (DHSS 1980).
39   Mildred Blaxter, *The Health of the Children* (Heinemann Educational Books 1981), p. 198.
40   J. Tudor Hart, 'The inverse care law', *Lancet, i* (1971), p. 405.
41   I. Douglas-Wilson and Gordon McLachlan, (eds.), *Health Service Prospects* (1973), cited in *New Society* (18 October 1973), p. 160.
42   *International Social Security Review*, vol. XXV, no. 1/2 (1972), pp. 562–4.
43   *Inequalities in Health*, foreword.
44   *Bulletin of International Social Security Association*, no. 9/10 (1966), p. 348.
45   Report of the Royal Commission on the National Health Service, para. 21.28.
46   *Economist* (18 December 1982).
47   Philip Chubb, Stuart Haywood and Paul Torrens, *Managing the*

Mixed Economy of Health, Health Services Management Centre, University of Birmingham, Occasional Paper no. 42 (1982).

10 The personal social services

1   Phoebe Hall, *Reforming the Welfare* (Heinemann 1976), p. xii.
2   Barbara Rodgers and Julia Dickson, *Portrait of Social Work* (Oxford University Press 1960), p. 31.
3   Report of the Assistance Board for 1944 (1945), p. 8.
4   Report of the Care of Children Committee (1946), paras. 62 and 32, Cmnd 6722.
5   Hubback Committee on the Neglected Child and his Family (1948).
6   Bleddyn Davies, *Social Needs and Resources in Local Services* (Michael Joseph 1968), p. 81.
7   Health Services and Public Health Act (1968), ch. 46, para. 45 (1).
8   Bill Jordan, *Poor Parents* (Routledge and Kegan Paul 1974).
9   *The Child, the Family and the Young Offender* (HMSO 1965), Cmnd 2742.
10 Longford Study Group, *Crime: a challenge to us all* (Labour Party, London 1964).
11 Quoted in Hall, *Reforming the Welfare*, p. 23.
12 ibid.
13 Colin Brewer and June Lait, *Can Social Work Survive?* (Temple Smith 1980), p. 63.
14 Hall, *Reforming the Welfare*, pp. 59–60.
15 Michael Brill, 'The local authority social worker', in Kathleen Jones (ed.), *The Year Book of Social Policy in Britain, 1971* (Routledge and Kegan Paul 1972), p. 81.
16 Eileen Younghusband, *Social Work in Britain, 1950–1975*, vol. 1, (Allen and Unwin 1978), p. 35.
17 Report of the Royal Commission on the National Health Service (1979), table 2.1, p. 163, Cmnd 7615.
18 A. Howard and J. Briers, *An Investigation into the Effects on Clients of Industrial Action by Social Workers in Tower Hamlets – a Report by the Social Work Services of the Department of Health and Social Security* (DHSS, London 1979).
19 The Report of the Committee of Enquiry into the Care and Supervision Provided in Relation to Maria Colwell (DHSS, London 1974).
20 Barbara Wootton., *Social Science and Social Pathology* (Allen and Unwin 1959).
21 Adrian Sinfield, *Which Way for Social Work?* Fabian Tract no. 393 (Fabian Society 1969).
22 P. Corrigan and P. Leonard, *Social Work Practice under Capitalism, a Marxist Approach* (Macmillan 1978); Mike Simpkin, *Trapped within Welfare, Surviving Social Work* (Macmillan 1979).

23 Brewer and Lait, *Can Social Work Survive*.

24 E. Matilda Goldberg, *Helping the Aged* (Allen and Unwin 1970).

25 C. L. Mowat, *The Charity Organization Society 1869–1913* (Methuen 1961), pp. 70–1 and 112.

26 Wootton, *Social Science . . .*, pp. 284–97.

27 Brewer and Lait, *Can Social Work Survive?*, p. 37. Mrs Lait makes clear that her views differ somewhat from those of her fellow author.

28 Martin Davies, *The Essential Social Worker: A Guide to Positive Practice* (Heinemann 1981), p. 3.

29 Goldberg, *Helping the Aged*, p. 197.

30 Association of Social Workers, *New Thinking about Welfare, values and priorities* (1969), p. 81.

31 Phyllida Parsloe and Olive Stevenson, *Social Service Teams: the Practitioners' View* (DHSS 1978), para. 13.26, p. 304.

32 See Carole Satyamurti, *Occupational Survival* (Basil Blackwell 1981).

33 *Social Workers, Their Role and Tasks*, The Report of a Working Party under the Chairmanship of Mr Peter M. Barclay (Bedford Square Press 1982), paras. 7.5–7.6, p. 103.

34 Formerly the National Institute for Social Work Training.

35 Barclay Report, para. 3.27, p. 39.

36 ibid., para. 3.23, p. 38.

37 ibid., appendix B, p. 249.

38 *Health and Personal Social Services Statistics for England 1982* (HMSO), table 3.32, p. 58.

39 Barclay Report, para. 4.6, p. 53.

40 Philip Abrams, 'Community care: some research problems and priorities', in Jack Barnes and Naomi Connelly (eds.), *Social Care Research* (Bedford Square Press 1978).

41 Roy Parker, 'Tending and social policy', in E. Matilda Goldberg and Stephen Hatch (eds.), *A New Look at the Personal Social Services* (Policy Studies Institute 1981).

42 Muriel Nissel and Lucy Bonnerjea, *Family Care of the Handicapped Elderly: Who Pays?* (Policy Studies Institute 1982).

43 Mark Abrams, *Beyond Three-score and Ten: a first report on a survey of the elderly* (Age Concern Mitcham), p. 8, cited in Chris Rossiter and Malcolm Wicks, *Crisis or Challenge? Family Care, Elderly People and Social Policy* (Study Commission on the Family, June 1982).

44 Michael Bayley, *Mental Handicap and Community Care* (Routledge and Kegan Paul 1973).

45 Howard Glennerster, with Nancy Korman and Francis Marston-Wilson, *Planning for Priority Groups* (Martin Robinson 1983), p. 155.

46   *The Government's Expenditure Plans, 1980–81*, Cmnd 7746 (HMSO, November 1979).

47   Audrey Hunt, *The Home Help Service in England and Wales* (HMSO 1970).

48   Social Services Committee, Second Report, Session 1981–2, *1982 White Paper: Public Expenditure on the Social Services, Vol. II*, HC 306 – II, (HMSO), p. 177.

49   The Conservative government has said that fresh funds will be made available for the emptying of the big old hospitals, which will continue even after the ending of the period of transition, but it is not clear how this will be done.

50   Adrian L. James, 'Policies into practice: intermediate treatment and community service compared', *Journal of Social Policy*, 10:2 (April 1981), p. 152.

51   D. Thorpe, J. Paley and C. Green, 'Ensuring the right result', *Community Care*, 263, (10 May 1979) p. 26; cited in James, 'Policies into practice', p. 153.

52   Peter Mitchell, 'Putting teeth into the act', *Disability Rights Handbook for 1983* (Disability Alliance 1982), pp. 102–3.

53   Peter Townsend, 'The objectives of the new social service', in *The Fifth Social Service* (Fabian Society 1970).

Chapter 11   Housing

1   General Household Survey, 1982 (HMSO 1984), table 5.1. The figures from *Housing and Construction Statistics 1972–82*, which are derived from the 1981 Census but are not broken down in such detail, show rather greater proportions of owner-occupiers. The GB figures for December 1982 are 20.3 per cent renting from local authorities or New Town Corporations, 59.0 per cent in owner-occupation, and 11.7 per cent in other tenures (HMSO 1983), Table 9.3.

2   D. Eversley, 'Demographic change and the demand for housing', in M. Buxton and E. Craven (eds.), *Demographic Change and Social Policy: the uncertain future* (Centre for Studies in Social Policy 1976); A. E. Holmans, 'A forecast of the effective demand for housing in Great Britain in the 1970s', *Social Trends*, no. 1 (1970).

3   Housing and Construction Statistics, no. 32, 4th quarter (HMSO 1979), table 16.

4   ibid.

5   W. Randolph and S. Roberts, 'Population redistribution in Great Britain 1971–1981', *Town and Country Planning* (September 1981), pp. 227–31.

6   *Inner London: policies for dispersal and balance*, Final Report of the Lambeth Inner Area Study (HMSO 1977).

7   D. Donnison and C. Ungerson, *Housing Policy* (Penguin Books 1982), pp. 49, 52.

8   Christian Wolmar, 'Picking up the pieces', *Roof* (March/April 1982), pp. 16–18.

9   N. Dennis, *People and Planning, the Sociology of Housing in Sunderland* (Faber and Faber 1970).

10   *Housing Policy, Technical Volume*, no. III (HMSO 1977), table X27, p. 118.

11   *Housing Policy, Technical Volume*, no. I (HMSO 1977), para. 82, p. 33.

12   Stephen Merrett, *State Housing in Britain* (Routledge and Kegan Paul 1979), p. 117.

13   *Housing Policy, Technical Volume*, no. I, (HMSO 1977), para. 85, p. 34.

14   ibid., paras. 20–3, pp. 59–60.

15   J. Perry and M. Gibson, 'Pause for renewal', *Roof* (July/August 1981), pp. 23–4.

16   *Housing Policy, Technical Volume*, no. III (HMSO 1977), table X23, p. 113.

17   Merrett, *State Housing in Britain*, p. 111.

18   Quoted in David Donnison, *The Government of Housing* (Penguin 1967), p. 164.

19   *The Labour Way is the Better Way*, reproduced in *The Times* Guide to the House of Commons (May 1979).

20   *Housing* (1963), Cmnd 2050, p. 2.

21   J. B. Cullingworth, *Essays on Housing Policy* Allen and Unwin 1979).

22   N. McIntosh, 'Owning up: housing finance – reform at last?', *Roof* (March/April 1982).

23   *Housing Policy, Technical Volumes I, II and III* (HMSO 1977).

24   A. Murie, 'Not so much a housing policy . . .?', in P. M. Jackson (ed.), *Government Policy Initiatives 1979–80: some case studies in public administration* (RIPA, London 1981), p. 152.

25   ibid., p. 150.

26   *Social Trends* (1972), table 113.

27   National Dwelling and Housing Survey (HMSO 1978), part I, table 41.

28   Cited in McIntosh, 'Owning up . . .'.

29   Merrett, *State Housing in Britain*, p. 16.

30   Family Expenditure Survey (1979), table J.

31   *Roof* (May/June 1982), p. 8.

32   George Boyne, 'The privatization of public housing', *Political Quarterly* (April–June 1984), pp. 180–7.

33   General Household Survey (1978), table 3.43.

34   *New Society* (28 June 1973).

35   V. Karn, 'Public sector demolition can seriously damage your health', *Roof* (January/February 1981), p. 15.

36   George Boyne, 'The privatization of public housing', p. 183.
37   EEC, *Exposé sur la situation sociale dans la Communauté* (1959), p. 259; (1961), pp. 214–16.
38   Lord Beveridge, *Voluntary Action* (Allen and Unwin 1948), p. 110.
39   J. B. Cullingworth, *Essays on Housing Policy*, p. 131.
40   George Boyne, 'The privatization of public housing', p. 187.

12 Poverty

1   *Research on Poverty* (Social Science Research Council Review of Current Research 1968), p. 5.
2   Peter Townsend, *Poverty in the United Kingdom* (Penguin Books 1979), pp. 248–62.
3   See David Piachaud, 'Is Peter Townsend wrong about poverty?', *New Society* (10 September 1981), pp. 419–21.
4   Townsend, *Poverty in the United Kingdom*, p. 560.
5   A. H. Halsey, 'The dilemma of educational priority areas', *Encounter* (May 1969), pp. 93–6.
6   Eric Midwinter, 'The strategy of the EPA Movement', *Year Book of Social Policy in 1972* (1973).
7   In the first seven years to 1975 total expenditure on the Urban Programme amounted to £55.5 million – still small, of course, in relation to total expenditure in the urban policy area. See Clare Demuth, *Government Initiatives on Urban Deprivation* (Runnymede Trust Briefing Paper 1977).
8   John Edwards and Richard Batley, *The Politics of Positive Discrimination* (Tavistock Publications 1978), p. 218.
9   The National Community Development Project (Inter-Project Report 1973), p. 26, para. 4.11.
10   Graeme Shankland, Peter Willmott and David Jordan, *Inner London: Policies for Dispersal and Balance: Final Report of the Lambeth Inner Area Study* (HMSO, London 1977); Hugh Wilson and Lewis Womersley, Roger Tym and Associates, Jameson Mackay and Partners, *Change on Decay; Final Report of the Liverpool Inner Area Study* (HMSO, London 1977); Llewelyn Davies, Weeks, Forestier-Walker and Bor, *Unequal City: Final Report of the Birmingham Inner Area Study* (HMSO, London 1977). The other three studies commissioned (of Rotherham, Sunderland and Oldham), had a rather different focus on local authority management of urban environmental problems.
11   Family Service Units, 25th Annual Report (1974).
12   *Social Assistance: A Review of the Supplementary Benefits Scheme in Great Britain* (Department of Health and Social Security 1978), para. 1.14, p. 5.
13   R. Walker, R. Lawson and P. Townsend (ed.), *Responses to Poverty: Lessons from Europe* (Heinemann 1984).

14 *Social Security Operational Strategy, a brief guide* (DHSS 1982), p. 2.

15 Ruth Lister, *Actions Not Words* (CPAG 1981).

16 Jonathan Bradshaw, 'An end to differentials?', *New Society*, (9 October 1980). In this article Bradshaw suggests that it is now more appropriate to talk of a 'poverty plateau' rather than a 'poverty trap'. He also demonstrated, however, the plight of a three-child family whose income then went up from £80 to £81: with the loss of the last slice of family income supplement and free school meals, they stood to be £5.61 a week worse off.

17 Douglas Wood, *Men Registering as Unemployed – a longitudinal study* (Department of Employment 1982).

18 Audrey Hunt, Judith Fox and Margaret Morgan, *Families and their Needs, with particular reference to one-parent families*, vol. 1 (HMSO 1973), pp. 31, 36, 81.

19 *Social Assistance, a Review of the Supplementary Benefits Scheme in Great Britain*, para. 2.14, p. 16.

20 David Barker, 'Negative income tax', in David Bull (ed.), *Family Poverty – Programme for the 70's* (Duckworth 1971), ch. 5.

21 *Proposals for a Tax Credit System* (1972), Cmnd 5116.

22 J. E. Meade, *Poverty in the Welfare State*, Oxford Economic Papers, vol. XXIV, no. 3 (1972), p. 305.

23 A. W. Dilnot, J. A. Kay and C. N. Morris, *The Reform of Social Security* (Institute of Fiscal Studies 1984), p. 132.

24 ibid., p. 134.

25 R. M. Titmuss, *Commitment to Welfare* (Allen and Unwin 1968), p. 122.

26 Barbara N. Rodgers, John Grere and John S. Morgan, *Comparative Social Administration* (Allen and Unwin 1968), p. 237.

27 Commission of the European Communities, *The Perception of Poverty in Europe* (Brussels 1977).

28 Townsend, *Poverty in the United Kingdom*, p. 429.

29 Peter Townsend, *Why are the Many Poor?* (Fabian Society 1984), p. 13.

30 *The Economist*, (14 April 1984).

31 Louie Burghes and Ray Stagles, *No Choice at 16: a study of Education Maintenance Allowances* (Child Poverty Action Group 1983).

32 *The Economist* (14 April 1984).

Chapter 13   Problems and prospects of the 1980s

1 Raymond Plant, 'The resurgence of ideology', in Henry Drucker, Patrick Dunleavy, Andrew Gamble and Gillian Peele (eds.), *Developments in British Politics* (Macmillan 1983), p. 12.

2   See Andrew Gamble, *Britain in Decline* (Macmillan 1981), pp. 17–23.

3   Richard Rose and Guy Peters, *Can Government go Bankrupt?* (Macmillan 1978).

4   Bleddyn Davies (with Mike Reddin), *Universality, Selectivity and Effectiveness in Social Policy* (Heinemann 1978), p. 251.

5   C. A. R. Crosland, *The Future of Socialism* (Jonathan Cape 1956).

6   A. J. Culyer, R. J. Lavers, A. Williams, 'Health indicators', in A. and S. Shaw (eds.), *Social Indicators and Social Policy* (Heinemann 1972).

7   J. Bradshaw, 'A taxonomy of social needs', in Gordon Maclachlan (ed.), *Problems and Progress in Medical Care*, seventh series (Nuffield Provincial Hospital Trust, Oxford 1972).

8   Robert Sugden, 'Hard-luck stories: the problem of the uninsured in a laissez-faire society', *Journal of Social Policy*, 11:2 (1982).

9   Alan Williams, '"need" as a demand concept', in A. J. Culyer (ed.), *Economic Policies and Social Goals* (Martin Robinson 1974).

10   Cmnd 7746 (HMSO 1979).

11   Susan Crosland, *Tony Crosland* (Jonathan Cape 1982), p. 295.

12   James E. Alt and K. Alec Chrystal, *Political Economics* (Wheatsheaf Books, Brighton 1983), p. 187.

13   Robert Bacon and Walter Eltis, *Britain's Economic Problem: Too Few Producers* (Macmillan 1976).

14   Maurice Wright, 'The restraint of public expenditure', in Christopher Hood and Maurice Wright (eds.), *Big Government in Hard Times* (Martin Robertson 1981).

15   Alan Walker, Steve Winyard and Chris Pond, 'Conservative economic policy; the social consequences', in David Bull and Paul Wilding (eds.), *Thatcherism and the Poor* (Child Poverty Action Group 1983).

16   Alt and Chrystal, *Political Economics*, pp. 220–37.

17   ibid., p. 237.

18   Arthur Midwinter, Michael Keating and Peter Taylor, '"Excessive and unreasonable": the politics of the Scottish hit list', *Political Studies*, 31:3 (September 1983).

19   Jim Bulpitt, 'Conservatism, unionism and the problem of territorial management', in Peter Madgwick and Richard Rose (eds.), *The Territorial Dimension in United Kingdom Politics* (Macmillan 1982).

20   Total expenditure grew from £10 million in 1979 to £90 million in 1983 and more than £200 million in 1984. *Sunday Times* (21 October 1984).

21 Regulation was duly tightened up – including new requirements for local authority inspection – in the Registered Homes Act 1984.

22 Brian Abel-Smith, 'Whose welfare state?', in Norman Mackenzie (ed.), *Conviction* (MacGibbon and Kee 1958), p. 57.

23 See Julian le Grand, *The Strategy of Equality: redistribution and the Social Services* (Allen and Unwin 1982).

24 Richard Titmuss, 'Equity, adequacy and innovation in social security', *International Social Security Review*, vol. xxiii, no. 2 (1970), pp. 259–67.

25 Margaret Wynn, *Fatherless Families* (Michael Joseph 1964), p. 45.

26 Herman Miller, in Howard S. Becker (ed.), *Social Problems: A Modern Approach* (Wiley 1966), p. 472.

27 Titmuss, 'Equity, adequacy and innovation . . .', p. 265.

28 *The Economist* (8 October 1983).

29 J. P. Martin, *Hospitals in Trouble* (Basil Blackwell 1984), pp. 17–27.

30 Robert Pinker, *Social Theory and Social Policy* (Heinemann 1971), p. 141.

31 W. H. Beveridge, *Voluntary Action* (Allen and Unwin 1948), p. 31.

32 R. M. Titmuss, *Problems of Social Policy* in 'History of the Second World War' (UK Civil Series 1950), pp. 261–2.

33 *New Society* (2 May 1974).

34 Bill Jordan, *Paupers: the making of the new claiming class* (Routledge and Kegan Paul 1973).

35 Davies, *Universality, Selectivity* . . ., pp. 126–9.

36 *Social Security Operational Strategy: a brief guide* (DHSS 1982).

37 David Lipsey, 'Lawson taxes our patience', *Sunday Times* (16 October 1983).

38 Clément Michel, in 'Current Issues in Social Security Planning', International Social Security Association, Study and Research Report no. 4, 1973.

Select bibliography

Historical background

Bruce, Maurice, *The Coming of the Welfare State*, Batsford 1961
Fabian Essays, Jubilee Edition, Fabian Society 1945
Flora, Peter and Heidenheimer, Arnold J., *The Development of the Welfare State in Britain and America*, Transaction: New Brunswick New Jersey 1981
Fraser, Derek, *The Evolution of the British Welfare State* (2nd edn), Macmillan 1984
Gilbert, Bentley R., *The Evolution of National Insurance in Great Britain*, Michael Joseph 1966
Gilbert, Bentley R., *British Social Policy 1914–1939* Batsford 1970
Thane, Pat, *The Foundations of the Welfare State*, Longman, 1982
Webb, Sidney and Beatrice, *English Poor Law History*, part 2, vol. 2, Longman 1929

General

Heidenheimer, Arnold J., Heclo, Hugh, and Adams, Carolyn Teich, *Comparative Public Policy: The Politics of Social Choice in Europe and America* (2nd edn), Macmillan 1983
Hill, Michael, *Understanding Social Policy*, Basil Blackwell and Martin Robertson 1980
Jones, Kathleen, Brown, John and Bradshaw, Jonathan, *Issues in Social Policy* (revised edn), Routledge and Kegan Paul 1983
Mishra, Ramesh, *The Welfare State in Crisis*, Wheatsheaf Books 1984
Pinker, Robert A., *Social Theory and Social Policy*, Heinemann 1971
Pinker, Robert A., *The Idea of Welfare*, Heinemann 1979
Robson, William A., *Welfare State and Welfare Society: illusion and reality*, George Allen and Unwin 1976
Titmuss, Richard M., *Essays on The Welfare State*, George Allen and Unwin 1958
Titmuss, Richard M., *Commitment to Welfare*, George Allen and Unwin 1968
Weale, Albert, *Political Theory and Social Policy*, Macmillan 1983

Economic and financial

Alt, James E. and Chrystal, Alec K., *Political Economics*, Wheatsheaf
   Books 1983
Culyer, A. J., *The Political Economy of Social Policy*, Martin Robertson
   1980
Glennerster, Howard, *Paying for Welfare*, Basil Blackwell 1985
Gough, Ian, *The Political Economy of the Welfare State*, Macmillan 1979
Hauser, M. M., *The Economics of Medical Care*, George Allen and
   Unwin 1970
Sandford, Cedric, *Social Economics*, Heinemann 1977

Social insurance

Beveridge, W. H. (Lord), *Insurance for All and Everything*, *Daily
   News*, 1924
Dilnot, A. W., Kay, J. A. and Morris, C. N., *The Reform of Social Security*,
   Clarendon Press, for the Institute of Fiscal Studies 1984
George, Victor, *Social Security, Beveridge and After*, Routledge and
   Kegan Paul 1968
Fogarty, Michael (ed.), *Retirement Policy: The Next Fifty Years*, Heine-
   mann, for Policy Studies Institute 1982
Social insurance and allied services (Beveridge Report) 1942
Walley, Sir John, *Social Security: Another British Failure?* Charles Knight
   1972

Poverty

Abel-Smith, Brian and Townsend, Peter, *The Poor and the Poorest*,
   Occasional Papers on Social Administration, no. 17, Bell 1965
Beltram, Geoffrey, *Testing the Safety Net*, Occasional Papers on Social
   Administration, no. 74, Bedford Square
Deacon, Alan and Bradshaw, Jonathan, *Reserved for the Poor: the Means
   Test in British Social Policy*, Basil Blackwell and Martin Robertson 1983
Donnison, David, *The Politics of Poverty*, Martin Robertson 1982
George, Victor and Lawson, Roger (eds.), *Poverty and Inequality in
   Common Market Countries*, Routledge and Kegan Paul 1980
Lower Incomes, Royal Commission on the Distribution of Income and
   Wealth, Report no. 6, 1978
Marris, Peter and Rein, Martin, *Dilemmas of Social Reform: Poverty and
   Community Action in the United States*, Routledge and Kegan Paul 1967
Townsend, Peter, *Poverty in the United Kingdom*, Allen Lane 1979

Health

Ham, Christopher, *Health Policy in Britain*, Macmillan 1982
Inequalities in Health, Report of a Research Working Group (The Black
　Report), DHSS 1982
Klein, Rudolf, *The Politics of Health*, Longman 1983
Lindsey, Almont, *Socialised Medicine in England and Wales*, University of
　California Press and Oxford University Press 1962
Office of Health Economics, *Understanding the National Health Service in
　the 1980s*, 1984
Powell, Enoch, *A New Look at Medicine and Politics*, Pitman 1966
Watkin, Brian, *The National Health Service: The First Phase*, George Allen
　and Unwin 1978

Social welfare and social work

General

Glennerster, Howard, Korman, Nancy and Marslen-Wilson, Francis,
　Planning for Priority Groups, Martin Robertson 1983
Goldberg, E. Matilda and Hatch, Stephen (eds.), *A New Look at the
　Personal Social Services*, Policy Studies Institute 1981
Hall, Phoebe, *Reforming the Welfare*, Heinemann 1976
Hallett, Christine, *The Personal Social Services in Local Government*,
　George Allen and Unwin 1982
Knapp, Martin, *The Economics of Social Care*, Macmillan 1984
Report of the Committee on Local Authority and Allied Personal Services
　(Seebohm Report), Cmnd. 3703, HMSO 1968
Rodgers, Barbara and Stephenson, June, *A New Portrait of Social Work*,
　Heinemann 1973

Voluntary action

Aves, Geraldine M., *The Voluntary Worker in the Social Services*, National
　Council of Social Service Report 1969
Beveridge, Lord, *Voluntary Action: A Report on Methods of Social
　Advance*, George Allen and Unwin 1948
The Future of Voluntary Organisations (Report of the Wolfenden
　Committee), Croom Helm 1978
Hadley, Roger and Hatch, Stephen, *Social Welfare and the Failure of the
　State*, George Allen and Unwin 1981

Social casework

Davies, Martin, *The Essential Social Worker*, Heinemann 1981

Goldberg, E. Matilda *et al.*, *Helping the Aged*, George Allen and Unwin 1970

Mayer, J. E. and Timms, Noel, *The Client Speaks: Working Class Impressions of Casework*, Routledge and Kegan Paul 1964

Social Workers: Their Role and Tasks, (Report of a Committee chaired by Mr P. M. Barclay), Bedford Square Press 1982

The old and disabled

Bayley, Michael, *Mental Handicap and Community Care*, Routledge and Kegan Paul 1973

Hunt, Audrey, *The Elderly at Home*, HMSO 1978

Shanas, Ethel *et al.*, *Old People in Three Industrial Societies*, Routledge and Kegan Paul 1968

Topliss, Eda, *Provision for the Disabled* (2nd edn), Basil Blackwell and Martin Robertson 1969

Family and children

Brown, Muriel and Madge, Nicola, *Despite the Welfare State*, Heinemann 1982

Blaxter, Muriel, *The Health of Children*, Heinemann 1982

Madge, Nicola, *Families at Risk*, Heinemann 1983

Wilson, Harriett and Herbert, G. W., *Parents and Children in the Inner City*, Routledge and Kegan Paul 1978

Race relations

Cheetham, Juliet, *Social Work with Immigrants*, Routledge and Kegan Paul 1972

Rose, E. J. B. (ed.), *Colour and Citizenship: A Report on British Race Relations*, part iv, Oxford University Press 1969

Housing

Bowley, Marian, *Housing and the State 1919–1944*, George Allen and Unwin 1945

Cullingworth, J. B., *Essays on Housing Policy*, George Allen and Unwin 1979

Donnison, David and Ungerson, Clare, *Housing Policy*, Penguin 1982

Housing Policy, Technical Volumes, parts I, II and III, HMSO 1977

Merrett, Stephen, *State Housing in Britain*, Routledge and Kegan Paul 1979

Merrett, Stephen and Gray, Fred, *Owner Occupation in Britain*, Routledge and Kegan Paul 1982

Murie, Alan, Niner, Pat and Wilson, Christopher, *Housing Policy and the Housing System*, George Allen and Unwin 1976

Nevitt, Adela A., *Housing, Taxation and Subsidies: a study of housing in the United Kingdom*, Nelson 1966

Periodical publications

Among the many periodicals carrying articles on social policy the following are the ones likely to be most useful.

British Journal of Social Work
International Social Security Review
Journal of Social Policy
New Society (weekly)
Policy and Politics
Political Quarterly
Social Policy and Administration (formerly *Social and Economic Administration*)

And the following annual publications:

Social Trends 1970– , published by Central Statistical Office (HMSO)
Year Book of Social Policy in Britain 1972– , edited first by Kathleen Jones, subsequently by other editors, Routledge and Kegan Paul.

Index